Rebuilding the Ark

Rebuilding the Ark

New Perspectives on Endangered Species Act Reform

Jonathan H. Adler, Editor

The AEI Press

Publisher for the American Enterprise Institute

WASHINGTON, D.C.

Distributed by arrangement with the Rowman & Littlefield Publishing Group, 4501 Forbes Boulevard, Suite 200, Lanham, Maryland 20706. To order, call toll free 1-800-462-6420 or 1-717-794-3800. For all other inquiries, please contact AEI Press, 1150 Seventeenth Street, N.W., Washington, D.C. 20036, or call 1-800-862-5801.

Library of Congress Cataloging-in-Publication Data

Rebuilding the ark: new perspectives on Endangered Species Act reform
Jonathan H. Adler, editor.

p. cm.

Includes bibliographical references and index.

ISBN-13: 978-0-8447-4391-2 (cloth)

ISBN-10: 0-8447-4391-7 (cloth)

ISBN-13: 978-0-8447-4393-6 (ebook)

ISBN-10: 0-8447-4393-3 (ebook)

1. Endangered species—Law and legislation—United States—Congresses.

2. United States. Endangered Species Act of 1973—Congresses. I. Adler, Jonathan H.

KF5640.A75R43 2011

346.7304'69522—dc22

Printed in the United States of America

Contents

Acknowledgments

Projects of this magnitude are rarely sole endeavors, and this book is no exception. Numerous individuals, not least the contributing authors, helped make this possible. Special thanks are owed to Henry Olsen and the National Research Initiative at the American Enterprise Institute for suggesting and supporting this project from its inception. Tremendous thanks are also due to Emily Batman for her attention to detail and tireless efforts to keep things on track for the book and September 2009 conference at which the chapters were first presented. Thanks also to the commentators and discussants at the conference who provided useful feedback to the paper authors, including Michael Bogert, Jeffrey Bossert Clark, Ken Green, Steven Hayward, Rafe Petersen, Lynn Scarlett, David Schoenbrod, William Snape, and David Sunding. In addition, I would like to thank Robert Rawson, Interim Dean at the Case Western Reserve University School of Law, for his support of my work on this and other projects, and my wife Christina, for her love and patience. Finally, a word to my daughters and the endless inspiration they provide. Whether we learn to protect environmental values in a more effective and equitable fashion matters more for them than for me; they will live with the result of our efforts. It is my hope that this book, in some small way, will leave them a better world than otherwise would have been.

Jonathan H. Adler, December 2010

Introduction:
Rebuilding the Ark

Jonathan H. Adler

The Endangered Species Act (ESA) was enacted in 1973 to conserve animal and plant species threatened with extinction and the ecosystems upon which they depend. Few quarrel with this goal, yet many quarrel with the Act. The ESA is among the most criticized and controversial of all environmental laws: landowners and private businesses have long decried the Act's regulatory burdens, while conservationists increasingly question the Act's environmental effectiveness.

Well over 1,200 species have been listed as needing the Act's protection, but few have been restored to healthy status. The law appears to have prevented some species from falling over the brink into extinction. Yet there is little evidence it has restored many species populations to health. Moreover, the Act may have done more harm than good for some species because it has discouraged conservation and antagonized those upon whom species' survival depends.

The ESA's failures have not been due to a lack of enforceable provisions. The Act is arguably the most powerful environmental law in the U.S. Code. One environmental activist likened the law to a pit bull because it is "short, compact, and has a hell of a set of teeth."[1] The law prohibits actions that may harm species or their habitat, and it imposes lengthy and extensive planning and consultation requirements on federal agencies. In some cases, the regulatory requirements of the Act are so severe as to discourage species conservation on private land and may even encourage landowners to harm endangered species or destroy valuable species habitat. Today the Act is the source of extensive litigation in federal courts as environmental activists, regulated interests, and government agencies spar over its implementation, including its application to greenhouse gas emissions and other regulatory programs.

The Supreme Court, in *Tennessee Valley Authority v. Hill*, declared that the ESA sought to prevent species extinction "whatever the cost," and costs rarely come into play under the Act. Fittingly, then, there is no comprehensive study of the ESA's economic costs or its benefits.[2] There is not even a full accounting of how much the federal and state governments spend to implement, enforce, and comply with the Act.[3] Existing government reports are incomplete, and there has been no meaningful effort to account for the costs the ESA imposes on the private sector.

Whatever the total costs of the ESA, they are far greater than has been accounted for in government reports. But this is only part of the story. Perhaps ironically, it appears the ESA is "underfunded," in that appropriations for species-related activities are insufficient to meet the needs of the Fish and Wildlife Service (FWS) and other conservation agencies (let alone individual species' needs).[4] A further problem is that federal spending is not driven by neutral scientific assessment of what species are in greatest need or where government support will be most helpful.[5] As New York University law professor Katrina Wyman observes, "limited amounts of public funding available for species recovery are allocated primarily based on political and bureaucratic considerations" instead of species-related or ecological factors.[6] FWS recovery expenditures, for instance, are "poorly correlated" with species priority rankings.[7] Political and institutional incentives as well as outside litigation combine to distort species funding priorities.[8] Responding to litigation can be particularly expensive and consumes large portions of available funds.[9]

Despite the ESA's failings, Congress has not revised the law in over twenty-five years. Legislative proposals have succumbed to partisan infighting and interest group pressure. Administrative reforms advanced by the Clinton and Bush Administrations may have done some good, but they are insufficient. Unless Congress acts to reform the ESA, the Act is unlikely to preserve many more species and thus fulfill its statutory mandate.

This volume seeks to contribute to the cause of ESA reform by expanding the debate over the Act's failings and possible avenues for reform. The contributors to this volume present a range of reform proposals from a wide range of perspectives. Not every contributor embraces the ideas put forward by the others, but all share a genuine interest in making species conservation more effective.

In chapter 1, I survey the Act's conservation record with a particular focus on private land. The vast majority of endangered and threatened species dwell on private land, and private land conservation is necessary for their survival. Yet there is evidence the ESA's primary regulatory provisions discourage private land conservation and are in particular need of reform.

Section 10 of the ESA authorizes the Fish and Wildlife Service to permit "incidental takes" of listed species in conjunction with approved habitat conservation plans (HCPs). Numerous HCPs are approved, but we know little about how they are working. To address these shortcomings, in chapter 2, David A. Dana proposes a series of reforms to the HCP process to enhance transparency, accountability, public participation, and, most of all, conservation.

There is a growing consensus that economic incentives could encourage greater conservation on private land but disagreement about what form such incentives should take. In chapter 3, R. Neal Wilkins summarizes recent incentive efforts and assesses the promise of incentive systems, including conservation banks and recovery crediting. Wilkins argues that the latter, in particular, are a promising tool for encouraging greater habitat protection on private land.

Instead of separating property rights and government permissions, Jamison E. Colburn in chapter 4 calls for greater integration of the two, treating regulatory permissions more like property to enhance assessment and certainty. Although nature is infinitely variable, a more standardized regulatory framework could enhance nature's conservation.

The tax code provides a modest incentive for conservation by allowing income tax deductions for the donation of conservation easements. In chapter 5, Jonathan Remy Nash suggests the conservation value of this policy could be increased if the value of the deduction were calibrated to the ecological value of the easement.

Species conservation affects owners of water no less than owners of land. Species-driven conflicts over water use and disposition would appear to place species conservation and water rights at odds. In chapter 6, James L. Huffman suggests this conclusion is misplaced, and that greater protection for property rights in water could improve regulatory incentives and actually enhance species conservation efforts.

Some ESA reform proponents argue that better science will produce better regulatory decisions under the ESA. Drawing on his experience in both state and federal regulatory agencies, Brian F. Mannix suggests in chapter 7 that the problem is less inadequate science than the way the Act applies science to its regulatory decisions. Enhancing species conservation requires improving the law more than improving the science.

Even if the ESA has yet to reach its limits, global climate change could overwhelm it. However well the ESA works to address traditional threats to species and the ecosystems upon which they depend, J. B. Ruhl explains in chapter 8 why the Act is completely unsuited to address the threat to endangered species posed by climate change, and how the Act could be reformed to address climate-driven concerns.

The ESA is concerned not only with species in the United States, but with species conservation internationally as well. Yet as Michael De Alessi explains in chapter 9, the Act's regulatory measures may inhibit the development of more effective incentive-driven conservation strategies in other nations. As at home, ESA reform could enhance the prospects for species conservation overseas.

This collection is not comprehensive. Worthy reform proposals could fill several more volumes, as could thoughtful responses and honest disagreement. The prospect of ESA reform provokes strong responses. Past debates over ESA reform have been quite contentious. But if species are to be conserved, it is a debate that must be joined again, for the ESA's ambitious goals cannot be achieved without significant reform. If we are to conserve a greater proportion of the earth's imperiled plants and animals, we must place saving endangered species ahead of saving the Endangered Species Act.

Notes

1. Timothy Egan, "Strongest U.S. Environment Law May Become Endangered Species," *New York Times*, May 26, 1992, quoting Donald Barry of the World Wildlife Fund.

2. Jason F. Shogren, "Benefits and Costs," in *The Endangered Species Act at Thirty, Volume 2: Conserving Biodiversity in Human-Dominated Landscapes*, ed. J. Michael Scott, Dale D. Goble, and Frank W. Davis (Washington, D.C.: Island Press, 2006), 186; and Katrina Miriam Wyman, "Rethinking the ESA to Reflect Human Dominion Over Nature," *NYU Environmental Law Journal*, 17 (2008): 502 ("While there is data on governmental spending on endangered species, there is no data on the costs that the ESA imposes on society at large.").

3. Randy T. Simmons and Kimberly Frost, *Accounting for Species: The True Costs of the Endangered Species Act* (Bozeman, Montana: Property and Environment Research Center, 2004), http://www.perc.org/pdf/esa_costs.pdf (showing how FWS reports dramatically understate ESA-related costs to federal agencies).

4. Mark W. Schwartz, "The Performance of the Endangered Species Act," *Annual Review of Ecology, Evolution, and Systematics* 39 (2008): 281; see also Wyman, "Rethinking the ESA," 499–500 ("There is no doubt" existing appropriations "are insufficient to recover the species that have been listed, let alone the many other imperiled species that remain unlisted.").

5. Marco Restain and John M. Marzluff, "Funding Extinction? Biological Needs and Political Realities in the Allocation of Resources to Endangered Species Recovery," *Bioscience,* 52, no. 2 (Feb. 2002):170. The priority rank is based upon the degree of threat to the species, potential for recovery, and taxonomic distinctness. Ibid.

6. Wyman, "Rethinking the ESA," 501–2.

7. Restain and Marzluff, "Funding Extinction?"

8. Schwartz, 287 ("social interest and politics retain the capacity to trump strict biological consideration when it comes to recovery expenditures.").

9. Wyman, "Rethinking the ESA," 496.

1

The Leaky Ark:
The Failure of Endangered Species
Regulation on Private Land

Jonathan H. Adler

The Endangered Species Act (ESA) was enacted with much fanfare and little opposition. In 1973, few anticipated how broadly the law would affect both government and private activities.[1] Yet ever since its celebrated passage, the nation's premier wildlife conservation law has been a source of conflict and controversy; it has been rightly described as "one of the most contentious of our federal environmental laws."[2] The ESA is controversial in part because of its strength. Indeed, the ESA may be the most powerful environmental law in the nation.

For all the Act's strength, it has not been particularly effective at conserving species. Although it is the "most comprehensive of all our environmental laws,"[3] it is not, by any measure, the most successful. Even strong advocates of regulatory measures to protect endangered species habitat acknowledge that "no one...suggests that the federal ESA is realizing Congressional intent or that it has been implemented rationally or responsibly."[4] A 2008 review concluded that the best one could say is that "the scientific question of whether the ESA works effectively to protect species remains open."[5]

One of the primary reasons that the ESA has failed to realize its objectives is that it is ineffective at preserving habitats that are found on private land. Habitat loss is the primary threat to endangered species in the United States.[6] At present, most endangered and threatened species' habitat is privately owned: over three-quarters of threatened and endangered species rely upon private land for some or all of their habitat.[7] Thus, even if all federal lands were managed exclusively for species conservation, this would be insufficient to save many imperiled species, because a significant percentage is not even found on federal lands.[8] Private land is also often (though not always) ecologically superior to government lands of the same type.[9] If the ESA is to be effective at conserving species by preserving their habitats, it must be effective at doing so on private land. However, the ESA's greatest failing has been species conservation on private land.[10]

As originally written and implemented, the ESA sought to conserve endangered species found on private land by regulating land use so as to prevent the adverse modification or destruction of species habitat. Land-owners were limited in their ability to make potentially harmful land use changes and threatened with civil or criminal prosecution for violating the Act's strictures. Only by regulating land use in this fashion, many believed, could endangered species be saved. Yet this approach has proven largely ineffective. Whatever successes the ESA has had in other contexts, such as by forcing federal agencies to consider how their actions affect imperiled species, the regulatory model has failed on private land. As *Science* reported in 2005: "It's become clear over three decades that its regulatory hammer isn't enough."[11] There is little question that "a purely regulatory approach will never be able to maximize the value of the working landscape for biodiversity."[12] The question today is what, if any, role regulation can play in encouraging conservation on private land.

The Endangered Species Act

The groundwork for the Endangered Species Act was laid in the 1960s, as the modern environmental movement came of age and the federal government began to flex its regulatory muscles in environmental policy.[13] In 1966, Congress passed the Endangered Species Preservation Act, which authorized the Secretary of the Interior to establish a list of endangered and threatened species and to purchase land deemed important for conserva-tion purposes. A prohibition on the import of endangered species for most purposes followed shortly thereafter in 1969; other limits on trade in endangered species and their products were established in the 1973 Convention on International Trade in Endangered Species of Wild Fauna and Flora (CITES).

Congress enacted the Endangered Species Act in 1973 by a wide margin. "Nothing is more priceless and more worthy of preservation than the rich array of animal life with which our country has been blessed," declared President Nixon when he signed the bill into law.[14] He proclaimed that "countless future generations" would have their lives enriched and the nation would be "more beautiful in the years ahead" due to the Act.[15]

The 1973 Act built upon Congress' prior enactments by incorporating the endangered and threatened species lists already established. It also established new procedures for listing species, designating critical habitat, and developing species recovery plans. Most significantly, the new law included powerful provisions designed to limit government and private actions that could imperil listed species. Under Section 7, federal agencies are required to consult with the Fish and Wildlife Service (FWS) or National Marine Fisheries Service (NMFS) to ensure that no action "authorized, funded, or carried out" by that agency will "jeopardize the continued existence of any endangered species or threatened species" or destroy critical habitat for such species.[16] Section 9 prohibits anyone to engage in the unpermitted "taking" of any endangered species.[17] Violators are subject to civil and criminal penalties. As defined in the Act, "taking" an endangered species not only includes killing, wounding, or capturing an endangered species, but also otherwise harming the species, including by destroying or adversely modifying its habitat.[18] Section 10 provides for the granting of "incidental take permits" to authorize activities that would be otherwise prohibited under Section 9.

In 1978, the Supreme Court held in *Tennessee Valley Authority v. Hill* that the ESA explicitly placed endangered species conservation above other social goals when in conflict.[19] Specifically, the Court held that the consultation requirement of Section 7 "admits of no exceptions" and prohibited completion of the Tellico Dam in Tennessee lest the dam's construction and operation push a small endangered fish, the Tennessee snail darter, over the brink of extinction. Explained the Court, "The plain intent of Congress in enacting this statute was to halt and reverse the trend toward species extinction, whatever the cost."[20]

Congress responded with amendments to impose greater procedures on the listing of new species, to require consideration of economic effects during the designation of critical habitat, as well as to authorize a special cabinet-level committee, subsequently known as the "God Squad," to exempt important projects from the ESA's prohibitions. This latter provision was intended to permit completion of the Tellico Dam, although it did not work out that way: Congress had to come back again and explicitly approve the dam's construction. Congress amended the law again in 1982, further revising the procedures for listing species and expanding the power of the FWS and NMFS to authorize incidental "takes" of endangered species that would be otherwise prohibited under Section 7 or Section 9 pursuant to habitat conservation plans (HCPs). The Act was last reauthorized in 1988, and that authorization expired in 1992. Though numerous reform proposals have been introduced and debated since, the law has yet to be reauthorized.

Assessing the ESA's Performance

Nearly four decades after the ESA's adoption, there is ample reason to doubt whether the law has fulfilled its promise. The number of species listed as endangered and threatened has increased exponentially, with no end in sight.[21] In 1973 there were only seventy-eight species on the endangered and threatened lists; by 1994 there were over one thousand. In just two decades the list had increased more than twelvefold and continues to climb.

As of August 2009, there were 1,320 species listed as threatened or endangered within the United States (1,011 and 309, respectively).[22] Of these, 573 are animals and 747 are plants. An additional 573 foreign species are listed, bringing the grand total of listed species to 1,893.[23] Of the 1,320 species listed within the United States, the FWS reports that 1,134 are covered by active recovery plans.[24]

The ESA's stated purpose is to "conserve" threatened and endangered species.[25] As defined by the law, to "conserve" means "to use…all methods and procedures which are necessary to bring any endangered species or threatened species to the point at which the measures provided pursuant to this Act are no longer necessary." In other words, the express aim of the Act is to recover all imperiled species to the point at which the Act's protection is no longer necessary.[26] As succinctly stated by wildlife law expert Michael Bean: "In a word, the Act's goal is recovery."[27] This goal may not be realistic with regard to all listed species. Some species are "conservation-reliant" and will require some degree of active support, such as predator control or regular habitat maintenance or modification.[28] Nonetheless, conservation-as-recovery is what Congress enacted into law.

Are species recovering? Alas, the aim of species recovery "has been reached in distressingly few cases."[29] As of August 2009, forty-seven species had been removed from the endangered and threatened species lists.[30] Of these, the FWS identified twenty-one as "recovered." Seventeen were delisted due to data errors of one sort or another, and nine were delisted because they went extinct. An additional twenty-five species had been reclassified as threatened from endangered, reflecting a significant improvement in their status, while another nine had been reclassified to endangered from threatened.[31] The FWS believes another twenty-eight listed species may have actually gone extinct but have yet to be delisted,[32] and at least forty-two additional species have gone extinct awaiting listing under the Act.[33]

Of the recoveries, several are foreign species, including three species of kangaroo, and thus not subject to the ESA's primary regulatory measures. Several others benefited from measures wholly independent of the ESA, such as limits on hunting or the Environmental Protection Agency's 1972 ban on domestic use of DDT. There is little doubt this latter action was essential to the recoveries of the bald eagle, Arctic peregrine falcon, American peregrine falcon, and brown pelican. The ESA's role is less clear. Several other species recovered on the island of Palau, including the Palau owl, Palau ground dove, and Palau fantail flycatcher, but this too was largely independent of the ESA.

Where the ESA has led to the recovery of endangered species, it has typically been because there was a specific identified threat that could be readily addressed through direct management measures rather than through the ESA's primary regulatory provisions. Recovery of the Aleutian Canada goose, for instance, was facilitated by the removal of predators from nesting grounds, largely on federal lands, and hunting limitations.[34] The Robbins' cinquefoil, an endangered plant, recovered due to changes in land management by the U.S. Forest Service and agreements with a local conservation organization to protect intact populations.[35] Thus, it appears the ESA is more effective at addressing some threats to species populations, such as extractive resource use (which primarily occurs on federal land), hunting, and natural threats (e.g., predators), than others.[36] As noted above, the law has successfully altered federal land management practices and raised the salience of species conservation in many federal agencies, but it does not appear to have done much to help species on private land.

Defenders of the Act argue that "counting only the number of recovery related delistings does not give a true measure of the Act's success."[37] Considering the extent to which the ESA has slowed some species' slide into extinction, stabilized threatened populations, or otherwise increased some species' chances of survival, provides a more complete picture of the Act's performance. A 1999 study estimated that the ESA prevented 192 domestic species extinctions during its first twenty-six years. Using this methodology, the ESA is estimated to have saved 227 species from going extinct in its first thirty years.[38] If this estimate is accurate, more species have been saved from extinction than are believed to have gone extinct while under the Act's protection. The FWS claims that the ESA is having a beneficial effect on some imperiled species: it reported that as of 2007 just over 40 percent of listed species were "doing better" since their initial listing.[39]

It may take several decades more before we can completely evaluate the ESA's effect. Species recovery is not necessarily a quick process. Most listed species were not suddenly imperiled overnight, and recovery may take as long, if not longer, due to a wide range of ecological and reproductive factors. However, although it may be too early to assess the overall performance of the ESA, it is possible to assess how the ESA's regulatory protections help species. Endangered animal species receive greater regulatory protections under the ESA than endangered plants. Yet this does not appear to translate into improved performance.[40] A recent study found endangered species are less likely to be improving than threatened species, despite the increased level of regulatory protection. Perhaps the fact that endangered species populations were likely to be in worse condition in the first place explains the better outcome for threatened species.[41]

The ESA requires the designation of critical habitat when a species is listed as endangered, but such designations have only limited legal import, particularly on private land. Whether designating critical habitat improves a species status is disputed. One study found that species for which critical habitat was designated were more likely to be improving.[42] Yet a subsequent study found no effect from designation once researchers accounted for recovery spending.[43] Indeed, there is some evidence that critical habitat designations can increase development pressure on private land.[44]

Several recent studies suggest that listing species and funding recovery efforts are beneficial to species, and increasingly so over time. For instance, one study concluded that the longer a species is listed under the ESA, the more likely it is to be stable or improving.[45] It also found that the completion of a recovery plan has a similar effect.[46] There also appears to be a positive relationship between species recovery and the percentage of recovery goals set out in a species' recovery plan achieved for that species.[47] Yet another recent study found evidence that species-related spending correlates with preventing continued deterioration of a listed species' status.[48] Yet insofar as these studies rely upon FWS assessments of species "status trends," they may be questioned. The data upon which status trends are based are "inconsistent and of questionable accuracy" and "trends for some species are simply the best guesses of USFWS personnel."[49] FWS assessments of species status are somewhat subjective, lack transparent criteria, and "may be manipulated to achieve agency objectives."[50]

With that caveat in mind, there is evidence that ESA-related spending helps at least some species. A 2007 study in *Ecological Economics* found, consistent with prior research, that "spending is correlated with improved status."[51] This study also found that "ESA-related spending is more effective in preventing deterioration than in promoting improvements in recovery status."[52] As the authors explained, "increased spending reduces the probability that FWS will classify a species as extinct or declining" but "evidence does not support the hypothesis that increased spending leads to increases in the probability that a species is stable or improving."[53] That is, insofar as the ESA helps, it is more effective at preventing extinction than fueling recovery. Yet this result could be explained by the fact that those species identified as having "high recovery potential" are less likely to be declining or extinct, and slightly more likely to be classified as improving.[54] This same study found no effect from designation of critical habitat.[55]

Other recent research casts doubt on the claim that listing species, in itself, is helpful for species. Indeed, a 2007 study found that listing a species can actually be detrimental if the listing is not followed with significant funding on species recovery.[56] Consistent with some prior studies, it found that the ESA can be effective at improving species status with substantial resource commitments, at least in some cases. Specifically, this study found that listing a species alone has no positive effect, but listing combined with funding has a positive effect, and listing with little or no funding has a significant negative effect.[57] On this basis, the authors concluded that "the ESA works when it is backed up with money, and not otherwise."[58] As the authors explained: "Our analysis suggests that it is not the act of listing itself that matters, but rather high levels of expenditures for recovery combined with listing. Simply listing a species in the absence of such expenditures appears to lead to a decline."[59] The authors could not conclude that the ESA is ineffective, as there is no counterfactual group of unlisted species that receive substantial funding.[60] The authors of this study hypothesize that the negative effect of listing without funding is due to perverse incentives on private landowners, and that species-specific funding is a likely proxy for increased monitoring and enforcement of the ESA's strictures. "Seen in this light, it is only the credible potential of enforcement that renders the ESA effective."[61]

Yet a closer look at the data, and especially the fact that different government agencies achieved varying degrees of success in protecting species, may suggest a different conclusion than that only the credible threat of enforcement makes the ESA effective. The study looked at species-related expenditures aggregated by agency, and the results are interesting: "Forest Service spending has the strongest positive effect, followed by the Bureau of Land Management and the Fish and Wildlife Service."[62] In other words, spending by land management agencies appears to be more effective than spending by the primary regulatory agency (which also has some land management responsibilities of its own). This would suggest that spending on species conservation on federal lands is more effective than spending to protect species on private land, or that spending on direct conservation measures is more effective than spending on regulatory programs aimed at controlling private behavior.

While only suggestive, this interpretation is consistent with other research showing that the ESA is more effective on federal land than on nonfederal land. Prior research has found that "species found exclusively on federal lands are more likely to be improving than those with mixed or private ownership."[63] One study in particular found that "the ratio of declining species to improving species is 1.5 to 1 on federal lands, and 9 to 1 on private lands."[64] As Robert Bonnie of the Environmental Defense Fund summarized: "Species that occur exclusively on non-federal lands (the majority of which are in private ownership) appear to be faring considerably worse than species reliant upon the federal land base."[65] These findings should not be a surprise, as the ESA can induce affirmative conservation measures on federal lands but can do little more than prevent harm to species on nonfederal land, often at the cost of discouraging voluntary conservation. Insofar as many listed species are conservation dependent, this can make a real difference.

The Private Land Problem

As noted above, habitat modification is the greatest threat to endangered species, and the lion's share of endangered species habitat is privately owned. Therefore, if endangered species habitat is not preserved on private land, many endangered species will not survive. There are many species, like the red-cockaded woodpecker, that rely upon private land and are not effectively protected. "We have too many cases like it, where a species is listed for years, but the population continues to go straight down the tubes in spite of this allegedly stringent and restrictive law," according to Bean.

Why is the ESA failing to conserve species on private land? The most likely culprit is the structure of the ESA itself and the incentives it creates for private landowners. In the simplest terms, the ESA penalizes owners of species habitat and so discourages habitat creation and conservation on private land. Under Section 9 of the Act, it is illegal for a private landowner to engage in activities that could "harm" an endangered species, including habitat modification, without first obtaining a federal permit. Acquiring permits may be costly and time consuming, and can be the source of substantial uncertainty, particularly for smaller landowners, notwithstanding recent efforts to provide landowners with regulatory assurances and facilitate habitat conservation planning. "Taking" a species without a permit, including by adverse habitat modification, can lead to fines of up to

$25,000 and even jail time. While not always stringently enforced, the threat remains, and the FWS is notoriously slow to approve activities that could harm species habitat.

Section 9 is not the only portion of the Act that affects private landowners. Section 7 constrains other actions on private land that are subject to federal permitting requirements. For instance, the U.S. Army Corps of Engineers will not grant a permit to fill a wetland under Section 404 of the Clean Water Act if the wetland is potential endangered species habitat unless it can ensure the action will not jeopardize a listed species or its habitat. To meet this requirement, a landowner may be required to mitigate her development by acquiring and conserving multiple acres of wetlands for each one she seeks to develop.

These requirements can reduce private land values and antagonize private landowners who might otherwise cooperate with conservation efforts. As several prominent conservation biologists observed in *Conservation Biology*: "The regulatory approach to conserving endangered species and diminishing habitats has created anti-conservation sentiment among many private landowners who view endangered species as economic liabilities."[67] They further explained:

> Landowners fear a decline in the value of their properties because the ESA restricts future land-use options where threatened or endangered species are found but makes no provisions for compensation. Consequently, endangered species are perceived by many landowners as a financial liability, resulting in anticonservation incentives because maintaining high-quality habitats that harbor or attract endangered species would represent a gamble against loss of future opportunities.[68]

As FWS Director Sam Hamilton observed in 1993, when he oversaw FWS efforts in Texas: "The incentives are wrong here. If I have a rare metal on my property, its value goes up. But if a rare bird occupies the land, its value disappears."[69]

As a consequence of these negative incentives there is less and lower-quality habitat available to endangered species on private land.[70] Such regulations may even encourage landowners to destroy or degrade potential habitat on their land. It is not illegal to modify land that might become endangered species habitat some day in the future, nor are landowners required to take affirmative steps to maintain endangered species habitat. Yet even if such actions are not taken, the Act creates substantial incentives for private landowners to *discourage* species conservation on their own land.

There are numerous accounts of landowners engaging in preemptive habitat destruction—that is, perfectly legal measures to make their land less hospitable to current or potential listed species before it is subject to regulation. These accounts have been a staple of debates over the ESA for years and are not confined to a handful of species or one region of the country. In the Pacific Northwest, for instance, the FWS found that land-use restrictions imposed to protect the northern spotted owl scared private landowners enough that they "accelerated harvest rotations in an effort to avoid the regrowth of habitat that is usable by owls."[71] Meanwhile, down in Texas, landowners razed hundreds of acres of juniper tree stands after the FWS listed the golden-cheeked warbler as an endangered species.[72] At the same time, landowners in California destroyed vegetation helpful for endangered species to prevent potential occupation, even at great personal expense. Said one: "The risk of not doing it is too great."[73]

Several recent empirical studies confirm the negative effects of the ESA on private land conservation. Two such studies found evidence of preemptive habitat destruction by forest landowners in the eastern United States due to the listing and presence of red-cockaded woodpeckers. The first found that private landowners engaged in preemptive habitat destruction when the presence of endangered red-cockaded woodpeckers placed the landowners at risk of federal regulation and a loss of their timber investment.[74] Providing habitat for a single woodpecker colony could cost a private timber owner as much as $200,000 in forgone timber harvests.[75] To avoid the loss, those landowners at greatest risk of restrictions were most likely to harvest their forestlands prematurely and reduce the length of their timber harvesting rotations.[76] The ultimate consequence of this behavior was the loss of several thousand acres of woodpecker habitat, a major habitat loss for a species dependent upon private land for its survival.[77]

The second study of landowner responses to red-cockaded woodpeckers confirmed the existence of widespread preemptive habitat destruction in southeastern forests.[78] Specifically, this study found that "regulatory uncertainty and lack of positive economic incentives alter landowner timber harvesting behavior and hinder endangered species conservation on private lands" and that "a landowner is 25% more likely to cut forests when he or she knows or perceives that a red-cockaded woodpecker cluster is within a mile of the land than otherwise."[79] Thus, this study concluded, "at least for the [woodpecker], the ESA has a strong negative effect on the habitat," and the effect appears to be "substantial."[80]

The perverse incentives of the ESA unfortunately do not affect only the woodpeckers and other species dependent upon private timberland. A 2003 study published in *Conservation Biology* found that listing a species could undermine other species and habitat conservation on private land.[81] Based on surveys of private owners of habitat for the Preble's Meadow jumping mouse, this study found that a substantial percentage of landowners would respond to a species listing by making their land less hospitable for it, and that "the efforts of landowners who acted to help the Preble's were cancelled by those who sought to harm it."[82] This led the study's authors to conclude that "as more landowners become aware that their land contains Preble's habitat, it is likely that the impact on the species may be negative."[83]

These studies, taken together and combined with the wealth of anecdotal accounts, provide powerful evidence that the ESA has the potential to discourage species conservation on private land. Worse, they suggest that the net effect of the ESA on private land could be negative, at least for some species. Recent administrations have sought to offset these effects through various programs and initiatives designed to encourage voluntary conservation efforts and provide landowners with greater regulatory certainty. Yet such regulatory assurances and "safe harbors" can only go so far to reduce the economic consequence of species listings for private landowners, and there is only so much flexibility in the law itself. Such reforms may ameliorate the anti-environmental incentives created by the Act, but they do not eliminate them.[84] So long as privately owned habitat is subject to greater regulatory burdens than other land, there will be an incentive against owning and maintaining land with habitat characteristics.

The threat of regulation can also affect the willingness of landowners to participate in voluntary conservation agreements.[85] As Michael Bean has observed, there is "a simple unwillingness to do the mundane management activities that could create or enhance habitat for rare species" due to fears of potential ESA regulation.[86] This is a problem because, "in numerous cases, the absence of harmful behavior may not be enough" to conserve and recover endangered species.[87] A large percentage, if not an absolute majority, of listed species subsist on land where active management is necessary for their conservation.[88] This means effective conservation requires either the imposition of greater regulatory requirements on private landowners or innovative ways to encourage voluntary conservation efforts on private land.

Ending Anti-Conservation Incentives

Species listings trigger the regulation of government activities and private land. As a consequence, the ESA inevitably penalizes private owners of species habitat and thus discourages the creation and maintenance of habitat conditions. Eliminating these negative incentives requires eliminating the economic burdens imposed by species listings.[89] Easing permit conditions or providing modest assurances for good behavior may be all that the current statute allows, but any lasting solution to the private land problem in species conservation requires much more.

Protecting private landowners from potential negative consequences of owning endangered species habitat—either by ending the regulation of habitat modification or ensuring that landowners are compensated when their ability to make reasonable use of their land is limited for the benefit of an endangered species—would remove the largest obstacle to greater landowner participation in conservation efforts. Many landowners are very willing to cooperate with conservation goals so long as they are not forced to bear the lion's share of the cost. Many landowners are often naturally willing to learn about, and even enhance, the ecological value of their land. Again, however, this must be something for which they will not be punished economically if landowners are to be drawn into conservation efforts.

There are many different tools available for the promotion of conservation objectives. Although rarely relied upon by regulatory agencies, "voluntary mechanisms (such as fee simple purchase, easements, conservation banking, and subsidies) are an effective and flexible method for targeting low-cost land with high-quality habitat."[90] Other forms of financial incentives could also improve species conservation on private land by offsetting the costs of regulation.

Government agencies have begun to create incentives for species and habitat conservation. In addition to various federal incentive programs, there are an estimated four hundred state incentive programs covering approximately seventy million acres of private land.[91] These programs range from straightforward financial incentives and easement purchases to landowner education programs and the provision of technical assistance.[92] Such programs have significant promise. The experience with non-regulatory wetland conservation programs suggests that it is often possible to save more land at lower economic (and political) cost through voluntary, cooperative efforts than through coercive regulation.[93] Yet despite the proliferation of incentive programs, such approaches remain grossly under-utilized and their effectiveness compromised by the underlying incentive structure created by the Act.

A compensation requirement is one way to eliminate nearly entirely the ESA's anti-environmental incentives on private land. It could also improve the incentives faced by conservation agencies.[94] Yet compensation is not a cure-all for the failings of the ESA's regulatory provisions. A compensation requirement, if not paired with broader programmatic reforms, may reduce the perverse incentives faced by landowners, but it would be insufficient to encourage greater consideration of species conservation on private land or enhance the effectiveness of government agencies. Nonetheless, requiring compensation would provide a firmer foundation for successful species conservation on private land.

Endangered Science

The punitive nature of the ESA's restrictions on private land not only undermine conservation, but they also appear to be undermining the science upon which successful species conservation efforts depend as well. This occurs in two ways. First, landowners increasingly resist allowing biologists and others onto their land to conduct research, survey species populations, and the like. Second, because the listing of a species as endangered automatically triggers burdensome regulatory consequences, landowners and others exert themselves to influence the outcome when a listing decision is to be made. These efforts are guided by self-interest rather than by science.

The threat of land-use regulation discourages private landowners from disclosing information and cooperating with scientific research on their land, further compromising species conservation efforts.[95] Some landowners fear that the discovery of endangered or threatened species populations will lead to the imposition of regulatory controls.[96] Perhaps as a consequence, most research on endangered species occurs on government land, despite the importance of private land for species preservation.[97] This can have broad consequences due to the importance of private land for species conservation.

Consider that, in some cases, "a private landowner might be the only individual who knows a listed species is on his or her land."[98] This information asymmetry makes government efforts to conserve species on private land particularly difficult.[99] Insofar as the ESA discourages landowner cooperation with scientific research, current estimates may actually underestimate the presence of endangered species on private lands.[100] The aforementioned *Conservation Biology* study of the effect of listing the Preble's Meadow jumping mouse on landowner behavior found that most landowners would refuse to give biologists permission to conduct research on their land to assess mouse populations, out of fear that land-use restrictions would follow the discovery of a mouse on their land.[101] Yet information about the location and status of species populations is essential to the development of effective species recovery plans.[102] The lack of more complete data on endangered species and their habitat greatly complicates species conservation efforts.[103]

With so much at stake when a species is listed, the scientific integrity of the listing process is put under enormous pressure. The ESA requires that decisions to list endangered and threatened species should be determined by the "best available" scientific evidence. Yet there is ample empirical evidence that political and other non-scientific factors influence listing decisions.[104] Early listing decisions in particular were driven by politics and preferences.[105] Species that were more "charismatic"—that is more "warm and fuzzy" or politically popular—were more likely to be listed and to receive funding.[106] Other recent studies have found that the political and environmental attitudes of legislators on relevant congressional committees appears to influence listing decisions as well.[107] These findings should not surprise. Listing decisions can force the federal government to adopt various regulatory measures with significant economic consequences. With so much at stake, it would be surprising if political and other factors did not influence listing decisions.

Given the structure of the ESA, various interest groups seek to manipulate the listing process so as to trigger or preempt the imposition of land-use restrictions.[108] Property owners who own potential habitat for a given species are likely to oppose listing of the species so as to prevent regulation of their land.[109] Opponents of development are likely to take the opposite view. Interest group activity also appears to influence how quickly species move through the ESA listing process.[110] Interest group opposition to species listing proposals increases as listings threaten development.[111] At the extreme, this has produced incentives to manipulate the scientific evidence supporting species listing.[112]

Delay in the listing of a species can benefit those landowners and economic interests that would have borne the costs of the ESA's regulatory limitations. At the same time, it can be harmful to conservation.[113] Delay in listing a species increases the opportunity for landowners to respond to the perverse incentives created by the Act.[114] It also deprives biologists, environmental groups, conservation-minded landowners, and others of the information that a given species is in need of assistance if it is to survive.

Not only may delay allow for the preemptive destruction of habitat, but it also may enable those in the regulated community to marshal scientific evidence that may suggest the listing is unwarranted.[115] As a listing is delayed, there is a possibility that the scientific data upon which the potential listing was based could become outdated.[116] Empirical research confirms that the longer it takes for a species listing to be proposed, its chances for eventual listing appear to decline.[117] If listing is the first step toward a species' recovery—a debatable proposition for reasons discussed above—political opposition to listing is environmentally worrisome.[118]

Groups opposing development or resource extractive industries also have an incentive to manipulate the listing process and identify potentially endangered species that can serve as a proxy for their other goals. Environmentalist groups have acknowledged that some species listings are sought out of a desire to control land use. For example, Andy Stahl of the

Sierra Club Legal Defense Fund acknowledged that "the ultimate goal" of litigation to list the northern spotted owl was "to delay the harvest of old growth forests so as to give Congress a chance to provide specific statutory protection for those forests." According to Stahl, the owl was a "surrogate" that could ensure "protection for the forests" under the Endangered Species Act.[119] The spotted owl litigation was not without its environmental costs, however. In order to respond to environmentalist lawsuits, the FWS was forced to divert resources from more pressing needs, compromising overall recovery efforts.[120] This does not appear to be an isolated instance, as the pattern of environmentalist litigation challenging FWS listing decisions does not appear to align with species conservation priorities. During the 1990s, outside groups sued to list threatened species three times as often as for endangered species.[121]

Insofar as such litigation sets listing priorities, it threatens to divert resources away from those species most in need. The FWS reports that it has spent "essentially all" of its listing appropriations on litigation-related and administrative costs.[122] As Professor Katrina Wyman of New York University explains: "The FWS has lost control over the listing process as decisions about whether to list species are largely made in response to citizen petitions for listing and litigation."[123] Both environmentalist groups and development interests wage legal wars over the listing and delisting of individual species as a proxy for fights over policy and regulatory priorities.

The above suggests that the ESA's current regulatory structure both discourages conservation and compromises conservation science. For these reasons, Professor Wyman recommends "decoupling" the listing decision from mandatory conservation measures.[124] This would enable federal agencies "to develop protections tailored to the needs of each species and its circumstances."[125] At present, however, the ESA's "protections" are triggered once a species is listed, regardless of their value for that particular species.[126] Decoupling would also "reduce the contentiousness of listing decisions by reducing the momentousness of listing."[127] While it would still make sense for listing to trigger a legal obligation for the FWS to develop a conservation strategy and recovery plan, it would not force the imposition of specific regulatory controls. This would mean that outside organizations would no longer be able to use endangered species as a proxy for other battles. As Professor Wyman explains, "One of the advantages of decoupling the listing of a species from decisions about how it should be protected is that there should be greater room for developing creative measures tailored to species' needs and circumstances."[128]

Foundational Reforms

If the ESA, as currently constituted, cannot do the job of conserving species, what would do the trick? Three foundational reforms, suggested above, are necessary, combined with the funding to carry them out. First, the ESA must no longer penalize landowners for owning endangered species habitat. If anything, owning habitat should be rewarded. This requires greater use of non-regulatory measures and compensating landowners for the costs of habitat regulation.

Second, the listing process should be insulated from political and economic pressure. The surest way to accomplish this is to "decouple" listing from mandatory regulatory measures. Such a reform would necessarily increase agency discretion in selecting among conservation policy options, but this is a feature, not a bug. Not every species will benefit from the same set of conservation tools, and enabling conservation agencies to pick from a menu of tools—and even develop new ones—is preferable to an automatic regulatory hammer triggered by a precautionary scientific finding. Conservation policy measures should be chosen by politically accountable regulators, and not be a function of triage or outcome of litigation in federal courts.

Third, Congress should recognize that, insofar as species habitat is a public good of value to the nation, it should be provided like any other public good through government subsidy, direct or indirect. This could well mean that federal resources devoted to species conservation increase; if so, that is simply the cost of this nation's conservation commitment. In 1973, the country declared it would take the measures to conserve the nation's biodiversity. Substantial ESA reform and adequate funding are the only way that promise can be fulfilled.

Notes

1. Michael J. Bean, "The Endangered Species Act: Science, Policy, and Politics," *The Year in Ecology and Conservation Biology, 2009: Annals of the New York Academy of Sciences*, 1162 (2009): 369.

2. Ibid.

3. Gardner M. Brown Jr. and Jason F. Shogren, "Economics of the Endangered Species Act," *Journal of Economic Perspectives* 12, no. 3 (1998): 3.

4. Lynn E. Dwyer, Dennis D. Murphy, and Paul R. Ehrlich, "Property Rights Case Law and the Challenges to the Endangered Species Act," *Conservation Biology* 9 (1995): 736. See also Daniel J. Rohlf, "Six Biological Reasons Why the Endangered Species Act Doesn't Work—And What to Do About It," *Conservation Biology* 5, no. 3 (1991): 274 ("the Act has had very limited success in achieving its stated goal of halting and reversing the trend toward species extinction.").

5. Mark W. Schwartz, "The Performance of the Endangered Species Act," *Annual Review of Ecology, Evolution, and Systematics*, 39 (2008): 280.

6. David S. Wilcove, David Rothstein, Jason Dubow, Ali Phillips, and Elizabeth Losos, "Quantifying Threats to Imperiled Species in the United States," *BioScience* 48 (1998): 607 ("scientists agree that habitat destruction is the primary lethal agent"); ibid. at 609 (finding that habitat destruction and degradation contributed to the endangerment of 85 percent of species analyzed).

7. U.S. General Accounting Office, *Endangered Species Act: Information on Species Protection on Nonfederal Lands* (1994). See also David S. Wilcove and Joon Lee, "Using Economic and Regulatory Incentives to Restore Endangered Species: Lessons Learned from Three Programs," *Conservation Biology* 18 (2004): 640 (Wilcove and Lee say the estimate that "private lands harbor at least one population of two-thirds of all federally listed species...is almost certainly an underestimate"); Jodi Hilty and Adina Merenlender, "Studying Biodiversity on Private Lands," *Conservation Biology* 17 (2003): 133 (noting 95 percent of endangered plant and animal species have some habitat on private land); and Barton H. Thompson, Jr., "Conservation Options: Toward a Greater Private Role," *Virginia Environmental Law Journal* 21 (2002): 249 (noting "much of the key riparian land in the West is in private hands" and that "some valuable ecosystems are found only on private lands").

8. David S. Wilcove, "The Private Side of Conservation," *Frontiers in Ecology and the Environment* 2, no. 6 (2004): 326 ("between one-third and one-half of all species protected under the US Endangered Species Act [ESA] do not occur on federal lands; many of these species presumably reside on private lands.").

9. See Hilty and Merenlender, "Studying Biodiversity," 133 ("Although there are exceptions, private lands tend to be more productive, better watered, and higher in soil quality than public land."); and Victoria L. Dreitz and Fritz L. Knopf, "Mountain Plovers and the Politics of Research on Private Lands," *Bioscience* 57 (2007): 681 ("In general, private lands are more productive, better watered, and higher in soil quality than public lands."). Both papers cite J. Michael Scott, Frank W. Davis, R. Gavin McGhie, R. Gerald Wright, Craig Groves, and John Estes, "Nature Reserves: Do They Capture the Full Range of America's Biological Diversity?" *Ecological Applications* 11 (2001): 999–1007.

10. Martin B. Main, Fritz M. Roka, and Reed F. Noss, "Evaluating Costs of Conservation," *Conservation Biology* 13 (1999): 1263 ("Regulatory mechanisms such as the U.S. Endangered Species Act of 1973 [ESA] are controversial and have not been particularly effective at preventing the loss of wildlife habitat, especially on private lands.").

11. Erik Stokstad, "What's Wrong with the Endangered Species Act?" *Science* 30 (2005): 2152.

12. Barton H. Thompson, Jr., "Managing the Working Landscape," in *The Endangered Species Act at Thirty, Volume 1: Renewing the Conservation Promise*, ed. Dale D. Goble, J. Michael Scott, and Frank W. Davis (Washington, D.C.: Island Press, 2006), 125.

13. The modern environmental movement should be distinguished from the prior conservation movement, which began decades earlier. See Jonathan H. Adler, *Environmentalism at the Crossroads: Green Activism in America* (Washington, D.C.: Capital Research Center, 1995), 1–5.

14. Quoted in Michael J. Bean, "Historical Background to the Endangered Species Act," in *Endangered Species Act: Law, Policy, and Perspectives*, ed. Donald C. Baur and William Robert Irvin (Chicago: American Bar Association, 2002), 16–17.

15. Ibid.

16. 16 U.S.C. §1536.

17. 16 U.S.C. §1538.

18. See *Babbitt v. Sweet Home Chapter of Communities for a Great Oregon*, 515 U.S. 687 (1995).

19. 437 U.S. 153 (1978).

20. Ibid., 184.

21. J. Michael Scott, Dale D. Goble, John A. Wiens, David S. Wilcove, Michael Bean, and Timothy Male, "Recovery of Imperiled Species under the Endangered Species Act: The Need for a New Approach," *Frontiers in Ecology and the Environment*

3, no. 7 (2005): 384 ("Since the inception of the Endangered Species Act in 1973, the number of endangered and threatened species listed has risen steadily.").

22. U.S. Fish & Wildlife Service, "Summary of Listed Species, Listed Populations and Recovery Plans," http://ecos.fws.gov/tess_public/TESSBoxscore (accessed August 23, 2009).

23. According to the FWS, eleven domestic and five foreign species are counted more than once because distinct populations are listed separately.

24. According to the FWS, there are 591 draft and final recovery plans, some of which cover more than one species.

25. 16 U.S.C. § 1531.

26. Scott et al., "Recovery," 383.

27. Bean, *ESA: Science, Policy, and Politics*, 387.

28. Scott et al., "Recovery," 387.

29. Joe Kerkvliet and Christian Langpap, "Learning from Endangered and Threatened Species Recovery Programs: A Case Study Using U.S. Endangered Species Act Recovery Scores," *Ecological Economics* 63 (2007): 500.

30. U.S. Fish & Wildlife Service, "Delisting Report," http://ecos.fws.gov/tess_public/DelistingReport.do (accessed August 23, 2009).

31. U.S. Fish & Wildlife Service, "Reclassified Species," http://ecos.fws.gov/tess_public/ReclassifiedSpecies.do (accessed August 23, 2009).

32. Martin Miller, "Three Decades of Recovery," *Endangered Species Bulletin* 28, no. 4 (July/December 2003): 4.

33. D. Noah Greenwald, Kieran F. Suckling, and Martin Taylor, "The Listing Record," in *The Endangered Species Act at Thirty, Volume 1: Renewing the Conservation Promise*, ed. Dale D. Goble, J. Michael Scott, and Frank W. Davis (Washington, D.C.: Island Press, 2006), 51.

34. Dale D. Goble, "Recovery in a Cynical Time—With Apologies to Eric Arthur Blair," *Washington Law Review* 82 (2007): 586–88.

35. Ibid., 589–90.

36. Julie K. Miller, J. Michael Scott, Craig R. Miller, and Lisette P. Waits, "The Endangered Species Act: Dollars and Sense?" *Bioscience* 52, no. 2 (February 2002): 164–66.

37. Krishna Gifford, "Measuring Recovery Success," *Endangered Species Bulletin* 32, no. 3 (Fall 2007): 4.

38. J. Michael Scott, Dale D. Goble, Leona K. Svancara, and Anna Pidgorna, "By the Numbers," in *The Endangered Species Act at Thirty, Volume 1: Renewing the Conservation Promise*, ed. Dale D. Goble, J. Michael Scott, and Frank W. Davis (Washington, D.C.: Island Press, 2006), 31.

39. Gifford, "Measuring," 4.

40. Martin F. J. Taylor, Kieran F. Suckling, and Jeffrey J. Rachlinski, "The Effectiveness of the Endangered Species Act: A Quantitative Analysis," *Bioscience* 55 (2005): 365.

41. Ibid., 365.

42. Ibid., 361 .

43. Kerkvliet and Langpap, "Learning," 499–510.

44. Jeffrey E. Zabel and Robert W. Patterson, "The Effects of Critical Habitat Designation on Housing Supply: An Analysis of California Housing Construction Activity," *Journal of Regional Science* 46 (2006): 67-95.

45. See Taylor, Suckling, and Rachlinski, "Effectiveness," 360–67.

46. Ibid., 364.

47. R.J.F. Abbit and J.M. Scott, "Examining Differences Between Recovered and Declining Endangered Species," *Conservation Biology* 15 (2001): 1274–84.

48. Kerkvliet and Langpap, "Learning,"

49. J. Alan Clark, Jonathan M. Hoekstra, P. Dee Boersma, and Peter Kareiva, "Improving U.S. Endangered Species Act Recovery Plans: Key Findings and Recommendations of the SCB Recovery Plan Project," *Conservation Biology* 16 (2002): 1514; see also P.D. Boersma, "How Good Are Endangered Species Recovery Plans?" *Bioscience* 51 (2001): 643–49.

50. Paul J. Ferraro, Craig McIntosh, and Monica Ospina, "The Effectiveness of the U.S. Endangered Species Act: An Econometric Analysis Using Matching Methods," *Journal of Environmental Economics and Management* 54 (2007), 247.

51. Kerkvleit and Langpap, "Learning," 506.

52. Ibid.

53. Ibid., 508.

54. Ibid.

55. Ibid., 506.

56. Ferraro, McIntosh, and Ospina, "Effectiveness," 246.
   "Our results indicate that success can be achieved when the ESA is combined with substantial species-specific spending, but listing in the absence of funding appears to have adverse consequences for species recovery. This implies that using scarce conservation funding in the contentious process of listing a species may be less effective than using this funding to promote recovery directly."

57. Ibid., 252.

58. Ibid., 256.

59. Ibid.

60. It is possible that efforts to conserve candidate species through so-called "candidate conservation agreements" might eventually provide data that could be used for such a comparison.

61. Ferraro, McIntosh, and Ospina, "Effectiveness," 256.

62. Ibid.

63. Schwartz, "Performance," 293

64. Brown and Shogren, "Economics," 10.

65. Robert Bonnie, "Endangered Species Mitigation Banking: Promoting Recovery through Habitat Conservation Planning under the Endangered Species Act," *The Science of the Total Environment* 240 (1999): 12.

66. Rudy Abramson, "Wildlife Act: Shield or Sword?" *Los Angeles Times* (December 14, 1990).

67. Main, Roka, and Noss, "Evaluating Costs," 1263.

68. Ibid. 1265.

69. Betsy Carpenter, "The Best-Laid Plans," *U.S. News & World Report*, October 4, 1993, 89.

70. Michael J. Bean, "Overcoming Unintended Consequences of Endangered Species Regulation," *Idaho Law Review* 38 (2002): 415.

71. 60 *Federal Register* 9507–8 (February 17, 1995).

72. See David Wright, "Death to Tweety," *New Republic*, July 6, 1992, 9–10; and James V. DeLong, *Property Matters* (New York: The Free Press, 1997), 103.

73. David Parrish, "Environmental dilemma," *Los Angeles Daily News*, March 19, 1995, 10. Similarly, in California's Central Valley, farmers plow fallow fields to destroy potential habitat and prevent the growth of vegetation that could attract endangered species. Jennifer Warren, "Revised Species Protection Law Eases Farmers' Anxiety," *Los Angeles Times* (Oct. 11, 1997).

74. Dean Lueck and Jeffrey Michael, "Preemptive Habitat Destruction under the Endangered Species Act," *Journal of Law and Economics*, vol. 46 (2003); 27–60.

75. Ibid., 33.

76. Ibid., 51–52.

77. Ibid., 53–54.

78. Daowei Zhang, "Endangered Species and Timber Harvesting: The Case of Red-Cockaded Woodpeckers," *Economic Inquiry*, 32 (2004): 150.

79. Ibid., 151, 160.

80. Ibid., 162.

81. Amara Brook, Michael Zint, and Raymond De Young, "Landowners' Responses to an Endangered Species Act Listing and Implications for Encouraging Conservation," *Conservation Biology* 17 (2003): 1638.

82. Ibid., 1643.

83. Ibid., 1644. A fourth study, looking at yet another species in another part of the country, found further evidence that species listing can accelerate the rate of habitat loss, albeit not conclusively. See John A. List, Michael Margolis, and Daniel E. Osgood, *Is the Endangered Species Act Endangering Species?* NBER Working Paper No. 12777 (December 2006).

84. Richard A. Epstein, "*Babbitt v. Sweet Home Chapters of Oregon:* The Law and Economics of Habitat Preservation," *Supreme Court Economic Review* 5 (1997): 33.

85. Christian Langpap and JunJie Wu, "Voluntary Conservation of Endangered Species: When Does No Regulatory Assurance Mean No Conservation?" *Journal of Environmental Economics and Management* 47 (2004): 435.

86. Bean, "Overcoming," 415.

87. Langpap and Wu, "Voluntary Conservation," 436.

88. Wilcove, "The Private Side," 326.

89. It can also be argued that simple fairness requires the elimination of these disproportionate burdens as well, but such normative considerations are beyond the scope of this chapter.

90. Gregory M. Parkhurst and Jason F. Shogren, "An Economic Review of Incentive Mechanisms to Protect Species on Private Lands," in *Species at Risk: Using Economic Incentives to Shelter Endangered Species on Private Lands*, ed. Jason F. Shogren (Austin: University of Texas Press, 2005), 121.

91. Jason F. Shogren, introduction to *Species at Risk*, 10.

92. Ibid.

93. See Jonathan H. Adler, "Money or Nothing: The Adverse Environmental Consequences of Uncompensated Land Use Controls," *Boston College Law Review* 49, no. 2 (2008): 354–61; and David Sunding, "An Opening for Meaningful Reform," *Regulation* (Summer 2003): 31–33.

94. Adler, "Money or Nothing," 337–51.

95. Stephen Polasky and Holly Doremus, "When the Truth Hurts: Endangered Species Policy on Private Land with Imperfect Information," *Journal of Environmental Economics and Management* 35 (1998): 41.

96. Hilty and Merenlender, "Studying Biodiversity," 136; and Dreitz and Knopf, "Politics of Research," 681.

97. Hilty and Merenlender, "Studying Biodiverstiy," 133.

98. Jason F. Shogren, Rodney B.W. Smith, and John Tschirhart, "The Role of Private Information in Designing Conservation Incentives for Property Owners," in *Species at Risk: Using Economic Incentives to Shelter Endangered Species on Private Lands*, ed. Jason F. Shogren (Austin: University of Texas Press, 2005), 217.

99. Barton H. Thompson, Jr., "The Endangered Species Act: A Case Study in Takings and Incentives," *Stanford Law Review* 49 (1997): 315; see also James Salzman, "Creating Markets for Ecosystem Services," *N.Y.U. Environmental Law Review* 80 (2005): 916 (noting information asymmetry between government regulators and private landowners).

100. Wilcove and Lee, "Using Economic and Regulatory Incentives," 640 (noting likely underestimate due to "the reluctance of many private landowners to cooperate with surveys for endangered species").

101. Brook, Zint, and De Young, "Landowners' Responses," 1644.

102. Ibid. ("Without this information, formulating conservation plans is difficult, and those that are formed may be inaccurate, perceived as illegitimate, or challenged in the courts because of a lack of supporting data.").

103. Shogren, Smith, and Tschirhart, "Role," 217 (noting that "imperfect information" complicates conservation efforts).

104. Ferraro, McIntosh, and Ospina, "Effectiveness," 246.

105. Holly Doremus, "Listing Decisions Under the Endangered Species Act: Why Better Science Isn't Always Better Policy," *Washington University Law Quarterly* 75 (1997): 1029–153.

106. Deborah Dawson and Jason F. Shogren, "An Update on Priorities and Expenditures under the Endangered Species Act," *Land Economics* 77 (2001): 527–32; and Andrew Metrick and Martin L. Weitzman, "Patterns of Behavior in Endangered Species Preservation," *Land Economics* 72 (1996): 1–16; See also Andrew Metrick and Martin L. Weitzman, "Conflicts and Choices in Biodiversity Preservation," *Journal of Economic Perspectives* 12 (1998): 21–32.

107. Bonnie Harllee, Myungsup Kim, and Michael Nieswiadomy, "Political Influence on Historical ESA Listings by State: A Count Data Analysis, *Public Choice* 140 (2009): 21–42. Harllee, Kim, and Nieswiadomy survey the relevant academic literature at 23–24.

108. Epstein, "*Babbitt*," 34 ("designation systems have two substantial costs: one is destruction before designation, and the other is the use of the political process to deny, delay or deflect the designations that might come.").

109. Thompson, "ESA," 350.

110. Amy Whritenour Ando, "Waiting to Be Protected under the Endangered Species Act: The Political Economy of Regulatory Delay," *Journal of Law and Economics* 42 (1999): 52.

111. Amy Whritenour Ando, "Economies of Scope in Endangered-Species Protection: Evidence from Interest Group Behavior," *Journal of Environmental Economics and Management* 41 (2001): 312; and Amy Whritenour Ando, "Do Interest Groups Compete? An Application to Endangered Species," *Public Choice* 114 (2003): 137 (finding interest group involvement in species listings increases with the expected costs and benefits of such listings).

112. For a recent example of such manipulation see Juliet Eilperin, "Report Faults Interior Appointee; Landowner Issues Trumped Animal Protections, IG Says," *Washington Post*, March 30, 2007 (senior Bush Administration official altered scientific field reports to minimize protections for imperiled species).

113. Ando, "Waiting," 34 ("Long delay in the addition of a species to the endangered species list can reduce the likelihood that the species will escape extinction; species have even been thought to have become extinct while waiting for final action from the agency. Thus, delay diminishes the benefits of a listing. It also reduces the costs.").

114. Ando, "Waiting," 36 ("delay can enable private citizens and firms to take preemptive irreversible actions [harvesting trees, developing land] on the land that will be protected once the listing is made.").

115. Ibid. ("Timing may also influence outcome" because "delay in the early stages of the process probably makes it more likely that a candidate species is sent back in the process rather than being moved forward during listing.").

116. Ibid.

117. Ibid., 45.

118. Thompson, "ESA," 350.

119. Ike C. Sugg, "Caught in the Act: Evaluating the Endangered Species Act, Its Effects on Man and Prospects for Reform," *Cumberland Law Review* 24 (1993): 53.

120. Marco Restain and John M. Marzluff, "Funding Extinction? Biological Needs and Political Realities in the Allocation of Resources to Endangered Species Recovery," *Bioscience* 52, no. 2 (Feb. 2002): 175.

121. Ibid., 174

122. Katrina Miriam Wyman, "Rethinking the ESA to Reflect Human Dominion Over Nature," *NYU Environmental Law Journal*, 17 (2008): 497.

123. Ibid., 496.

124. Ibid., 516.

125. Ibid.

126. Bean, "Endangered Species Act," 373 (noting that species are listed without regard for whether the Act's prohibitions "address the threats that imperil a species").

127. Ibid.

128. Wyman, "Rethinking," 519.

2

Reforming Section 10
and the Habitat Conservation Program

David A. Dana

One of the central dilemmas of the Endangered Species Act (ESA) is how to foster species conservation and recovery on private land. Much of the habitat occupied by endangered species is on private land: according to some estimates, more than two thirds of listed endangered species can be found on private land.[1] Even in areas where there is substantial federal land that contains critical habitat, the federal land often is part of a patchwork of federal, state, local, and purely private holdings. Moreover, the Act treats land owned by states and localities as private land. Thus, for many endangered species, any comprehensive recovery plan must extend to private land.

In theory, the ESA powerfully addresses the risks posed to endangered species by private development and other economic activity on private land in Section 9 of the Act. That section prohibits the "taking" of endangered species on private land. "Take" is broadly defined to "harass, harm, pursue, hunt, shoot, wound, kill, trap, capture, or collect, or to attempt to engage in any such conduct."[2] The Fish and Wildlife Service's regulation that implements Section 9 clearly encompasses private development activity that kills or prevents the reproduction of protected species members,[3] and the United States Supreme Court upheld that regulation in *Babbitt v. Sweet Home Chapter of Communities for a Greater Oregon*.[4]

In practice, however, there have been relatively few Section 9 enforcement actions brought by the government or Section 9 citizens' suits. One reason that government regulators and citizen groups have brought few Section 9 actions is that there generally is much less information available to the government or the public regarding what is happening on private land than there is about what is happening on federal land. In addition, aggressive regulation of private land generally is much more controversial politically and troubling to judges than aggressive regulation of federal land. Indeed, the United States Supreme Court in *Sweet Home* expressed some concerns about the legality of any aggressive applications of Section 9 pursuant to the Fish and Wildlife Service (FWS) regulation.[5] Moreover, the sheer number of private holdings with endangered species populations, when coupled with the high costs of government enforcement or citizen suit litigation, means that only a fairly small percentage of plausible Section 9 actions could ever be brought.

Perhaps because there have been relatively few Section 9 actions, most of the attention with respect to the preservation of species on private land has focused instead on Section 10. Enacted as part of amendments to the Act in 1982, Section 10 allows the Secretary of the Interior to permit "incidental takings" of endangered species that otherwise would be illegal under Section 9. An incidental take is one where the harm to the species is not intentional—that is, it is not the goal of the landowner's action—but is rather incidental to the landowner's activities on the land (such as clearing scrub with habitat as part of an effort to build a new residential subdivision). According to Section 10, the Secretary may grant an incidental take permit only in conjunction with an approved habitat conservation plan (HCP).[6]

Section 10 anticipates a two-part process: an application by a landowner that includes a conservation plan and the discretionary approval of the conservation plan by the Secretary based on certain required findings. The landowner's submitted conservation plan must specify, among other things, "the impact which will likely result from [the] taking," "what steps the applicant will take to minimize and mitigate such impacts," "the funding that will be available to implement such steps," and "what alternative actions to such taking the applicant considered and the reasons why such alternatives are not being utilized." The Secretary may grant the permit only upon finding that the "taking will be incidental," "the applicant will, to the maximum extent practicable, minimize and mitigate the impacts of such taking," "the applicant will ensure that adequate funding for the plan will be provided," and, it would seem most critically, "the taking will not appreciably reduce the likelihood of the survival or recovery of the species in the wild."[7]

What is not in the text of Section 10 is important, and (as discussed below) the Section could benefit from more specific directives by Congress to the federal regulators regarding the content of HCPs. Section 10 does not mandate serious public participation in the HCP formation and approval process but merely mentions the need for "public comment" prior to a final decision by the Secretary. Nor is there any provision regarding the quality of the scientific review needed for an HCP to be approved or the role of any scientific advisory committees. The funding provision does require that the landowner/applicant demonstrate adequate funding to execute the plan, but says nothing about funding for measures *not* included in the plan that may prove necessary to secure the species' survival or recovery. For example, where a plan just prohibits a landowner from draining or contaminating a wetland on his land that provides habitat to an endangered bird population, Section 10 would not seem to require that the landowner reserve funds to finance the replenishment of the wetland or creation of substitute wetlands in the event it dries up during an extended heat wave or drought.

Section 10, indeed, says almost nothing about what happens *after* the plan is approved. There is no cap on the length of the permit, and the Secretary is not required to review periodically compliance with a plan or, perhaps even more important, the actual condition of the species population (regardless of whether there is compliance with the plan). The Act provides only that "the Secretary shall revoke a permit issued under this paragraph if he finds that the permittee is not complying with the terms and conditions of the permit."[8] That provision does not require the Secretary to take measures to find out if there is compliance or to find out whether compliance has been sufficient to assure species survival and recovery.

Section 10 and the entire concept of incidental permits and habitat conservation plans had little practical impact prior to the Clinton Administration: only a dozen or so HCPs were approved in the first decade after the passage of Section 10 in 1982. Almost all of these involved relatively small parcels of land and had a single-species focus. Then, during the Clinton

Administration, Secretary of the Interior Bruce Babbitt made HCPs a center-piece of species conservation. Approximately 300 HCPs had been approved by the end of 2000, including a number of large-scale HCPs encompassing vast areas of land. HCP activity continued during the Bush Administration, such that more than 200 additional HCPs had received approval by the end of 2007.[9] It does appear, however, that there were fewer proposals for ambitious HCPs during the Bush Administration and there was less attention in policymaking and academic circles to HCPs and their merits.

This may change: we may be at a moment of renewed attention to the HCP process and HCP outcomes and perhaps fundamental HCP reform. The HCP program is an example of what I have elsewhere called "contractarian regulation"—regulation in which the government and an entity that would otherwise be subject to command-and-control regulation contract into an alternative regulatory arrangement that allows the entity to avoid some formal requirements while allowing the government to require actions on the part of the entity that go beyond the scope of current formal legal mandates. In contractarian regimes, the private actors are willing to enter into "voluntary" contract-like binding arrangements because the threat of the imposition of command-and-control regulation is real enough that it is worthwhile to contract out of that threat.[10] To the extent that "the Services"—the FWS of the Department of the Interior (DOI) and the National Oceanic and Atmospheric Administration (NOAA) at the Department of Commerce—under the Obama Administration credibly can communicate a greater willingness to consider Section 9 enforcement actions than they could under the Bush Administration (which is plausible), landowners may well be more willing to engage in the HCP process. From the perspective of environmental groups and concerned policymakers and citizens, moreover, renewed attention to HCPs also makes sense because the general limitations in achieving preservation via Section 9 and other provisions of the ESA remain (e.g., lack of information about private land, formal limitation of regulatory authority to habitat of listed species only). Moreover, climate change and continuing urbanization mean that the threats of species extinction are greater than they ever have been.

This chapter provides a framework for HCP reform. I first briefly review the history of HCP regulations and guidance and what we know about HCPs in practice (which is limited). I offer a range of reforms to address problems in the current HCP approach, including requirements that the Services assemble a better database regarding current HCPs and report to Congress on the program periodically; greater reliance on programmatic regulations adopted after notice and comment; development of guidelines for assessing the likely or possible environmental impacts of HCPs upfront, at the time an HCP is proposed, and the development of separate rules, processes, and requirements for HCPs depending on the possible range of impacts; enhanced citizen enforcement of at least high-impact HCPs by means of explicit authorization of citizens' suits to enforce HCPs; reliance on scientific advisory boards to provide scientific legitimacy with respect to high-impact HCPs; development of public-private insurance to address the long-term uncertainty posed by high-impact HCPs; and development of rules and plans for greater reliance on conservation banks to address the long-term uncertainty posed by smaller-scale, lower-impact HCPs.

The last two reforms would probably be the most controversial but perhaps the most important. There is extraordinary uncertainty as to whether HCPs will really work in stabilizing species populations let alone achieving recovery, and that uncertainty is not simply an artifact of flaws in how particular HCPs may have been put together to date. We really know surprisingly little about how particular species populations in particular settings will fare under different circumstances; even when we know a great deal, achieving species conservation and recovery can be daunting. The federal government has spent billions on salmon recovery, and the very limited success so far may soon be undone by climate change.[11] Uncertainties abound not just as to how species populations will fare but as to our understanding of the importance of a given species for different ecosystems. There are limits to how much any program can deal with this long-term uncertainty but, so far, the HCP program has basically just ignored it.[12]

HCP Programs: A Brief History of
Administrative Regulations and Guidance

It is unclear whether Congress intended to transform the ESA when it enacted Section 10 in 1982. On the one hand, the House Conference Committee Report for the Amendments does suggest that the HCP process will "measurably reduce conflicts…and will provide the institutional framework to permit cooperation between the public and private sectors in the interest of endangered species and habitat conservation" and directs the Secretary of the Interior to "encourage creative partnerships between the public and private sectors and among governmental agencies…."[13] On the other hand, the legislative history indicates that HCPs are not intended to weaken the (very strong) mandates of the ESA, and the language of Section 10 itself does not codify a new or expanded vision for the ESA. The modest experience with HCPs in the ten or so years after the adoption of the 1982 amendments, moreover, tends to underscore how modest these amendments on their face appear to be.

Beginning in 1994, however, Secretary Babbitt undertook a remarkable transformation of the HCP program that had as its apparent mission transforming the ESA itself from a single-listed-species management tool to a multi-species, ecosystem management tool. This new approach was meant to encompass species and species clusters that had not yet diminished to the point of qualifying as endangered as well as species that were imperiled but had not, for whatever reason, made it onto the government's lists of threatened and endangered species. Secretary Babbitt's approach reflected a consensus that had emerged regarding species preservation, a consensus that the singular focus of the ESA on a single species at a time—and then only on a single species once it was on the verge of extinction and had been listed after an arduous and often litigious process—was untenable, from a biological point of view, from an economic point of view, and, ultimately, from a political point of view. According to Secretary Babbitt, the ESA's "train wreck" approach to ecological interventions was akin to a transportation safety regime that only came into play moments before two speeding trains were about to collide (the two trains being a species on the brink and human economic development at odds with preservation of the remnant population of that species).[14]

Under the new approach, intervention was to be made earlier rather than later and to be broad in terms of the number of species and natural conditions that garnered attention. In the new consensus, too, isolated animal populations on tiny fragments of land were unsustainable and hence undesirable. What was needed instead, according to the new consensus, were large tracts of habitat or, where that was impossible, smaller areas connected by protected habitat corridors. The DOI focused on providing incentives for landowners whose land harbored species that were not yet listed. In these arrangements, landowners would receive protection against any future regulatory interventions in return for their efforts to enrich habitat for species that were not yet listed or to create habitat that would be suitable for new populations of listed species.

As the HCP program was developed, landowners were concerned about the cost of preparing and complying with an HCP, but many were more concerned about the uncertainties of future regulatory treatment. In 1994, the DOI acted forcefully to address their concern about the uncertainty of future regulatory treatment by announcing and then adopting the so-called No Surprises Rule. This rule, adopted without any meaningful opportunity for public comment, has been controversial since its adoption.[15] It has been subject to a series of legal challenges, which later compelled DOI to accept public comments and codify the rule in regulations (it is also part of the HCP handbook). But throughout the protracted, multipart litigation, the substance of the rule has remained the same: that landowners who participate in an HCP receive a guarantee that even if the plan fails to result in the survival (let alone recovery) of a species population on the affected land, the landowners will not be asked to do more except "under extraordinary circumstances." Even then, what the landowners can be asked to do is quite limited, and any costs must be borne by the government. Under the rule, the government cannot ask for the dedication of new land or other conservation measures of a sort not already provided for in the plan, even upon a showing of extraordinary circumstances. Only if the government can show extraordinary circumstances can it ask for modifications on land already dedicated for conservation, and, even then, the government must pay for such modifications. Moreover, the protections for landowners apply to both listed and non-listed species that are included in the habitat conservation plan. And compliance with the plan—and hence receipt of No Surprises protection—is presumed on the part of the holder of a valid incidental take permit under Section 10. Finally, the DOI maintained that there is no maximum time limit on HCPs—and indeed, HCPs that last decades have been approved—and also that there is no time limit on the No Surprises guarantee.

Genuine questions can be raised as to whether the courts should have permitted the No Surprises Rule to stand and whether the questionable legal legitimacy of the No Surprises Rule has undermined the legitimacy of the HCP program to date. The plain text of the ESA does not seem to authorize the Secretary of the Interior to promise no surprises, no matter what, as the No Surprises Rule does. Moreover, as a matter of basic democratic theory, it is arguably troubling for regulators at any given point in time to promise, in what purports to be a contractually binding way, that the same regulatory treatment will be afforded ten or twenty or even fifty years hence.[16]

The No Surprises Rule is a helpful prism through which to understand key areas of controversy about HCPs: the controversy over the scientific grounding for HCPs; over the inclusion (or not) of biological goals, metrics, and adaptive management as part of the plans themselves; and the quality (or lack thereof) of monitoring and reporting on compliance. First, given the No Surprises guarantee, it seems especially important that HCPs be based on good data collection and the best scientific knowledge, as it will be costly or impossible for the government to force a departure from the plan. Yet there is significant evidence that some HCPs, including ones with potentially great environmental consequences, have been based on little or inadequate biological data.

Second, given that No Surprises means in effect that landowners cannot be asked to take any new measures outside the plan, it would seem very important that the plan itself build in measures that take into account possible changes in conditions and uncertainties, such as plan requirements of meeting biological goals and undertaking adaptive management. However, clear biological goals and metrics for meeting the goals and meaningful adaptive management requirements appear to be the exception rather than the rule in HCPs, even major HCPs. At best, the empirical evidence on how frequently these measures are built into HCPs is incomplete.

Finally, if compliance with the plan is to a large degree all the government can ever demand and compliance is presumed, it would seem key that landowners be required to engage in close monitoring and report the results in a way that would allow enforcement actions to be taken despite the presumption of compliance. Although all HCPs contain monitoring requirements, monitoring of compliance with HCPs appears to be highly inconsistent.[17] Enforcement by means of citizens' suits (or the threat of such suits) is undermined by the fact that HCP agreements generally have not identified citizens or citizen groups as third-party beneficiaries of the agreements, and hence it is doubtful whether citizen groups have standing to sue to enforce the terms of an HCP and to implement agreements entered into by the federal government and the landowner.[18]

Criticisms of HCPs in the wake of the No Surprises Rule crystallized around a 1998 report from Defenders of Wildlife, the title of which, *Frayed Safety Nets*, summarizes its central thesis regarding the reliability of HCPs in ensuring species protection.[19] In 1999, the DOI reportedly expressed a willingness to reform the HCP program to address concerns that had been raised by these studies and other reports of problematic HCPs.

At the very end of the Clinton Administration, the DOI did adopt some very general, informal "guidelines" that addressed some of the concerns raised by environmentalists. These guidelines were never adopted as formal agency regulations (although they were added as an addendum to the Department's HCP handbook after receipt of public comment[20]). Moreover, the guidelines are vague and aspirational, not prescriptive: the guidelines emphasize the importance of including biological goals in plans, adaptive management mechanisms, monitoring mechanisms, and public participation provisions, but they do not commit the agency to include any particular kinds of provisions or measures in all or some categories of HCPs. Similarly, the guidelines acknowledge concerns about the long duration of some HCPs, but do not commit the agency to any particular duration limit for all HCPs or any categories of HCPs.

Moreover, we have absolutely no way of knowing whether the DOI has changed any of its practices with regard to new or existing HCPs since 2000. Congress has not required reports about the HCP program, and no reports have been forthcoming. Private nongovernmental organizations (NGOs) and academics have not filled the void. Perhaps one reason this is so is that the DOI has not facilitated public or NGO assessments by making what data it does have readily available: there is no good, easy, accessible source on the specifics of each HCP, including the specifics of any HCP amendments or any data on how well or poorly the plan is working. The only centralized database for HCPs, the DOI's Environmental Conservation Online site,[21] is inadequate. It includes many approved HCPs, but for each

HCP, only the barest information—the name, the date of approval, the duration, and at best a few words of description—is provided. There is no way to discern the actual contents of any HCP, including the biological bases and goals of the HCP (to the extent there are any clearly stated in the plans) and the required conservation measures. Nor is there any way to discern how HCPs within a single region geographically and ecologically relate to one another.

Is Stakeholder Participation the Answer?

Some commentators seem to suggest that the lack of mandatory, sustained public participation in HCPs is the primary problem with them.[22] They argue that HCPs should move from a bilateral negotiation model to a multilateral consensus or collaboration model. Absent such participation, the argument goes, it is simply too easy for agency officials to be, if not captured, unduly influenced by and too easy on landowners. And collaboration will produce useful information and insights that otherwise would have been ignored.

Certainly, more public participation would be valuable on the level of individual HCPs, and below I make one suggestion of statutory and regulatory requirements that would enhance public participation. But the emphasis on public participation as the key reform is mistaken for several reasons. First, who constitutes the "public" and legitimate public representatives is extremely contested. If environmental NGOs are part of the public, is the local Chamber of Commerce as well? Even as among NGOs, there are often a range of viewpoints and concerns, so that it is impossible to equate any single, given NGO with the "environmentalist" point of view or certainly with "the public interest."

Second, any inclusion of a broad range of "stakeholders" in land-use outcomes may make agreement extremely difficult to achieve or at least too costly to achieve for landowners to tolerate, and inclusion without agreement or consensus may add nothing but delay and hard feelings. As Brad Karkkainen has observed, it is "highly unrealistic" to assume that we can put a group of "stakeholders" in a room and have them reach a win-win solution "insofar as it assumes that a Pareto-superior solution will be available for every problem."[23] Moreover, even when intensive public participation would not disrupt and delay plan development, it will be hard for landowners to feel assured, ex ante, that complications and delays will be avoided. As a result of this uncertainty, they may avoid participating in the HCP process.

Third, in some cases there will not be strong local stakeholders who want to and are equipped to engage in meaningful public participation. Some proposed HCPs will be in parts of the country with relatively weak local NGOS and which have not received attention from national NGOs; NGOs also may not be available or willing or able to commit to sustained participation in the many proposed HCPs that may involve very small land areas or arcane technical issues or decidedly non-charismatic fauna. Indeed, it may be that reforms in the HCP process are most critical for the category of HCPs that involve beneath-the-NGO/public-radar locations and natural resources. Even where there is a great deal of NGO interest, some NGOs may lack the sophistication and resources to provide key technical and scientific information and argue on the basis of such information, or to explain effectively why more scientific information and analysis are required. And even when an NGO can produce such information, the information may be tainted by the perception that the NGO is biased against any economic development or resource extraction.

The problem with looking to public participation as the key reform is illustrated by imagining what I am supposing (but certainly cannot prove) is a reasonably typical HCP negotiation scenario: the agency officials want to pursue, pragmatically but aggressively, conservation aims through an HCP but they also need to obtain the consent from landowners who may drive a hard bargain. In such a scenario, sustained public participation could be helpful in generating information regulators could use and in giving regulators some support as they seek concessions from the landowners. But other things would be helpful too, and perhaps much more helpful, namely: Congressional or agency regulatory requirements that make certain kinds of provisions mandatory (and hence something the regulators may insist upon), and mandatory review of the proposed plan by scientific experts. Such experts have the training public participants may well lack and whose analysis landowners cannot dismiss as biased, unlike the analysis of public participants that landowners can label (and genuinely may perceive as) nothing more than NIMBY-ists or environmental extremists.

What Congress Can and Should Do

One essential category of Congressional reforms of the HCP program would be to mandate the collection of information. The first thing Congress can do is amend Section 10 to require the Services to collect and make public a complete database on HCPs. Congress, too, should require the Services to report to Congress on a periodic basis on both the provisions of individual HCPs and the performance or results of HCPs. By requiring performance reporting, Congress would encourage the agency to pay more attention to monitoring and reporting by permittees, and to demand data in support of permittee reports. Government agencies such as the FWS invariably have more tasks than their resources allow them to pursue, and they therefore have a tendency to defer efforts and investigations that could show that plans they approved have caused environmental damage without producing offsetting or indeed any environmental benefits. No organization seeks out criticism, which is why a statutory mandate to report to Congress periodically on HCP performance is needed. Reports to Congress also could result in more effective participation by NGOs in ongoing debates over substantive reforms in the HCP program.

Congress should also require that HCPs include data-gathering and monitoring provisions that specify biological goals and metrics and describe adaptive management mechanisms. Such requirements might be too expensive to be sensible for all HCPs, so Congress should also direct the DOI to develop regulations for categorizing HCP proposals upfront according to possible environmental impacts, and to develop different tiers or grades of goal-setting and adaptive management depending on the impact categorization.

Prioritizing HCP proposals by likely or possible environmental impact would be a substantial and important reform in and of itself. The DOI has established some special processes for very-small-scale, very-low-impact HCPs, but otherwise has formally applied the same requirements to massive regional HCPs and ones that affect relatively few parcels of land.

The one-size-fits-all approach does not suit the real heterogeneity of the subject matter of HCPs. Moreover, assigning all HCPs to a tier based on possible impacts and rooted in actual evidence will help ensure that every HCP proposal is formulated around some kind of initial biological survey or data collection—which should always be the case but has not necessarily always been so. Finally, as in the National Environmental Policy Act (NEPA) impact review process, it is critical that HCP proposals be assessed based on likely or possible impacts, taking into consideration not just the land at issue but also cumulative effects and related effects (such as the precedent the HCP will set for the management of parcels with similar conditions, and interactions between private land and federal land).[24]

Congress should also require that high-impact HCPs include a provision authorizing citizen groups to bring a suit against the HCP permittee for substantial, continuing noncompliance with HCP requirements.[25] Citizens' suits have been a central part of American environmental law and enforcement, but the ESA does not on its face authorize citizens' suits for HCP noncompliance, and (as noted above) HCP plans and implementing agreements have not authorized them. The possibility of a citizen suit is a powerful incentive for compliance and provides an important recourse for the contingency of regulatory failure due to lack of resources or political pressures. By the same token, however, allowing citizens' suits may discourage landowners from participating in the HCP program. That is why citizens' suits should be limited to high-impact HCPs (where landowners have the most to gain from the HCP process and compliance is the most important to ensure). It is also why suits should be limited to substantial noncompliance (defined in as clear statutory language as possible, to discourage dubious litigation and cabin judicial discretion) and why the presumption of compliance under the No Surprises Rule should continue to apply, such that a citizen group must have some hard evidence of substantial negative impact beyond its first court pleading.

Scientific Advisory Board Review

Mandatory review by a scientific advisory board (SAB) should be instituted by statute for approval of a habitat conservation plan. This requirement should apply at least to any plan that is categorized as having moderate or high likely or possible impact. Periodic SAB review (perhaps every five or ten years) also may be appropriate for a statutory mandate. SAB review would not fully address the concerns of some critics that the HCP process does not contain enough opportunities for public participation and is not "democratic" enough,[26] but it would allow a certain degree of highly valuable participation by independent, non-agency actors and would address the fundamental concern about HCPs that they sometimes are not well-founded on basic scientific principles and data.

SAB members could not plausibly be discounted as NIMBY types or professional environmental activists; at the same time, they would have independence from both the government and landowners/permittees and hence could be expected to give expression to some of the same concerns that the most sophisticated NGOs would be able to articulate. Moreover, because each SAB member would serve for a term of perhaps two to five years and would therefore review multiple HCPs, SAB members could develop an understanding of the HCP program as a whole and a working relationship with agency officials. SAB reviewers could not be expected to do substantive scientific studies regarding proposed HCPs but they could raise questions, voice criticisms, and ask for clarifications. This should produce better HCPs and screen out the most plainly problematic HCP proposals.

SAB review, moreover, could facilitate meaningful public participation, just as could mandatory reports to Congress. SAB reviews of proposals would be made public, including negative, split, or qualified reviews. Using those reviews, NGOs and others could press their case against approval of a proposed HCP or for cancellation or revision of approved HCPs. One potentially useful statutory or regulatory mandate would be that the DOI would be required to explain why it was not adopting an SAB recommendation as part of its approval of an HCP and would be required to solicit public comments on the decision not to follow an SAB recommendation. Taken as a collective over time, moreover, SAB reviews may provide the public with a more candid picture of the HCP program than (inevitably somewhat self-serving) agency reports.

There are precedents for using SABs in the conservation context. NOAA's fish recovery efforts in the Columbia River basin are reviewed by a standing SAB that also reports to various Indian tribes.[27] Moreover, some individual HCPs have utilized scientific advisory boards. A study by Harding et al. suggests that HCPs that were approved after SAB review had a higher degree of scientific quality than those that employed steering committees that were not dominated by scientists. The study concluded that:

> One means of ensuring that current scientific information and approaches are used within the HCP process is through the increased use of independent scientists. When scientists, especially experts on the species covered by the plan, were consulted, adequate and even high-quality plans were often developed....At present, scientific input is not required...and is often lacking in the conservation planning process, yet it seems both reasonable and feasible to include scientists in the HCP process.[28]

Harding et al. do suggest, however, that SAB review may have modest impact overall because the SAB cannot effectively evaluate HCP proposals that are not accompanied by adequate data about the species population on the affected land. SAB review, however, would be more effective if there were also (as I have proposed) specific, clear requirements for data collection as part of all HCP proposals. With these requirements as a backdrop, a SAB could strongly recommend against acceptance of a proposal until the required data were collected and, after they were collected, the SAB would be able to make an informed assessment.

There are, to be sure, some risks with SAB review. SAB review will add to the expense of the HCP process and delay HCP approvals, which may mean that some landowners who might otherwise participate in the HCP process would instead engage in quiet, preemptive destruction of habitat. Making the SAB process efficient, with reasonably quick turnovers during each review phase, is important to mitigate this risk. There is also a risk that SAB review will frame the question of HCP approval as one of science only when we know that normative questions beyond scientific analysis are implicated by HCPs. But attention to what the available science can tell us—and that is always limited to some degree—is a helpful grounding for debate and discussion of these normative questions, and SAB review can help prompt the generation and understanding of the available science.

Public-Private Insurance and Time Limits on HCPs

The No Surprises Rule responds to the plausible belief that landowners will not participate in HCPs if they face the possibility of crushing regulatory costs if approved plans do not secure species survival or recovery or otherwise meet political demands for conservation actions in the future. But the No Surprises Rule goes too far: it creates perverse incentives on the part of landowners and government regulators alike.

For landowners, the No Surprises Rule creates a powerful incentive to exclude from plans biological goals that should be part of plans, because landowners are not financially responsible for any conservation measures that may be required later that are outside or inconsistent with the original plan. The No Surprises approach also creates an incentive on the part of landowners not to invest and not to take actions voluntarily that may go beyond the strict terms of the plan but that may help it succeed in its basic goals, because, at most, landowners can be held responsible only for non-compliance with the plan. Where ongoing compliance with the plan may be hard for regulators to detect, the No Surprises Rule also may allow landowners who wish to save on their costs to get away with intentional non- or sub-compliance with requirements that are plainly part of the plan.

At the same time, the No Surprises approach creates an incentive on the part of government actors *not* to know about plans that fail and species populations that are at risk. It encourages an ostrich's head-in-the-sand posture. Government agencies like the DOI work within annual budgets, and those budgets are fully allocated before the fiscal year starts; there is no extra money lying around. To the extent the No Surprises approach puts the full financial responsibility on the federal government for any conservation failures without providing any realistic funding resource for new conservation measures, the approach seems to ask regulators to go out and discover how plans they approved have imperiled species and then declare that there is nothing they can do to rectify the conservation failure. It is not realistic to expect that regulators will want to do that, and, even if they did, there still would remain the question of how new conservation measures could be funded.

What is needed is a tool or institutional device that limits and mitigates the financial risks for both private and public actors while providing some incentive for landowners to take the extra step on their own to prevent failure (where that is possible) and for government regulators to pay attention to cases in which new conservation measures, outside of current plans, really may be justifiable. One such mechanism would be publicly supported but privately operated insurance. Landowners would pay a premium for conservation-failure insurance, and a private insurer that operated the program would calibrate the annual premium (within a pre-set range, to limit financial uncertainty for landowners) based on the quality of the plan and quality of monitoring reports and the substantive meeting of biological goals. The private market has not developed and would not develop reasonably affordable insurance on its own given the nature of the risks involved, but private insurers have worked in conjunction with government re-insurance guarantees and underwriting in other contexts, such as in the context of insurance against the risk of nuclear accidents and terrorism.[29] In effect, landowners and the government would make investments toward a pool of insurance proceeds that could fund new conservation measures. Getting premiums rights and ensuring an adequate pool of insurance funds would not be easy, but some efforts in this regard would be an improvement over the No Surprises approach.

Finally, the DOI should establish some criteria for time limits on HCPs through notice and comment rulemaking. There should be some effort to connect levels of long-term uncertainty with time limits and a flat ban on plan lengths such as fifty years (the length of the massive Plum Creek HCP), which are almost certainly longer than can be defended, given our current understandings, and almost certainly longer than is needed to elicit cooperation from landowners.

Conservation Banking

Smaller-scale, lower-impact HCPs pose special regulatory challenges for several reasons. First, unless cost-pooling arrangements can be made, economies of scale and investment values are such that the landowners in such cases will not invest too much in developing or implementing an HCP. They may be unable to afford reasonable plan mitigation and conservation measures, let alone the insurance premiums I have just suggested. And these smaller plans also pose huge enforcement and compliance issues: neither regulators nor NGOs can be expected to pay much attention to them or perhaps even keep track of them, and, as a result, the temptations on the part of some landowners to skimp on compliance investments may be very powerful.

One response to the small-scale-plan challenges is to suggest that the DOI simply should not develop small-scale HCPs.[30] Another, preferable approach would be to allow reasonable, smaller-scale HCPs and seek to ensure compliance through selective auditing, while also openly recognizing that the uncertainties of achieving biological goals through these sorts of plans can be managed only to a limited extent through formal monitoring requirements. To offset the biological "slippage" inherent in small-scale plans, the DOI could require landowners with such plans to make one-time financial contributions to a conservation mitigation bank, preferably in the same region and preferably containing similar mixes of species.

A conservation mitigation bank typically has been and would be a large landholding managed for conservation purposes. Because such bank holdings are extensive and largely, if not necessarily exclusively, dedicated to conservation, they are an ideal site for the application of adaptive management techniques and relatively easy for regulators to oversee. As Ruhl et al. explain: "Conservation banks, in comparison to the piecemeal approach [to species mitigation], generally can be expected to result in larger preserves and thus better habitat connectivity."[31] Conservation banks, in effect, can serve as insurance for failure or lack of conservation achievement in smaller-scale HCPs.

Conservation banks have a limited track record and there are many theoretical objections to their use. Like wetland mitigation banking, but even more so, conservation banking raises difficult questions of locality and incommensurability: one pair of endangered birds in one location is not, ecologically or in terms of benefits to the surrounding human community, necessarily the same as another pair hundreds of miles away. Nor are conservation banks free from the objection that the conservation they afford might have happened anyway because they invariably involve preservation of habitat rather than creation of it and they may be located in areas with low-development demand or where there are already other development restrictions. Assessing how many credits should be required and how much they should cost as a component of any given HCPs also may prove difficult.

The DOI has approved specific conservation banks, but there has been no attempt to develop regulatory criteria for judging bank success or efforts to measure and report on success or lack of it. There is not even an official, complete database of approved banks. As to the question of how and when conservation banking should be used as part of HCPs, there have been no notice-and-comment regulations, and the guidance documents that have been issued are incomplete and somewhat confusing, at least according to some critics. To the extent the guidance suggests anything, it suggests a restrictive attitude toward the use of conservation banks.[32] Adopting rules after notice and comment that clarify criteria for banks and the use of conservation banking in HCPs would help make conservation banking a helpful insurance policy element for small-scale HCPs. Conservation banking can be part of the response to the long-term uncertainty problem posed by some kinds of HCPs.

Conclusion

The HCP program is a major way that conservation on private land has been achieved in the United States, including conservation that moves beyond the limited approach of the ESA in focusing only upon train-wreck instances where a species is on the brink of extinction. We do not know how well or not HCPs are working, but we can find out with some straight-forward reforms, such as a mandated public database, and we can ensure that future HCPs are produced with scientific review and include key components such as biological goals and adaptive management. We can also address the neglect of issues arising from long-term uncertainty in the HCP program through insurance mandates and conservation banking.

These reforms must begin with legislative, not regulatory, action. The statutory basis of the HCP program as it is now is quite modest, and a reformed HCP program needs Congressional authorization to avoid the legal legitimacy questions that now surround the HCP program. Moreover, because some of the reforms proposed would force agencies to do what they are disinclined to do (e.g., engage in nondiscretionary reporting to Congress) and would require new government funding (e.g., the public funding for public-private conservation-failure insurance), one cannot expect the agencies to act without Congressional action. Moreover, the HCP program and the proposed reforms raise fundamental normative questions that deserve public debate and deliberation. While notice-and-comment rulemaking can be an important site of such debate and deliberation, Congress, for all its flaws, is the better suited for debate and deliberation because it is a nationally elected body. Much of the hard work of HCP reform will be done via agency rulemaking and other initiatives, but we need Congress to take on the project of HCP reform.

Notes

1. Jodi Hilty and Adina M. Merenlender, "Studying Diversity on Private Lands," *Conservation Biology* 17, no. 1 (2003): 133 (stating that 95 percent of endangered plant and animal species have some habitat on private land); and David S. Wilcove and Joon Lee, "Using Economic and Regulatory Incentives to Restore Endangered Species: Lessons Learned from Three New Programs," *Conservation Biology* 18, no. 3 (2004): 640 (explaining that an estimate that "private lands harbor at least one population of two-thirds of all federally-listed species…is almost certainly an underestimate").

2. 16 U.S.C.A. §§ 1532(19), 1538(a)(1).

3. The Department of Interior regulation defines "harm" to include "significant habitat modification or degradation where it actually kills or injures wildlife by significantly impairing essential behavioral patterns, including breeding, feeding or sheltering." 50 C.F.R. § 17.3.

4. 515 U.S. 687 (1995).

5. Of course, even a modest threat of a government or citizen suit under Section 9 may deter some landowners from "taking" or arguably taking species on their land. Thus, Section 9 certainly does have an impact beyond those cases in which litigation is initiated under Section 9. Measuring that impact, however, would be exceedingly difficult.

6. 16 U.S.C. §1539, (a) (2) (A)(2009).

7. 16 U.S.C. §1539, (a) 2 (B) (2009).

8. 16 U.S.C. §1539 (a) (2) (C)(2009).

9. Alejandro E. Camacho, "Can Regulation Evolve? Lessons from a Study in Maladaptive Regulation," *UCLA Law Review* 55 (2007): 308.

10. David A. Dana, "The New 'Contractarian' Paradigm in Environmental Regulation," *University of Illinois Law Review* 2000 (2000): 35–58.

11. See for example, Rocky Barker, "Efforts to save salmon may be undone by climate change," *Miami Herald*, May 12, 2009, www.miamiherald.com/news/environment/story/1044060.html; see also Matthew Daly, "Feds Seek Delay in Developing NW Salmon Plan," Associated Press, May 1, 2009, available at http://www.wildsalmon.org (describing ongoing controversy over federal recovery plan).

12. The problem of uncertainty is as applicable to species on federal land as it is to species on nonfederal, private land, but, at least to date, no one has claimed that the federal government is ever relieved under the terms of the Act from responding to uncertainty with new protective measures on federal land. The HCP program, as implemented, appears in some cases (via the No Surprises Rule) to have provided just such an assurance to private landowners.

13. H.R. Conf. Rep. No. 97-835, at 31 (1982).

14. Philip R. Berke, "Integrating Bioconservation and Land Use Planning: A Grand Challenge of the Twenty-First Century," *Vermont Journal of Environmental Law* 10 (2009): 412.

15. In brief, the No Surprises Rule assured landowners participating in an HCP that they would not be surprised with the expense of new conservation measures if the plan did not work as originally intended or the federal government for some other reason came to believe that different or more aggressive conservation measures were appropriate. For a good discussion of the history of the No Surprises Rule, see Karin P. Sheldon, "Habitat Conservation Planning: Addressing the Achilles Heel of the Endangered Species Act," *NYU Environmental Law Journal* 6 (1998): 279.

16. See generally David A. Dana and Susan P. Koniak, "Bargaining in the Shadow of Democracy," *University of Pennsylvania Law Review* 148 (1999): 473.

17. See Camacho, "Can Regulation Evolve?" 323 (explaining that the "program's monitoring and adaptation requirements have provided applicants and the Services considerable flexibility and incentives to ignore monitoring and evade adaptation"). The most comprehensive study to date, a study conducted by the American Institute of Biological Sciences and the National Center for Ecological Analysis and Synthesis based on a sample of 43 HCPs, found that only 22 of the 43 plans reviewed had a clear monitoring program and that monitoring of HCPs is generally inadequate. See http://www.fws.gov/Endangered/hcp/response.htm (describing the study and the FWS's comments on it).

18. In addition, the citizen suit provision of the Act itself refers to citizens' suits for violations of "any provision of [the Act] or regulation issued under the authority thereof," 16 U.S.C §1540(g)(2009), and it is unclear whether a provision in an HCP implementing agreement is a requirement within the meaning of Section 11.

19. See Laura C. Hood, "Frayed Safety Nets: Conservation Planning Under the Endangered Species Act" (1998), available at www.defenders.org/. A study in the *American Scientist* reached similar conclusions and found HCPs, overall, to be woefully lacking in scientific grounding. See Laura Watchman, Martha Groom, and John Perrine, "Science and Uncertainty in Habitat Conservation Planning," *American Scientist* 89 (2001): 351–59.

20. See http://www.fws.gov/endangered/pdfs/HCP/final_notice.pdf.

21. See U.S. Fish and Wildlife Service, Conservation Plans and Agreements Database, http://ecos.fws.gov/conserv_plans/public.jsp.

22. See for example, Holly Doremus, "Preserving Citizen Participation in the Era of Reinvention: the Endangered Species Act Example," *Ecology Law Quarterly* 25 (1999): 707–17; and Anne B. Hulick, "Habitat Conservation Plans: Protecting Species, Enhancing Democratic Legitimacy and Promoting Stewardship Are Not Mutually Exclusive Goals," *UCLA Environmental Law and Policy* 25 (2006): 441–71.

23. Bradley C. Karkkainen, "Collaborative Ecosystem Governance: Scale, Complexity, and Dynamism," *Virginia Environmental Law Journal* 21 (2002): 239.

24. On the problem of cumulative effects, see Laura C. Hood, "Frayed Safety Nets," 56–58; on NEPA, see L. W. Canter, "Cumulative Effects and Other Analytic Challenges of NEPA," in *Environmental Policy and NEPA*, ed. Ray Clark and Larry W. Canter (St. Lucie Press, 1997), 115–138.

25. See Donald Bauer and William Robert Irvin, *The Endangered Species Act: Law, Policy, and Perspectives* (Chicago, Ill.: ABA Section of Environment, Energy, and Resources, 2002), 356 (explaining the legal ambiguity surrounding citizen suits to enforce HCP provisions, and urging the adoption of "regulations requiring that HCPs identify citizens as third-party beneficiaries" in order to "ensure effective enforcement of the ESA.")

26. See Hood, "Frayed Safety Nets"; Doremus, "Preserving Citizen Participation," 707–17.

27. Independent Scientific Advisory Board background, http://www.nwcouncil.org/Fw/isab/background.htm.

28. Elaine K. Harding, Elizabeth E. Crone, Bret D. Elderd, Jonathan M. Hoekstra, Alexa J. McKerrow, John D. Perrine, Jim Regetz, Leslie Rissler, Amanda G. Stanley, Eric L. Walters, and NCEAS Habitat Conservation Plan Working Group, "The Scientific Foundations of Habitat Conservation Plans: a Quantitative Assessment," *Conservation Biology* 15, no. 2 (2001): 499.

29. See Terrorism Insurance Act of 2002, Pub L No. 107–297 (requiring insurers not to exclude terrorism-related claims and providing for the government to act as an excess insurer of terrorism-related claims); Price-Anderson Act, 42 USC Sec 2210, as amended by the Energy Policy Act of 2005 (requiring nuclear power providers to carry insurance and providing for federal payment of insurance claims in excess of the private insurance mandated by the statute)

30. See Doremus, "Preserving Citizen Participation," 716 (suggesting that "Congress should give serious thoughts to limiting the HCP process to regional or area-wide plans").

31. J.B. Ruhl, Alan Glen, and David Hartman, "A Practical Guide to Habitat Conservation Banking Law and Policy," *Natural Resources & Environment* 20 (Summer 2005): 28.

32. For a good overview of policies and data regarding conservation banks by

two DOI officials, see Edward Mailett and Benjamin Simon, Discussion Paper: Characteristics of Federal Conservation Banks (September 2007), available at http://docs.google.com/gview?a=v&q=cache:dzlEN-pX4wIJ:www.fws.gov/ economics/Discussion%2520Papers/Discussion%2520Paper%2520_%2520%252 0Conservation%2520Banks.pdf+Characteristics+of+Federal+Conservation+Banks &hl=en&gl=us.

3

Improving the ESA's Performance on Private Land

R. Neal Wilkins

The Endangered Species Act (ESA) was intended to defend against species loss and to promote the recovery of threatened and endangered species. The evidence suggests that the ESA functions as an adequate safety net against the extinction of threatened and endangered species but that it has not performed well in promoting the recovery of these species. Econometric analyses have demonstrated what some have learned from experience—listing a species under the ESA is not only ineffective in promoting recovery but is often harmful to the species and promotes recovery only when accompanied by substantial funding.[1] Other analyses conclude that recovery and delisting are not to be expected given the slight commitment of governmental resources for implementation.[2] Simply put, the ESA is not accomplishing its objective of recovering at-risk species, and reform is necessary to improve ESA performance with regard to promoting species recovery.[3] Unless implementation of the ESA becomes more effective, the ESA will not do better than ensure mere species survival.

Nowhere are there greater obstacles to better ESA performance than on private land. More rare, threatened, or endangered species rely on private lands than on lands held under any other class of ownership. In fact, the majority of listed species are estimated to have 80 percent or more of their habitat on private land,[4] and as much as one-third of the nation's at-risk species are thought to dwell exclusively on private lands.[5] However, private landowners have both opportunities and incentives to thwart the effective implementation of the ESA. Given the importance of private land as habitat for at-risk species and the challenges to working with landowners, the solutions to ESA performance must largely be found where the Act involves private land.

In what follows, I lay out some of the obstacles to, as well as opportunities for, a more effective and incentive-driven approach to endangered species recovery on private lands. While I focus particularly on private lands, some of the reforms suggested have broader implications. My purpose is not to lament the way in which the ESA has been implemented. Rather, I intend to concentrate attention on the obstacles to recovery efforts on private lands, draw some lessons from experiences on private lands, and then use those lessons to recommend simple reforms that could result in more innovative approaches to recovery on private lands through efficient incentives.

Private Lands and the ESA: Uncertainty and Fear

There is a growing body of empirical evidence that efforts to enforce ESA on private lands have been counter to the Act's purpose. At times, the threat of enforcement encourages landowners to apply political pressures to delay species listings,[6] preemptively destroy habitat,[7] and deny access for scientific study, which limits the reliable information on species status and distribution.[8] Fear and regulatory uncertainty of the ESA emerge as defiance on the part of private landowners, especially in the case of high-profile ESA listings that threaten to reduce future land values through land-use regulations. The example of the Lesser Prairie chicken illustrates these concerns.

The Lesser Prairie Chicken. On May 12, 2009, over 100 local farmers, ranchers, and business owners gathered at the Community Center in Hereford, Texas to hear from federal and state wildlife biologists about the future of the Lesser Prairie chicken and the potential to create partnerships for habitat restoration. The Lesser Prairie chicken now occupies less than 10 percent of its original range due to loss of native short-grass prairie habitat through agricultural conversion, fire suppression, excessive grazing, and petroleum development.[9] Some landowners in Deaf Smith County restored Lesser Prairie chicken habitat through participation in federal and state cost-sharing and technical assistance efforts and now are proud to provide some of the last habitat for the species.

The Lesser Prairie chicken is a candidate for listing under the ESA, and the official listing decision may be made in the next year. In the meantime, the species is on a collision course with another environmental objective: green energy. The southern high plains of Texas, part of the last refuge for the Lesser Prairie chicken, is also one of the nation's most active regions for wind-power development. Contracts for wind energy development are lucrative for local landowners, which could pose a problem for the Lesser Prairie chicken. While the specific ecological circumstances are unique to this case and the social and economic issues are complex, the conflict between preservation of the Lesser Prairie chicken and economic development are typical of many conflicts between conservation and economic development. Wind turbines, with their associated service roads and transmission lines, are likely further to reduce habitat quality for the species, thus resulting in a prohibited "take" of threatened or endangered species under ESA Section 9, which not only prohibits direct harm, but also prohibits indirect harm by modifying or degrading a species' habitat. Some private landowners, facing tough economic conditions, are anticipating economic windfalls through contracts for wind energy companies to erect turbines on their land. Unless provided with an incentive to do otherwise, many of these landowners will not likely enhance and restore endangered species habitat. In addition, the uncertainty created by an impending ESA listing may actually motivate some to do what wildlife biologists are afraid to mention—they might actually destroy habitat that could support the species in order to preempt a future ESA requirement that constrains their land use.

Resolving the conflict between protecting the Lesser Prairie chicken and building wind turbines could be relatively simple. The former range of the species is expansive, the ecology of the species is relatively well known, and the technology for habitat restoration is understood. Throughout the range, some lands will be more suited for installing wind turbines and transmission lines, others will be more suited to habitat restoration for prairie chickens, and still others will likely remain in some form of agriculture. Costs for conservation and recovery actions could be paid by those standing to benefit from the wind energy industry as a cost of doing business.

In short, in theory it should be possible to allow for both species recovery and wind energy development. But as ESA listing of the species becomes more likely, the focus shifts toward what can be done to either forestall the listing or reduce the uncertainty that arrives with a new listing. The complex implementation history, structure, and administrative process of the ESA complicates the picture. Because the species is not yet listed, the U.S. Fish and Wildlife Service (FWS) cannot use its regulatory authority to threaten action against the landowners and the wind energy industry. Landowners, even those who have contributed to conservation of the species, are now less certain that creating habitat for prairie chickens is a good idea.

This example of the Lesser Prairie chicken illustrates the challenges in implementing the ESA that are found in numerous other cases. These cases demand some simple but effective reforms to the ESA—reforms discussed later in this chapter. Such solutions would reward private landowners for measurable conservation outcomes, remove the disincentives of the current regulatory approach, and simplify the administrative procedures that occupy wildlife biologists who should be advising landowners about effective recovery measures. Until those reforms are implemented, the performance of the ESA on private lands will continue to be hindered by denial of access to land and information as well as preemptive actions to avoid constraints on land use.

Denial of access and information. In most cases, private landowners can control access to their property, and they can also choose to withhold information concerning the biological resources that exist there. This prevents the accumulation of reliable scientific information that is key to properly implementing the ESA. Species listings, critical habitat designations, status reviews, recovery plans, and enforcement actions all depend upon the reliability of accumulated, site-specific information for the species. In its annual reports to Congress, the FWS describes the status of listed species as "improving," "stable," or "declining." From 1988 to 2002, the FWS had insufficient information to assess status for about 40 percent of all listed species.[10] Much of the information required to determine the status of those species found largely on private lands remains either uncollected or underreported.

Denial of access thwarts efforts to determine a species' status and hinders legitimate recovery efforts. In order to plan for recovery efforts, wildlife ecologists seek basic information on habitat occupancy, life history traits, and the relationships between the species and its habitat. Most landowners' reasons for denying access have nothing to do with obstructing science. Instead, many private landowners simply deny access to scientists and researchers out of fear of creating a regulatory burden on their land use should an endangered species be found. The same information used to determine species status and aid in recovery planning is also used for designating critical habitat and ESA Section 9 enforcement action—and it is the threat of this enforcement action that often causes landowners to deny access to those collecting information. Under the current legal regime, information is the prerequisite to regulation of land use on private lands.[11] By denying access, many private landowners are simply reacting as expected given what is at stake when their property becomes a known location for endangered species. Within the FWS there is little or no separation of the personnel involved in permitting and enforcement from those overseeing the science and recovery of a species. Therefore, private landowners' fears are well founded.

Preemptive action and the take prohibition. Much of the problem with attaining meaningful endangered species conservation on private lands stems from the ESA's Section 9 take prohibition. In many cases the outcome of this prohibition is simply a failed attempt to protect individual animals at the expense of population recovery.[12] In practice, this prohibition is often unenforceable. The definition of "take" under the ESA is so broad that it is often difficult to determine clearly when the take prohibition has been violated. The legal definition of take includes actions that may result in "harm," including "significant habitat modification or degradation where it actually kills or injures wildlife by significantly impairing essential behavioral patterns, including breeding, feeding or sheltering."[13] The difficulty in deciding whether one or more individuals might be taken through such a broad definition of "harm" has rendered the take prohibition largely unenforceable in all but the most blatant of circumstances. However, the threat remains, and the uncertainty that it causes results in some interesting and counterintuitive outcomes.

From a private landowner's perspective, there are two basic strategies to address the prohibition on incidental take. The first is simply to identify existing suitable habitat, make some effort to determine if it is occupied, and then avoid any actions that disturb the habitat. This results in some passive conservation, but under Section 9 the landowner has no real incentive to enhance or restore habitats suitable for endangered species. The other approach is to identify habitats that are, or could become, suitable and occupied and then take preemptive action to reduce habitat suitability— at times this preemptive action might include actually refraining from certain activities that could enhance habitats. When met with the potential for incidental take, most private landowners strategically apply a combination of these two approaches to manage their risks. As a consequence, the techniques for avoiding a Section 9 regulatory burden are now well embedded in the culture and practice of private lands management. These strategies result in no real recovery actions on private lands, and the outcome is often worse for the species than if it had not been listed under the ESA.

Addressing Landowners' Concerns:
Habitat Conservation Plans and Compensation

Despite the self-defeating outcomes of the take prohibition, the ESA does not always shape landowners' incentives such that they will oppose efforts to protect at-risk species. The ESA allows voluntary conservation and recovery efforts on private lands that fall into the category of regulatory incentives, including habitat conservation plans (HCPs), candidate conservation agreements (CCAs), and compensation for lost property values. Before discussing ESA reform and new ways of addressing landowners' resistance to the ESA, I consider these tested mechanisms for voluntary conservation and recovery efforts under the ESA.

Relief from regulatory uncertainty. The ESA allows for agreements that address landowners' uncertainty about what burdens might be imposed on them under the ESA. These agreements may reduce uncertainty through an HCP for permitting incidental take, establish baselines above which future incidental take is allowable (so-called "safe harbor agreements"), or CCAs that encourage conservation actions for ESA candidate species. These binding agreements are often accompanied by no-surprises policies and other assurances that offer a level of certainty that no further conservation actions will be required through the term of the agreement. In fact, the successful negotiation and overall conservation value of such agreements are often contingent upon landowners being shielded from future changes in conservation requirements.[14] The significant investment of time, energy, and finances to endure the current administrative processes and arcane procedures required discourages general use of HCPs and CCAs.[15] But nevertheless, these agreements have demonstrated some utility as regulatory incentives.

Thus, just as fear of future regulation under the ESA has sometimes motivated landowners to destroy habitat,[16] fear of future regulation motivates some landowners to undertake voluntary conservation measures through HCPs and CCAs. It appears that both the chief successes and failures of the ESA on private lands originate from the same fear of future uncertainty. In its effect, an HCP can provide an indirect economic incentive by, for example, securing predictable rights to timber harvest and economic forest management.[17] However, if it is only the uncertainty of future conservation requirements—specifically the expectation that future requirements will be more restrictive than those at present—that is the primary "incentive" for private landowners to take conservation actions now, then it may be that much potential for conservation from private lands is yet left untapped.

Compensation. Compensating landowners for lost property values incurred when their lands are needed for protecting endangered species has been a controversial topic since the early days of implementing the ESA. Compensation programs have increasingly taken the form of public purchase of land, development rights, and conservation easements by local and state governments. In one such program in California, the conservation investments of $2.8 billion from 1990 to 2006 returned species conservation benefits that were substantially lower than what they could have been if funds had been more focused on areas of high value for conserving biological diversity as opposed to land acquisitions in popular coastal areas and population centers.[18] The California example (one of the largest conservation expenditures in the nation) illustrates one of the problems in relying on these compensation programs as a primary conservation tool. Moreover, there is some evidence that relying on purchase of full or partial rights in land as a conservation tool may actually undermine conservation outcomes. Without some accounting for market dynamics, purchase of land for conservation can actually accelerate the pace of development, or displace development into biologically valuable areas.[19]

Nevertheless, compensation programs do reduce some of the local resistance to ESA constraints,[20] and they may assist in maintaining habitats of last resort for some species. Programs whereby landowners in the path of development are assigned tradable development rights that may be bought and sold may enhance the efficiency of compensation programs.[21] The problems of inefficiency and unintended outcomes do not warrant the abandonment of compensation programs, but it is apparent that better-designed incentives are needed if substantial recovery efforts are to be expected from private lands. Turning private lands into public lands is seldom the best answer for implementing large-scale conservation efforts. The obvious financial and political costs of transferring enough private ownership into the public domain make a recovery-via-public-lands scenario viable for only a minority of currently listed species. In addition, there is growing evidence that private landowners are able and willing to contribute to species recovery, given appropriate incentives.

Addressing Landowners' Concerns: New Incentives

In 1991, several members of the U.S. Congress wrote to the National Research Council asking for a study of the ESA. The issues raised for study were broad and related to the overall purpose of the Act. The response, prepared by a committee of seventeen scientists, concluded with the following statement: "To conserve natural habitats, approaches must be developed that rely on cooperation and innovative procedures; examples provided by the ESA are habitat conservation plans and natural community conservation planning. But those are only the beginning. Many other approaches have been discussed in various forums. They include cooperative management (sharing decision-making authority among several governmental and nongovernmental groups), transfer of development credits, mitigation banks, tax incentives, and conservation easements."[22]

What is interesting, and perhaps hopeful, is that many of the approaches that were considered new and innovative two decades ago are now relatively well developed. For example, few HCPs were in effect at that time but now more than six hundred are in effect. In some cases, however, the science underlying these approaches has lagged behind the policy innovations. For example, a review of HCPs by the National Center for Ecological Analysis and Synthesis found serious shortcomings in the scientific data used in their development.[23] Other market-based innovations in species conservation have occurred since the early 1990s. For example, while market-based approaches to water conservation were discussed by some academics at the time,[24] there was limited discussion of market-based incentives for endangered species conservation. In contrast, now there is serious analysis of habitat trading and other market-based systems for endangered species conservation among both academics and practitioners.[25]

This new dialogue could create scenarios whereby private landowners could reap substantial benefits from the fact that they possess suitable habitat for an endangered species. Consider the conservation and recovery benefits of a scenario whereby landowners are provided with payments for identifying, enhancing, and restoring endangered species habitats. If such a program were market-based, landowners might actually compete to participate. Program costs could be aligned with conservation benefits and landowners' willingness to participate. Two such programs are conservation banking and recovery crediting.

Conservation banking. Why should a private landowner protect endangered species' habitats and participate in a recovery effort? As reviewed in the preceding sections, the structure and implementation of the ESA have often stifled any motivation for a conservation-minded landowner to contribute to species recovery. The recent success of safe-harbor agreements demonstrates that eliminating the threat of additional take prohibitions is enough to prompt some landowners to implement conservation efforts that could contribute to species recovery. Other landowners may need a more powerful motivation to participate in recovery programs. For this motivation, we need look no further than the entrepreneurs establishing new marketplaces for ecosystem services. Farmers, ranchers, and forest managers understand the process of developing products from their land and the value of having secure property rights to those products. If a product happens to be a tangible unit of conservation (i.e., a credit) for a particular endangered species and there is a market for accumulating such credits in anticipation of their value in offsetting habitat loss elsewhere, then a landowner might be motivated to protect, restore, and enhance habitats for endangered species.

This idea was the impetus behind the establishment of conservation banking. Conservation banks protect habitats and mitigate impacts on one or more species by permanent conservation easements. Conservation banking is a tool used largely for more efficiently meeting the mitigation requirements of Section 10 HCPs or Section 7 consultations. Following the pioneering of conservation banking in California, the U.S. Fish & Wildlife Service adopted guidelines for habitat conservation banks in 2003.[26]

Since guidelines were issued, the practice of conservation banking has expanded geographically but has been limited in its overall impact. Among the limitations is the fact that most banks receive credit only for preserving existing habitat, so there is little direct incentive for restoration. In addition, the guidelines require that habitat must be protected and managed "in perpetuity" through a conservation easement with an inexhaustible management endowment. Given these limitations, conservation banks, while representing an important opportunity for investing in conservation on private lands, are limited in their impact: they are primarily tools for facilitating development, and are not likely to contribute fundamentally to recovery for the species they target.[27] A conservation strategy that relies foremost on securing habitat with perpetual conservation easements assumes that habitat quality is static, or that it can be maintained as such forever. Evidence for most species clearly demonstrates that habitat quality is ephemeral. Thus the idea of permanently securing functional habitat begins to stumble when faced with the dynamic processes responsible for creating suitable habitat conditions in the first place.

Recovery crediting. A more recent innovation addresses some of the shortcomings of conservation banking. On July 31, 2008 the FWS issued guidelines for "Recovery Crediting." Recovery crediting provides additional means for federal agencies to meet their ESA Section 7 obligations arising from actions on private and other nonfederal lands. According to the guidelines, "a recovery credit is a quantifiable unit of measure recognized by the Service representing a contribution to the recovery" of a listed species.[28] The process allows recovery credits to be accrued through accomplishing recovery tasks for the species on nonfederal lands. The credits are then available to offset adverse impacts elsewhere to the same species. Accumulating credits to offset debits under a recovery credit system is to be conducted in such a manner as to yield a net benefit to recovery for the species. Biological monitoring is required for both the credit and debit phase of the program.

While the FWS guidelines for recovery crediting are substantive and wide-ranging, there is hardly any mention of the incentives required for motivating private landowners to participate in such a program. Recovery crediting was first developed for endangered golden-cheeked warblers in central Texas, and it was applied as a three-year "proof-of-concept" across a 2.5-million-acre area surrounding Fort Hood Military Reservation.[29] Fort Hood has a large population of golden-cheeked warblers, and training activities there often impact the species' habitat. While it is yet too early to assess the full ecological benefits of the recovery credit system (RCS) on golden-cheeked warbler populations, the response of private landowners demonstrates some of the principles that could be used to reform ESA.

The key features of the RCS program include:

- The RCS was designed mostly through the participation of nongovernmental actors: conservation nongovernmental organizations, state agencies, landowner groups, and university scientists. Federal agencies participated in the advisory and oversight functions.

- Species experts were convened to establish a method for determining a standard unit of recovery, a "credit" based on habitat protection, enhancement, and restoration using known species–

habitat relationships. This is a unit of habitat ecologically relevant to the species.

- A recovery credit is based on a 20-acre unit of suitable habitat (mature oak-juniper woodland) where at least 50 acres are under contract, and part of a patch of at least 250 acres of suitable habitat. Credits are adjusted upward for habitat in larger patches, where habitat is in close proximity to other known breeding populations of the bird, and for recovery regions where the species is not yet well represented. When competing for limited funds, these adjustments give an advantage to building conservation efforts aligned to the species recovery priorities. To earn credit, the function of the habitat must be enhanced through a series of habitat management and control practices designed by a team of species experts.

- University researchers were engaged to launch a monitoring program for the private lands across the 2.5-million-acre landscape. The monitoring program is designed to validate the credit criteria, establish habitat occupancy models, determine population baselines, and follow trends in habitat recovery and population response.

- Landowners are recruited into the RCS through an outreach team that includes Texas A&M Agrilife Extension, the Environmental Defense Fund, and the Texas Watershed Management Foundation.

- Landowner information and site-specific endangered species information are kept confidential and are not made publicly available—nor are they available to the FWS.

- A management plan that includes conservation and recovery actions is established for each private property where landowners identified themselves as potential participants in the program.

- Funding is made available through program sponsors that include the Department of Defense, U.S. Army, National Fish

and Wildlife Foundation, and U.S. Department of Agriculture–
Natural Resources Conservation Service.

- Landowner contracts and their implementation are adminis-
  tered by a local nonprofit foundation.

- Landowners are informed of program details, including contract
  terms, site-specific conservation and management practices
  required, and the number of eligible "credits" for their property.

- Landowners compete for participation in the program through
  a reverse auction process whereby they place bids that include
  their credits, amount of cost-share they are willing to contribute,
  contract length (ten to twenty-five years), and the amount of
  annual payment they expect.

- Competing bids are compared according to their cost-
  effectiveness at providing the most credits, for the longest
  contract term, at the lowest price.

The RCS process results in a market-based system whereby landowners
actually compete to provide tangible conservation benefits for a target
species. Following eight bid rounds over a three-year period, the program
now has 13,858 acres of private lands enrolled, including 2,201 acres of
occupied golden-cheeked warbler habitat. Approximately 33 percent of
the total area is enrolled in twenty-five-year contracts. The total cost of the
RCS thus far is $1,954,666.

Once recovery credits are established, they are held in trust for use by
the sponsor until they are needed to offset an adverse action by being
withdrawn from the trust (as debits). The FWS guidelines require that the
combined effect of crediting and debiting must provide a meaningful "net
benefit to recovery" for the species.

The science database emerging from the monitoring program for the
RCS is considerable. The primary goals of the monitoring program are
(1) to validate the reliability of the credits as a proxy for contributing to
recovery; (2) to determine the effectiveness of management practices in
enhancing habitat function; and (3) to develop a broader understanding
of the species. Through the RCS monitoring program the knowledge of

occurrence, distribution, abundance, and productivity has increased, resulting in a more reliable environmental baseline from which to inform future consultations between the FWS and the U.S. Army.

An important but controversial feature of the RCS at Fort Hood is that landowners may participate while maintaining confidentiality. In other words, site-specific information about endangered species is not released directly to the FWS. The information is used by researchers for monitoring, recovery planning, and understanding species–habitat relationships. The results, but not the raw data, become available. As a consequence of what many have called a "landowner friendly" approach, the RCS has garnered support from several local landowner associations, including the Texas Farm Bureau and Texas and Southwestern Cattle Raisers Association. As a result, the program has spurred enough interest in the species and enough trust among landowners that landowners are now willing to participate in conservation programs and real recovery efforts are being implemented.

Nevertheless, the Fort Hood proof-of-concept for the RCS has drawn criticism. The confidentiality agreements with landowners have created a perception of "secrecy," making the program a target among critics in the popular media.[30] Another major criticism is that the mechanism does not include a perpetual easement that obligates landowners to preserve habitat permanently.[31] The confidentiality and nonperpetual agreements are focuses for both critics and defenders of these programs.

A large fraction of private landowners avoid formalized conservation programs that require them to reveal site-specific information—especially when it concerns endangered species. As a case in point, private landowners in many parts of Texas had refused to allow wildlife biologists on their property until legislation was passed that shielded site-specific wildlife data from disclosure, even to federal agencies.[32] Many private landowners also avoid permanent surrender of land-use decisions. A poll of landowners in the Edward's Plateau of central Texas found that a perpetual conservation easement was the least preferred instrument for promoting conservation efforts on private lands. Performance contracts and lease agreements were the most favored.[33] Regardless of preference, however, the overall investment in conservation easements has grown exponentially in recent years.[34]

Evolution of effective market-based systems. Some of the lessons from recovery crediting are transferable to other landowner incentive programs. As mentioned in the previous section, however, the most important lessons for creating an incentive program that attracts and motivates landowners were not covered in the FWS guidelines for the program. These lessons may be addressed by some reforms to the ESA and its implementation.

The fact that the guidelines for conservation banking were already in place and operating was instrumental in the conceptual design of the RCS. In fact, without the existence of conservation banking and the 2003 guidance, it is unlikely that the RCS guidelines would have been established. But how does the RCS stack up against conservation banking? On one hand, the RCS seems to be more cost-effective. Using the example above, the equivalent cost would have been approximately $16.5 million to obtain a similar initial conservation impact under an existing conservation bank for the species—this is based on a cost of $7,500 per acre for credits under an existing conservation bank for the species.[35] In this single existing example, use of the RCS cost about 12 percent of a similar habitat area impact under conservation banking. Moreover, one of the features of the RCS is that the currency of trade is a credit that takes account of factors influencing habitat value. As a consequence, a unit that constitutes a recovery credit may more closely approximate a uniform measure of performance than the simple measure of land area that is common to conservation banking. But there are some important advantages of conservation banking over the RCS. Conservation banking requires that a permanent conservation easement be placed on the property, while RCS contracts are for limited terms. Finally, conservation banking is becoming a large and relatively well-established industry. Thus, one advantage of conservation banking is that there is growing educational effort and political support arising from the organized efforts of the National Mitigation Banking Association. Whether recovery crediting is to become broadly applied is yet to be known; the guidance for conservation banking had been in effect for over five years by the time recovery crediting guidelines were issued.

The above discussion is not to suggest that conservation banking using perpetual conservation easements should be abandoned in favor of instruments such as recovery crediting. While perpetual conservation easements have proven to be a valuable tool for protecting lands from development impacts, the financial expense and unfavorable reception by some landowners suggest that additional instruments may be needed for stimulating recovery action across large expanses of private land. In addition, there are cases where one approach is more practical than the other. Instruments such as recovery credits may be more cost effective where habitat is not under imminent threat of land use conversion or development but where the reduction of threats to a listed species requires habitat restoration, management of invasive species, or other management interventions across a large expanse. Conservation banking and perpetual easements might be preferred when long-term protection of rare habitats and unique physical features (e.g., karst features, riparian areas, unique wetlands, and talus slopes) is required for species conservation, especially in areas threatened by land use conversion. By having a variety of instruments available, conservationists are more likely to achieve a higher return on investment from available conservation funding.

In the same way that recovery crediting built upon some of the lessons and desirable attributes of conservation banking, it is likely that further innovation will build upon recovery crediting. The fact that a new innovation for endangered species incentives took over five years to emerge after conservation banking argues for a more active approach. The development of market-based conservation programs for endangered species is truly in its infancy. As new programs emerge, those that have organized in support of the prior innovations may fight newer ideas. This was the case with the guidance for recovery crediting. The national organization that supports mitigation banks actively opposed the development of recovery crediting, partly on the grounds that they anticipated competition. Comments in response to the draft guidance for recovery crediting actually included a recommendation that the FWS examine the economic effects that recovery crediting would have on the conservation banking industry.[36] Obviously, such resistance could stifle innovation. Similar concerns were expressed by LMI, a consultant to the U.S. Army environmental program. Its concern was that the RCS could compete for limited funding against Army Compatible Use Buffer (ACUB) proposals.[37] The ACUB uses perpetual conservation easements to protect against encroachment to Army installations.

While some of the resistance to the RCS and similar innovations appears to be rent-seeking efforts to avoid competition for funding (as in the above examples), there are concerns expressed in the interest of species conservation. For example, the Environmental Defense Fund and other national environmental groups have participated in development of the RCS and similar innovations, but they have encouraged rigorous evaluation to validate the instrument's likely impact on species recovery. Independent evaluation of policy innovations, followed by public disclosure of the evaluator's conclusions, may be the most productive means for speeding market-based innovations into application. Without independent evaluation, market-based systems for endangered species recovery may suffer criticisms similar to conservation programs in the U.S. Farm Bill. Criticisms aimed at Farm Bill conservation programs include claims of inadequate performance measures, lack of evaluation, and placing farm income support above the intended goal of natural resource protection.[38]

For endangered species recovery, a regulatory framework that encourages testing of a wide variety of market-based approaches but then requires independent evaluation and public scrutiny of results would be superior to the more cautious approach taken thus far. Inasmuch as financial costs may override other concerns, it is important that evaluations gauge cost-efficiency against the benchmark of prevailing programs. Finally, for an evaluation process to withstand scientific scrutiny, the process must rely on well-designed field monitoring for documenting actual recovery outcomes. In the end, an informed evaluation must include the collection of field data within a sampling scheme designed to yield reliable information on species status and trends.

Emerging concepts. Concepts for revolutionizing market-based incentives for endangered species conservation on private lands are emerging rapidly. Ecologists are developing spatially explicit and statistical models for more reliable alignment of credit metrics with conservation outcomes.[39] Because conservation actions for a species are not uniformly effective across a species' range, these new approaches will inform managers, scientists, and landowners on the areas where more reliable or cost-effective recovery results would be expected. These approaches should be used to develop more reliable metrics of species recovery. More reliable metrics should result in more reliable outcomes.

Business experts are beginning to tackle the technical concepts for establishing prospective restoration credits as a business framework for market-based incentives leading to proactive habitat restoration.[40] When investors are more confident that their conservation actions will be rewarded in the marketplace, they will be more likely to invest in species recovery in anticipation of a future return. When investments in conservation are made early, they are likely to yield more effective performance over time. As environmental entrepreneurs develop novel financial instruments to generate capital for private endangered species conservation efforts,[41] the marketplace could become more competitive as investors seek opportunities. Most of the potential for applying these emerging concepts are on private lands. For these and other innovations to move from concept to practice, the ESA must be adjusted to meet the emerging business, technology, and science of market-based incentives.

Lessons for Reform

By all evidence, the current ESA functions as an adequate "safety net" against species extinction. The social, economic, and political costs of the ESA are extremely high for an Act that does not yet serve its additional purpose of conserving threatened and endangered species through actions leading to recovery. Commenting on the organizational science of endangered species recovery efforts, Ron Westrum made a simple observation on the failure of recovery efforts: "Recovery efforts fail for four basic reasons: intention, incompetence, ignorance, and ill fortune."[42] So overcoming the obstacles to recovery requires motivation, skill, information, and luck. The history of failure on private lands demands some simple but effective solutions for overcoming Westrum's obstacles. Ideally, such solutions would engage private landowners in conservation actions through incentives rather than regulatory requirements. Such solutions must also include incentives for scientists, wildlife conservation interests, and the agencies responsible for administering the ESA.

While the recent calls to reform the ESA in the United States have not yet produced much in the way of a more effective statute, the lessons drawn from a history of the ESA's regulatory approach resulting in defiant private interests may have influence elsewhere. In neighboring Canada, the negative lessons of the ESA apparently influenced that nation's 2002 Species at Risk Act (SARA) such that the Canadian statute avoids imposing endangered species conservation costs on the private sector in favor of funding for voluntary stewardship and regulatory compensation.[43] Another important difference is that the Canadian statute defers implementation to provinces and territories (with the exception of aquatic species and migratory birds), while under the ESA, states may only be authorized to take implementation responsibility under strict federal terms.[44]

Separate regulatory and recovery duties. A separation of the permitting and enforcement obligations of the ESA from the science, monitoring, and recovery functions would likely result in more effective species recovery through increased access and information from private lands. Upon revision, the ESA should direct the Secretary of the Interior to defer the science, monitoring, and recovery functions to appropriate state wildlife agencies. Through cooperative agreements, data collected from private lands could then be made available to inform status reviews and monitor recovery efforts. Under the authority of the states, these data could be treated as confidential information. The benefits of this reform would be twofold: (1) landowners will be more likely to allow access and provide species information; and (2) personnel and resources for the important activities of coordinating monitoring efforts and planning recovery actions will be less likely to be overridden by the urgent activities of permitting and enforcement.

Authorize nongovernmental third parties to work with private landowners. The ESA should be revised to allow qualified third-party technical service providers to work with private landowners in the development and implementation of site-specific plans for recovery actions connected with conservation incentives. Landowners are more likely to trust nongovernmental organizations with site-specific information and property access. The FWS could use a registry program for qualified technical service providers similar to that used by the federal agencies responsible for implementation of Farm Bill Conservation Programs.

Modify the Section 9 prohibition on take. Section 9 of the ESA should be revised to give more specific guidance for allowing broad exemptions from Section 9 prohibition. Specifically, the guidance should call for exemptions for combined actions that demonstrate a net benefit to a species' population through habitat modification, even if this might cause harm to one or more individual organisms. Provisions for expedited exemptions from Section 9 should be authorized for actions that may risk some incidental take but will clearly provide long-term net benefit to species recovery. This provision would spur innovative conservation actions in concert with common land management practices (e.g., forest management, grazing, and agriculture) that do not permanently eliminate species habitat.

Stimulate the development of market-based conservation programs. The ESA should direct the Secretary of Interior to produce regulations for market-based conservation programs. The regulations should provide broad guidance that is developed specifically to stimulate the development of habitat trading and other crediting programs. When developing guidelines for such programs, the Secretary should consider measures that encourage use by the widest possible group of investors. If crediting programs are available uniformly for both federal and nonfederal actions, the investments in recovery actions would likely increase. In addition, policy that allows for federal investments in credits that are ultimately retired (i.e., not used to offset impacts to the species elsewhere) could accelerate recovery and actually be used as part of a recovery planning process. Maintaining a market-based approach such as the reverse auction feature of the RCS proof-of-concept described in this chapter should be a requirement for maintaining an efficient process.

Establish recovery goals at time of listing. In order to facilitate better planning and to create some certain targets for market-based programs, the ESA should direct the FWS to establish recovery goals at the time of species listing. Some exceptions (e.g., for emergency listings) should be established. Market-based incentives for conservation will also stimulate private investments in science and monitoring. As a consequence, the information required for developing recovery goals should become more readily available.

The mere existence of the ESA confirms that conservation of biological diversity is a public imperative. Much of the nation's biological diversity is on private lands, and thus depends on private actions for assuring its conservation. If the conservation actions that are expected from private lands are indeed important, then ESA reforms must be directed at improving the Act's performance on private lands. An ESA that provides a framework for innovative approaches to stimulating conservation on private lands will be much more effective than an ESA that approaches private lands as a regulatory problem.

Notes

1. Paul J. Ferraro, Craig McIntosh, and Monica Ospina, "The Effectiveness of the U.S. Endangered Species Act," *Journal of Environmental Economics and Management* 54 (2007): 256.

2. Mark W. Schwartz, "The Performance of the Endangered Species Act," *Annual Review of Ecology, Evolution, and Systematics* 39 (2008): 292

3. Michael J. Bean, "Second-Generation Approaches," in *The Endangered Species Act at Thirty: Renewing the Conservation Promise*, ed. Dale D. Goble, J. Michael Scott, and Frank W. Davis (Washington, D.C.: Island Press, 2006), 274.

4. U.S. Fish and Wildlife Service, News Release, June 6, 1997.

5. Dennis D. Murphy and Barry R. Noon, "The Role of Scientists in Conservation Planning on Private Lands," *Conservation Biology* 21, no.1 (2007): 26.

6. Amy W. Ando, "Waiting to Be Protected under the Endangered Species Act: The Political Economy of Regulatory Delay," *Journal of Law and Economics* 42 (1999): 52-53.

7. John A. List, Michael Margolis, and Daniel E. Osgood, "Is the Endangered Species Act Endangering Species?" *NBER Working Paper* No. 12777 (2006): 26–27, http://ssrn.com/abstract=953200; and Dean Lueck and Jeffrey A. Michael, "Preemptive Habitat Destruction under the Endangered Species Act," *Journal of Law and Economics* 46 (2003): 27–56.

8. Stephen Polasky and Holly Doremus, "When the Truth Hurts: Endangered Species Policy on Private Land with Imperfect Information," *Journal of Environmental Economics and Management* 35 (1998): 26-29.

9. Christian A. Hagen, Brent E. Jamison, Kenneth M. Giesen, and Terry Z. Riley, "Guidelines for Managing Lesser Prairie-Chicken Populations and Their Habitats," *Wildlife Society Bulletin* 32, no.1 (2004): 69–82.

10. Timothy D. Male and Michael J. Bean, "Measuring Progress in U.S. Endangered Species Conservation," *Ecology Letters* 8, no. 9 (2005): 988.

11. Polasky and Doremus, "When the Truth Hurts," 26–29.

12. For a discussion, see R. Neal Wilkins, "Wildlife Conservation on Private Lands: Habitat Planning and Regulatory Certainty" in *Sustaining the Forests of the Pacific Coast: Forging Truces in the War in the Wood*, ed. Debra J. Salazar and Donald K. Alper (Vancouver: University of British Columbia Press, 2001), 193–208.

13. 50 C.F.R. § 17.3.

14. Christian Langpap and JunJie Wu, "Voluntary Conservation of Endangered Species: When Does No Regulatory Assurance Mean No Conservation?" *Journal of Environmental Management* 47 (2003): 435–57.

15. Bean, "Second-Generation Approaches." 569.

16. Lueck and Michael, "Preemptive Habitat Destruction," 282.

17. Wilkins, "Wildlife Conservation on Private Lands: Habitat Planning and Regulatory Certainty," 193–208.

18. Emma C. Underwood, Kirk R. Klausmeyer, Scott A. Morrison, Michael Bode, and M. Rebecca Shaw, "Evaluating Conservation Spending for Species Return: A Retrospective Analysis in California," *Conservation Letters* 2 (2009): 130–37.

19. Paul R. Armsworth, Gretchen C. Daily, Peter Kareiva, and James N. Sanchirico, "Land Market Feedbacks Can Undermine Biodiversity Conservation," *Proceedings of the National Academies of Science* 103, no.14 (2006): 5403–8.

20. Robert Innes, Stephen Polasky, and John Tschirhart, "Takings, Compensation, and Endangered Species Protection on Private Lands," *Journal of Economic Perspectives* 12 (1998): 39.

21. Robert Innes, "Takings, Compensation and Equal Treatment for Owners of Developed and Undeveloped Property," *Journal of Law and Economics* 40, no. 2 (1997): 403–32.

22. National Research Council, *Science and the Endangered Species Act* (Washington, D.C.: National Academy Press, 1995), 271.

23. Peter Kareiva, Sandy Andelman, Daniel Doak, Bret Elderd, Martha Groom, Jonathan Hoekstra, Laura Hood, Frances James, John Lamoreux, Gretchen LeBuhn, Charles McCulloch, James Regetz, Lisa Savage, Mary Ruckelshaus, David Skelly, Henry Wilbur, Kelly Zamudio, and NCEAS HCP working group, "Using Science in Habitat Conservation Plans," National Center for Ecological Analysis and Synthesis, University of California, Santa Barbara, 1999, http://www.nceas.ucsb.edu/nceas-web/projects/2049/hcp-1991-01-14.pdf.

24. Terry L. Anderson and Donald R. Leal, "Free Market versus Political Environmentalism," *Harvard Journal of Law & Public Policy* 15, no. 2 (1992): 297–310.

25. Florian Hartig and Martin Drechsler, "Smart Spatial Incentives for Market-Based Conservation," *Biological Conservation* 142 (2009): 779–88; Douglas Bruggeman and Michael Jones, "Should Habitat Trading Be Based on Mitigation Ratios Derived from Landscape Indices? A Model-Based Analysis of Compensatory Restoration Options for the Red-Cockaded Woodpecker," *Environmental Management* 42, no. 4 (2008): 591–602; B. Kelsey Jack, Carolyn Kousky, and Katharine R. E. Sims, "Designing Payments for Ecosystem Services: Lessons from Previous Experience with Incentive-Based Mechanisms," *Proceedings of the National Academy of Sciences* 105, no. 28 (2008): 9465–70; and Martin Drechsler, Frank Watzold, Karin Johst, Holger Bergmann, and Josef Settele, "A Model-Based Approach for Designing Cost-Effective Compensation Payments for Conservation

of Endangered Species in Real Landscapes," *Biological Conservation* 140, no. 1-2 (2007): 174–86.

26. U.S. Fish & Wildlife Service, "Guidance for the Establishment, Use, and Operation of Conservation Banks," *Federal Register* 60 (2003): 58605–14.

27. Jessica Fox, Gretchen C. Daily, Barton H. Thompson, Jr., Kai M. A. Chan, Adam Davis, and Anamaria Nino-Murcia, "Conservation Banking," in *The Endangered Species Act at Thirty: Conserving Biodiversity in Human-Dominated Landscapes.* ed. J. Michael Scott, Dale D. Goble, and Frank W. Davis (Washington, D.C.: Island Press, 2006), 228–43.

28. U.S. Fish & Wildlife Service, "Endangered and Threatened Wildlife and Plants: Recovery Crediting Guidance," *Federal Register* 73 (2008): 44761–72.

29. For details, see R. Neal Wilkins, David Wolfe, Linda S. Campbell, and Susan Baggett, "Development of Recovery Credit Systems as a New Policy Innovation for Threatened and Endangered Species," *Transactions of the 73rd North American Wildlife and Natural Resources Conference* (2009): 1–12

30. "Pentagon Issues 'Credits' to Offset Harm to Wildlife: Payouts to Landowners Draw Criticism," *Washington Post*, February 9, 2009.

31. Michael E. Canes and Elizabeth S. Rohr, "Cost-Benefit Analysis of the Fort Hood Recovery Credit System," Unpublished Report CE710T2, LMI Government Consulting, 2008.

32. Texas Parks & Wildlife Code §12.0251. Disclosure of Information Collected During Technical Guidance to Private Landowner.

33. Keith L. Olenick, Urs P. Kreuter, and J. Richard Conner, "Texas Landowner Perceptions Regarding Ecosystem Services and Cost-Sharing Land Management Programs," *Ecological Economics* 53 (2005): 247–60.

34. Isla S. Fishburn, Peter Kareiva, Kevin J. Gaston, and Paul R. Armsworth, "The Growth of Conservation Easements as a Conservation Tool," *PLoS ONE* 4, no. 3 (2009): e4996, doi:10.1371/journal.pone.0004996.

35. Canes and Rohr, *Cost-Benefit Analysis of the Fort Hood Recovery Credit System*, 4.16.

36. U.S. Fish & Wildlife Service, "Endangered and Threatened Wildlife and Plants."

37. Canes and Rohr, *Cost-Benefit Analysis of the Fort Hood Recovery Credit System*, 4.16–4.17.

38. Sandra S. Batie, "Green Payments and the U.S. Farm Bill: Information and Policy Challenges," *Frontiers in Ecology and the Environment* (2009), doi:10.1890/080004.

39. Hartig and Drechsler, "Smart Spatial Incentives for Market-Based Conservation."

40. R. G. Stahl, R. Gouguet, A. DeSantis, J. Liu, and M. Ammann, "Prospective Environmental Restoration/Restoration Up Front: A Concept for an Incentive-Based Program to Increase Restoration Planning and Implementation in the United States," *Integrated Environmental Assessment and Management* 4, no. 1 (2007): 6–14.

41. James T. Mandel, C. Josh Donlan, and Jonathan Armstrong, "A Derivative Approach to Endangered Species Conservation," *Frontiers in Ecology and the Environment* (2009), doi: 10.1890/070170.

42. Ron Westrum, "An Organizational Perspective: Designing Recovery Teams from the Inside Out," in *Endangered Species Recovery: Finding the Lessons, Improving the Process*, ed. Tim W. Clark, Richard P. Reading, and Alice L. Clarke (Washington, D.C.: Island Press, 1994), 327–49.

43. Mary Illical and Kathryn Harrison, "Protecting Endangered Species in the U.S. and Canada: The Role of Negative Lesson Drawing," *Canadian Journal of Political Science* 40, no. 2 (2007): 367–94.

44. Ibid.

4

Permits, Property, and Planning in the Twenty-First Century: Habitat as Survival and Beyond

Jamison E. Colburn

In our legal tradition there are permits and there is property, and they are like oil and water. The norms, institutions, and agents of one seem antagonistic—even antithetical—to the other. Property is reliable, tangible, and intimately bound up with one's autonomy, one's severability from society. Excluding others from our assets supposedly just is what we do to express, secure, and comfort ourselves and the company we keep. Government permissions, by contrast, are fleeting, revocable—they are what we collectively use to express, secure, and comfort *society*. They are the mechanism of choice by which individual plans for assets are filtered and reconciled with collective needs.[1] If we are to get around the impasses we have reached today in protecting nature's composition and function, however, we must strive to better combine permits and property and leave behind exactly the sort of distinctions we now use in differentiating one from the other. This may seem about as easy as changing the laws of physics that separate oil and water, but I will argue that it is actually long overdue and perhaps much simpler than we think.

Of course if people were predictable, protecting nature would be easy. In reality, the range of human motivations is vast and complex, and hence behavior is unpredictable.[2] Some people are conscientious neighbors while

The author thanks Jonathan Adler for helpful comments on earlier drafts.

others are driven by quick profit. Most importantly, though, people hardly ever embody an archetype—a reality which unwinds even the richest behavioral models. Indeed, the pervasive threat of conscious (even strategic) preference adaptation makes our behavioral sciences decidedly under-informative. Thus, the further the federal government has undertaken the enterprise of regulating behavior to protect imperiled species or their habitats, the more this unpredictability has defined its efforts. The more the unpredictability of human behavior has defined national conservation policy, the more those who administer the Endangered Species Act (ESA) have favored an evidence-based approach to their work. Yet this evolution has now reached a threshold—one that conservation advocates and courts alike too often ignore—summed up in the following question. How deep is our commitment to biodiversity conservation, *really*?

In this chapter, I propose one answer to that question by examining the Act's treatment of the most serious and pervasive threat to biodiversity today: habitat disruption and loss.[3] This requires, first, a reconsideration of the Act as it has evolved. That leads directly to a prognosis and prescription for the ESA's continued dominance of biodiversity conservation in the United States. In essence, I argue that the ESA is beginning an uncertain process of "de-territorialization." The U.S. Fish and Wildlife Service (FWS) and National Oceanic and Atmospheric Administration's Fisheries Service (NOAA Fisheries Service) officers charged with administering the ESA are shifting their focus away from protecting particular lands or identifiably imperiled habitats and toward building capacities for conservation in themselves and others. Out of necessity, these agents of the ESA must strive to assemble a "resilient landscape" from a mixture of public and private lands. The only way they can do that is by devoting what little capacity they have to improving the physical and managerial connections between "owned" property and the public domain's different reserve systems. In short, they must learn how to integrate a variety of conservation practices, a shift in approach that will remain unlikely as long as conservation remains so spatially and conceptually scattered. Real ESA reform would, therefore, link up the disparate fits and starts that have brought us this far and pull them together into a larger, more intentional whole.

Habitat loss and disruption have been constants on Earth, geologically speaking. They have played formative roles in the processes of evolution and speciation.[4] But their rapid, anthropogenic acceleration in the past century now sets a stunningly broad and deep agenda for the ESA if its declared commitment to conservation is to be taken seriously. This should force us to do some hard thinking about several basic legal and social institutions—institutions like property, legal permissions, and land use planning—and how they must co-evolve if we are to synthesize the disparate methods of habitat protection we have into a better conservation system. Habitat is a concept encompassing a vast range of biological and physical attributes, only some of which are understood well enough to affect intentionally.[5] In this chapter, I assume that we seek collectively to protect as many of those attributes as we possibly can consistent with other, equally (or more) important priorities. I describe the history of the ESA and how it has been amended in order to protect habitat while also deferring to owners. I then detail the challenges we face when we attempt to shape human behaviors for the sake of habitat protection. Next, I contrast permits and property as means of shaping human behavior and offer several targeted reforms of the ESA's permits as components of a more integrative approach. I conclude the essay by offering what may seem like a counterintuitive proposal: that the best path to greater influence for already overburdened conservation actors may be to better standardize their programs that manage habitat and human behavior.

Statutory Evolution: From Categorical to Cost-Driven in Two Decades

How ought we to interpret a statute that began as one thing and evolved into something very different? Ascribing a coherent intent to the disparate collectives that gave us the Endangered Species Act in its current form—with changes that came in a jagged sequence—is a challenging exercise in synthesis, surely. The Endangered Species Act of 1973 famously declared that extinction was to be eradicated and that costs should play little-to-no role in that process.[6] After that richly symbolic act, however, things got more complicated. The scale and scope of this objective came into view and, eventually, came to dominate the statute and its administrators. By the 1990s, implementation of the ESA was affected by two very different imperatives. On the one hand was the original, largely symbolic imperative aimed at halting the loss of biological diversity. On the other hand was a growing skepticism of governance that marked the 1980s and 1990s, aimed at pitting each public objective against its peers and allocating (scarce) public resources according to the relative popularity and/or urgency of public objectives. As it happened, cost-conscious governance affected laws like the ESA deeply and led to their restructuring.[7] Significant amendments in 1978, 1979, 1982, and 1988 all combined to remake the ESA's simple, forceful declaration of principle into a labyrinthine framework serving first and foremost to empower a pair of administrative agencies, the FWS and National Marine Fisheries Service (NMFS) (collectively, the Services), to *govern* the almost limitless domain in which our extinction pandemic is unfolding.

At the same time, the public was becoming much more cognizant of environmental issues.[8] Today, most educated people realize that humanity is causing a "massive die-off"—a geological extinction event linked to our very existence.[9] And yet, the determination of whether a species is at risk of extinction and, therefore, should be listed pursuant to ESA Section 4's risk factors must be made without weighing the costs and benefits of that listing. Indeed, this is the *only* juncture where the relative costs and benefits of regulatory action remain categorically excluded from consideration in administering the ESA.[10] Moreover, that express exclusion of costs was *added* in the 1982 amendments by the same provision that directed the Services, in making their listing decisions, to "tak[e] into account those efforts, if any, being made by any State or foreign nation, or any political subdivision of a State or foreign nation, to protect [the candidate] species."[11] For virtually every other regulatory action carried out pursuant to the Act, it is either silent on the choice factors the Services may or must weigh or it expressly includes cost, feasibility, practicability, and other like considerations.

Extinction was supposedly viewed in 1973 as a relatively rare, discrete phenomenon—passenger pigeons, dodos, and the like. Existential threats to iconic wildlife like the grizzly or bald eagle catalyzed the enactment of statutes to deal with these threatened extinctions.[12] As our regulators examined the threats to species, though (and as citizens' suits forced regulators to act to protect species), the assumption that extinctions are rare crumbled.[13] We were learning how enormous our disturbance footprint had grown and would continue growing, just as risk regulation was confronting austere fiscal restraints during the economic turbulence of the 1970s. Looking back, the record implies that our society is willing to invest the resources needed to protect our iconic wildlife as long as it does not upset our basic structures of production, consumption, and governance. Curbing identifiable threats and carrying out extraordinary restorative work species-by-species, place-by-place have demonstrated plenty about our society and culture. The more charismatic and iconic a species, the better it has attracted scarce conservation attention and investment.[14] That past does not prove much at all about our society's possible *future* commitments to biodiversity conservation, though, and the following thematic sketch of the ESA's evolution to date should not be misinterpreted to imply anything of the sort. What it does seek to convey is an evolutionary record of legal development—a record that should serve as a cautionary tale as we look ahead to efforts better to protect habitats and biodiversity.

Today, the ESA is known for two notorious amendments, each of which seriously complicated efforts to assess the Act's overall commitment to biodiversity: (1) the 1978 creation of the so-called "God squad,"[15] and (2) the 1982 addition of permissions to "take" listed species.[16] The God squad was a cabinet-level committee designed to exempt federal actions otherwise prohibited by ESA Section 7[17] whenever, upon petition, it concluded that the risks of losing a species were outweighed by the expected benefits of the (challenged) federal actions.[18] These 1978 amendments followed *Tennessee Valley Authority v. Hill*,[19] a precedent that has preoccupied legal philosophers as much as it has conservation lawyers since its decision.[20] Over the years, though, the "committee" has been convened exactly twice and, in one of the matters, botched its proceedings so thoroughly that it was stayed by federal court order.[21] The actual results of the God squad, in short, have been decidedly modest.

The other notorious amendment, the 1982 injection of "incidental" take permissions, has been of much greater moment and will be considered below. Often overlooked, however, have been several less conspicuous amendments gradually transforming the Services' implementation of the Act into a set list of highly constrained actions and procedures driven by agency cost accounting and resource availability.[22] The 1978 amendments, for example, bound listed taxa to a presumption of eventual "recovery" and the development of taxon-specific plans to that end.[23] And the 1982 amendments further directed the Services to give "priority to those [listed] species most likely to benefit from [recovery] plans, particularly those species that are, or may be, in conflict with construction or other developmental projects or other forms of economic activity."[24] Finally, the 1988 amendments required the FWS to begin compiling and annually reporting to Congress "an accounting on a species by species basis of all reasonably identifiable Federal expenditures made primarily for the conservation of [listed] species" pursuant to the ESA.[25] The increasingly taut procedures and purse strings, in short, formalized Section 4 status changes and Section 7 consultations and made judicial review into a core facet of the Act.[26]

The key peak in the statute's developmental arc, however, was the permission now known as "incidental" takings.[27] Modern legislation is said to be replete with delegations of discretionary authority to permit, require, or forbid conduct. Legislation, they say, is now largely "intransitive."[28] Intransitive legislation, instead of setting the rights and duties of A and B, directs C to specify their rights and duties, often on an evolving basis. The 1978 amendments are at least weak confirmation of this thesis. At the same time the amendments injected more formality into the consultation process,[29] they empowered the FWS and NMFS to establish and recommend whatever "reasonable and prudent alternatives" (RPAs) they concluded "would avoid jeopardizing" the listed species in the event their Section 7 conclusions were that the subject federal actions might jeopardize the taxa or might "adversely modify" any designated "critical habitat."[30] These RPAs have since become the principal path *out* of consultation proceedings involving critically endangered taxa.[31] The Services have agreed that such RPAs must be "consistent with the purposes of the action" and "economically and technically feasible."[32] And they have allocated the burdens of collecting and assembling the requisite information to the action agency(s).[33] The courts have generally left them free to choose the best RPA(s) and/or incidental take level for the circumstances. However, in spite of this deference from the courts, consultation as a whole seems to have entrenched the Services in a reactive posture precisely because they must rely on others for the information needed to establish the "reasonable" and "prudent" alternative courses of action and move forward.[34] And RPAs soon became the model by which a whole variety of "take" forms would be permitted!

The creation of "incidental take permits" in 1982 arguably provided a robust confirmation of the intransitivity thesis. They empowered the Services to make action-specific determinations of permissible "take" and habitat destruction, thereby creating a vast practice of conduct-supervision by the Services. ESA Section 10(a) provides that the Services

> may permit, under [terms and conditions they prescribe] (A) any act otherwise prohibited by [ESA Section 9] for scientific purposes or to enhance the propagation or survival of the affected species, including, but not limited to, acts necessary for the establishment and maintenance of experimental populations...or (B) any taking otherwise prohibited by [ESA Section 9] if such taking is incidental to, and not the purpose of, the carrying out of an otherwise lawful activity.[35]

The operative notions are the *enhancing* of "propagation or survival" of the affected taxa and the notion of an "incidental" taking of listed taxa. While these might sound like real thresholds, the latter focuses on an actor's *intent*[36] while the former lacks any meaningful standard of proof. Thus, the decisive thresholds (if any) must be spelled out by the Services, and this has rendered "intransitive" virtually everything about the Act's control of habitat disturbance and loss. The evident motivation for the amendments was to allow the Services to reconcile owner/permittee autonomy with recognized conservation needs. This motive gripped the federal government in the era following the enactment of our major conservation statutes. Not surprisingly, the Services have struggled since 1978 to define acceptable levels of "take" associated with regulated actions. When a federal action governed by ESA Section 7 and some "taking" of the species may occur even under the control of RPAs, the Services have issued "incidental take statements" (ITSs) as a kind of "safe harbor" for the actors involved. Consequently, consultations have become like litigation, with RPAs and ITSs beginning to seem like the structural reform consent decrees of old.[37] Thus, in cases like *Arizona Cattle Growers' Association v. U.S. Fish & Wildlife Service*,[38] and *Oregon Natural Resources Council v. Allen*,[39] the Ninth Circuit held that ITS safe harbors—

where "incidental take" is likely to occur but *only* where it is likely to occur—must be predicated on facts found and evidence gathered.[40] Indeed, the *Allen* court held, citing the legislative history of the 1982 amendments, that an ITS safe harbor ought generally to include a numerical limit of some kind, i.e., how much take is *too* much.[41] When the cap is reached, consultation must be reinitiated.[42] Alas, with final documents being due at the conclusion of what amounts to a legal proceeding, and with their content, as well as the content of any related ITS, dictated by available evidence, consultation has become at best a litigious (and costly) check on government.[43] The Services and most action agencies now seek to avoid or to terminate consultations however they can.[44] This undoubtedly increases the costs involved, but the worst of it is that consultations are now dominated by highly strategic behaviors in which information flows become viscous immediately.

The statute's notion of "critical habitat" is one of the principal factors driving this evolution. While they do not alter private rights/obligations per se, critical habitat designations at least *seem* to encumber federal actors with more stringent precautions in designated areas by enjoining them to "insure" they do not adversely modify the designated habitat.[45] And given the ubiquity of federal permission requirements today, critical habitat designations have become high-profile events. Under the Act, however, critical habitat need only be designated where the Services find it "prudent," "determinable," and where its economic costs do not outweigh its benefits.[46] And the statute requires the Services to take affirmative steps to provide notice of designation proposals to the communities and landowners "within or adjacent to such habitat."[47] Conflict over both the hard-to-find facts and conflicted statutory standard is, therefore, the norm.[48] And what had been a rather accommodating interpretation of "adverse modification"—essentially collapsing it into the subject taxon's survival—was invalidated years ago and has never been replaced.[49] The Services apparently have no desire to rework so heavily strategized and contentious a crossroads. Amending what has become, virtually by default, one of the most broadly applicable standards in the ESA would be a time sink, to be sure.[50] Thus, *any* permission to take actions within designated critical habitats (including incidental take permits and candidate conservation agreements with assurances, both to be discussed below) can, at least in theory, trigger a consultation and activate the "jeopardy" and "adverse modification" standards along with it.[51]

The 1982 amendments also empowered the Services to permit "incidental" take wherever some applicant's "conservation plan" would, "to the maximum extent practicable, minimize and mitigate the impacts of such taking" and where the Services find that the taking would "not appreciably reduce the likelihood of survival and recovery of the species in the wild."[52] These conservation plans are usually known as *habitat* conservation plans (HCPs) because the approved activities almost always involve some form of habitat alteration.[53] Technically, though, the HCP is in exchange for an "incidental take permit" (ITP).[54] Before they may issue an ITP, the Services must find that each statutory criterion is met, including that "adequate funding for the conservation plan and procedures to deal with unforeseen circumstances will be provided."[55] HCPs are supposed to minimize the risks presented by their ITPs, though, and an "assurance" that an ITP will not be revoked just because the subject taxon is declining is a rather curious allocation of risk.[56] This assurance to the applicant raises the question of whether ITPs are a means to protect—or a means to disturb and destroy—habitat.

Widely vilified, celebrated, studied, and tweaked with things like "assurances," this sort of exchange is essentially a cipher if its overall efficacy is the question. No amount of evidence could be gathered to prove or disprove conclusively the instrumental value of this program—or these permissions.[57] What the program has done is further the transition of the ESA from a simple, declarative law into a system of intransitive norms governing a vast and expanding array of human behaviors. The substantive standard for the issuance of an ITP is as ambivalent toward habitat disturbance as it could be. It boils down to whether the mitigation is "practicable" for the applicant and whether or not his or her conduct "appreciably" reduces the species' survival chances.[58] Over the years, this combination of factors in the granting of ITPs has put the Services in an unenviable position. As many have observed, it turns the Services into a kind of ratchet permitting as much— but *only* as much—risk to listed species as they supposedly can bear.[59] But it assumes a precision the Services cannot possibly achieve. Several of their conservation plans and ITP findings have now been overturned in court, perhaps because of the ambiguous nature of the standard itself.[60]

Unsurprisingly, HCPs remained rare for years after the 1982 amendment that allowed them.[61] Not until the Clinton Administration introduced a "no surprises policy" (NSP)—the *assurance* that no further mitigations would be due from any "incidental take" permittee for the life of the permit—did these permits become central to ESA practice.[62] According to the NSP, any material enhancements a conservation plan might require must either be *volunteered* by the permittee or be supplied by the government.[63] Such assurances assign the risks of uncertainty inherent in any such enterprise to the public,[64] and a flawed conservation plan means excess risk. Yet habitat conservation today comes down to a bare "survival" standard in virtually every ESA context. The core finding the Services must make in issuing an ITP is that the permittee will not "appreciably" reduce the species' survival chances.[65] Indeed, even apart from RPAs and ITPs, a whole series of take permits—"safe harbor agreements" (SHAs) and "candidate conservation agreements" (CCAs)—are now backed by similar "assurances," aiming to entice would-be conservationists into partnerships for the benefit of at-risk taxa.[66]

The FWS has actively cultivated these SHAs and CCAs under ESA Section 10 by granting assurances like those in the NSP. An SHA can be completed wherever the Service finds that the owner's proposed plan will generate a "net conservation benefit" for listed taxa.[67] Typically, this involves an owner willing to improve habitat for listed taxa but *not* willing to do so if it means being bound not to alter or disturb that (enhanced) habitat indefinitely.[68] The assurances permit the owner(s) to return the land to some agreed-upon "baseline" without ESA liability if and when it suits them.[69] A candidate conservation agreement with assurances (CCAA) has a similar structure except that it involves taxa that are at risk but have not yet been listed pursuant to ESA Section 4.[70] Each of these mechanisms can be more or less challenging to negotiate depending on their scale, scope, and any related ESA "special" rules[71] or National Environmental Policy Act procedures.[72] SHAs and CCAAs must "enhance" the propagation or survival of listed taxa, a standard entirely divorced from the recovery of range or abundance but intimately bound up with the property being encumbered. Each of these permissions, moreover, can last for decades,[73] raising still further concerns about the propriety of what may turn out to be profoundly mistaken judgments.

A nationwide Freedom of Information Act request in mid-2009 yielded over 60 SHAs and over 30 CCAAs,[74] most of which had been done since these "assurances" were made available.[75] Averaging these deals would be pointless: each is entrenched in its own unique context. But as these mechanisms spread and as more owned land is encumbered with what amounts to a kind of regulatory *easement*, the persistence of resident wildlife is becoming a function of bilateral relationships between owners and government—a government that is increasingly cost-conscious and overburdened. Given the ESA's pronounced ambivalence toward habitat regulation, this growing intransitivity of its habitat protections is perhaps not surprising. But it is most definitely a central trope of conservation as a field of regulation today. Next I describe the difficulty inherent in shaping human behavior for the sake of habitat preservation.

Results-Based Regulation, Information Triage, and Owner Autonomy

Risk regulation today is defined by the defaults from which regulatory actions depart, along with the information bottlenecks that regulators must confront before taking action.[76] Most risk regulation in the United States today is carried out by administrative agencies that are governed by the principles of administrative law. And if our culture worships the virtue of self-interest and the profit motive, our administrative law celebrates the virtues of (1) accountability, (2) participation, and (3) means/ends rationality that can be demonstrated from record evidence. Consequently, U.S. regulators generally bear substantial proof and procedural burdens.

Of course, the trouble with this evidence-based approach when it comes to human behavior is the irreducibly cryptic nature of the evidence. The claim is often heard, for example, that the very structure of the ESA encourages the behaviors it is meant to control. An interval between the identification of a taxon at risk and the activation of the Act's protections, it is said, produces a sharp incentive for owners to destroy or degrade their land's habitat values for named taxa because of the profits that they might forgo if they fail to destroy the habitat before it becomes protected.[77] ESA Section 9 and the meticulous withholding of RPAs, ITPs, etc. both potentially impinge upon landowners' autonomy and, knowing this, landowners arguably have an incentive to act preemptively.[78] Lueck and Michael even put quantitative force behind the anecdotes and theoretical speculation. In 2003, they published a study of forgone and "preemptive" timber harvesting in connection with the designation of critical habitat for red-cockaded woodpeckers (RCW). By time-slicing forest plot data taken from the U.S. Forest Service's Forest Inventory and Analysis (FIA) database, Lueck and Michael sought to prove that landowners threatened by woodpecker colonization of their timber tended to cut that timber "prematurely."[79] The trouble with their calculations, apart from how little we know about this behavior as a harm to overall biodiversity or even to the RCW in particular,[80] is the vast array of simplifying assumptions they had to adopt in order to derive *anything* quantitative at all. From what constitutes a "forested" acre,[81] to what habitat "values" red-cockaded woodpeckers require,[82] to the dispersal threats woodpecker colonies supposedly represented to landowners,[83] to how "onerous" habitat regulations are actually perceived to be,[84] to the gross spatial imprecision of FIA data,[85] Lueck and Michael carried out a veritable odyssey of data-minded oversimplification. Indeed, they were forced to study "strategic" behaviors surrounding a "regulation" that is not even regulatory per se. While the intuition is plainly reasonable that incentives to act strategically often arise from the imperfect scaling and/or scoping of legal rules,[86] the quantitative evidence Lueck and Michael were able to marshal to support the intuition was weak at best. This kind of evidence can at best incompletely justify the practice of "paying" for habitat conservation on private lands through assurances. As a justification for the CCAAs, ITPs, and SHAs that "pay" for habitat conservation on owned lands, then, this one is at best incomplete.

More generally, though, creating prospective rules virtually entails such inaccuracies of scale or scope, if for no other reason than that natural languages are naturally imprecise. People constantly adjust their expectations and reorient their plans over time in view of others' behaviors and (likely) intentions, especially as to what we might call legislative over- and under-inclusion. So when the unavoidable flaws of legal processes are factored in, the probability that ends and means will be mismatched in laws that are enacted and applied mounts to a virtual certainty—and people know it. But this no more justifies the generalization that all regulation is ill-conceived than it does the flight from "reality" in the very scientific fields that might actually help us re-engineer our legal rights, privileges, and immunities rationally.[87] It underscores the potential that behavior-predicting tools would have for regulators. But where are those tools? They almost never guide the steps we take implicitly assuming we have such predictive powers.

Take the spread of "assurances" and other representations to would-be conservationist-owners by the Services. *Trust* in the owners being permitted and granted these assurances is the only conclusive reason to accept the risks we run in allowing them their autonomy where habitat loss is concerned. But whom *should* the Services trust? We resolve such questions without any hard metrics—intuitively, tacitly, and too often defectively. It is certainly not a matter for which the typical "agency" has expertise, at least not in any traditional sense.[88] Will the Services *develop* such expertise the more they engage in this kind of dealing? Judging by how they are structured, there is little reason to assume so. And, of course, the real test of these permits will only come when some private enforcer finally gets a valid "case" of ESA Section 9 liability before a court and the defendant claims a permit as a shield.[89]

In short, these instruments' factual complexities are being compounded by their normative ambiguities. They are making an already fragmented, fast-changing landscape more so. Piecemeal efforts of the sort—however virtuous on their own merits—almost always increase the risk of "gridlock" down the road, if for no other reason than that each is different from the others.[90] Of course, information triage like the Services' uses of best available information in the formation of these uniquely tailored deals is now part and parcel of risk regulation more generally. Regulators too often must choose which risks to investigate based on which risks are, from an information-gathering perspective, most feasibly investigated. And the rise of ecosystem services—the pricing of externalities that normally cannot be priced[91]—shows how intensely we are pursuing regulatory mechanisms that cope with the uncertainty and enormity of conservation today. Locating habitat "regulation" of this kind across our intermixed landscapes, though, was taken as a step toward a more "results-based" conservation practice. Yet the bilateralism of owner-to-government conservation is spreading according to no organizing principles other than resident wildlife's "survival" and the protection of owner autonomy. Next I argue that this is only further obstructing the paths toward a synthesis of our disparate conservation practices into a truly results-based whole.

Permits into Property?

"Because human beings are fated to live mostly on the surface of the earth," the conventional wisdom holds, "the pattern of entitlements to use land is a central issue in social organization."[92] "Real" property, especially, is standardized into relatively stable bundles of rights "off the rack" that change hands "as is."[93] Property rights, *unlike* contracts, are said to be *in rem*, i.e., they run with an asset and bind all subsequent claimants on that asset regardless of their specific relationship(s) to the right holder(s).[94] Government permissions, *like* contracts, are usually bilateral, imbricated in multifactored conditionals, and, most of all, are generally non-transferable.[95] Moreover, as Jerry Mashaw once argued, government permissions are shaped in good part by "bureaucratic imperatives":

> The quality of justice provided…depends primarily on how good the management system is at dealing with the set of conflicting demands that define rational, fair, and efficient adjudication. It must translate vague and conflicting statutory goals into administrable rules, without losing the true and sometimes subtle thrust of the program. It must attempt to ensure that decisions are consistent and that development is adequate, without impairing the discretion necessary [for] individualization.[96]

The Services' many bureaucratic imperatives, as suggested above, might be thought to leave little opportunity for standardization or the other hallmarks of property. Even with the advent of the NSP and other "assurances," these devices are still revocable in the strictest sense[97] and only "run with the land" as the Services permit.[98] In this light, the partnerships ITPs, ITSs, safe harbors, and CCAAs represent are just good old-fashioned leveraging of scarce resources.[99] To listen to the Services, the ESA's regulation of habitat is a framework in crisis. Congress cannot appropriate money fast enough to keep up with all the taxa that could or should be listed and managed as imperiled. So the Services use what they can always make more of: their permitting authority.

But the risks these tools introduce are asymmetrical: they can generate harmful externalities, both at present and in the future, and they are potentially serious notice/comprehension problems in the making, given their complexity. Treating these government permissions *as* property, thus, would be exceedingly tricky. It has only been in the context of due process adjudication that government permissions have been associated with property, and then only for limited purposes.[100] Of course, administrative agencies routinely *create* property and, even shy of the "property" threshold, government assurances often endorse private expectations in a way the Constitution can be invoked to protect. Contractual obligations, for example, encumber government just as surely as do various "property" liabilities.[101] Even supposing that the ESA habitat permits reviewed are regarded as mere contracts, the legal liabilities the government would face for breaching them are significant enough to give any administrator pause.[102]

This instinctual distrust of lumping property and permits together ought not to inhibit us from exploring why or how permissions and property are comparable, though. Property rights in our legal system are, in a sense, bimodal: they secure privileges, powers, and immunities against other agents within a legal jurisdiction while simultaneously doing so against the agents of that legal jurisdiction. Ownership works its magic in part by securing to owners a subordinate form of sovereignty: standard, recognizable forms of dominion that order behaviors without the need for constant recourse to fine print. Thus, not surprisingly, property's bimodality—its nature as right *in rem* and as right against government—invariably chills discussions of making government permissions more "like" property. Modeling ESA habitat permissions after property, however, might paradoxically empower the Services to protect more habitat more effectively over the long term and on a broader scale, in part because doing so could: (1) simplify the mechanics of creating, adjusting, and reordering these managerial permissions; (2) enhance market and non-market actors' capacities to assess, compare, and benchmark their own (often quite disparate) conservation actions; and (3) better standardize the risks being shifted by tools like CCAAs, SHAs, and ITPs.

Nevertheless, one kind of legal right should not be confused for another, and nothing that follows suggests otherwise. My argument is that the ESA's evolution—toward an instransitive normative system empowering the FWS and NMWF, two smallish bureaucratic agencies, to govern vast, expanding arrays of human conduct—has given us a view of how property and permissions actually interact in real time. Clearly, owner autonomy exerts powerful influences on systems like the ESA. But just as clearly, permissions are an increasingly pervasive constraint on owner autonomy. Next I argue that this view should persuade those shaping the Act's future to treat human systems as being every bit as variable and adaptive as natural systems and to start laying the foundation that will enable the agents *of*, as well as the agents *within*, our legal jurisdictions to pool their information, cognitive capacities, and cooperative innovations in ways that empower all of them to solve their own problems of scarcity and depletion.

The Intermixed Landscape

Given our diversity of owners and regulators, the core challenge we face in the looming crisis of habitat loss and disturbance is enabling (and prompting) broader-scale cooperation. Yet the permissions that the Services have been generating are too small, too customized, too opaque, and too bound up with the highly imperfect information that happens to be available at their origination. If they were modeled to function more like property, they would be more standardized, more recordable and searchable, more legally explicit, and likely more *exchangeable* as such. Such adjustments are both feasible and overdue.

In my view, reshaping habitat permissions to look and operate more like property would enable greater coordination across geographic regions and over time. In turn, this would enable the public better to protect itself against externalities like habitat loss. Like the proverbial "patent thicket," habitat permissions that are idiosyncratic, costly to generate, and hard to transfer can actually create more "frictions" than innovations.[103] Retooling them to function more like—and be *recognizable* as—relatively standardized bundles of "rights" and "duties," therefore, could yield both public and private benefits. As our opportunities to scale up arise from the modest beginnings in any particular parcel, protected area, or conservation deal, it is obvious that standardized versions of habitat maintenance could be more easily bundled, collapsed into larger composites, and eventually compared for their relative advantages. The transition to standardized habitat permissions would be aided by (1) standardized terminology, (2) measurable outcomes, and (3) temporal increments.[104]

To be sure, the biological evaluation of habitats is very difficult. What makes a habitat a habitat is often population- or species-specific. And, as things stand today, our individual efforts can be more or less specific to their own parties, conservation targets, and circumstances and, thus, more or less recognizable to others. Even standard protocols for monitoring or surveying or a requirement that Geographic Information System coordinates accompany any ESA habitat permit, for example, would be a significant improvement over current practices. Going forward, however, the deep structure of our biomes as created by geological and evolutionary processes must become much better known and much more of a driver in conservation planning. Were the Services able to synthesize standardizable units of the sort, a variety of intermediaries exists to ease the negotiation and exchange of habitat permissions for landowers.[105] In addition to standardizing biogeographic units, standardizing the kinds of "assurances" being granted would be an improvement, too. At present, assurances vary among ITPs, SHAs, and CCAAs in how, when, and on what grounds they can be revoked[106] or amended,[107] in their duration,[108] and in their transferability.[109] More standardized forms of assurances, we can imagine, might be more readily assembled (or disassembled) as necessity dictates and would certainly change hands more easily among points of contact within the Services.

Finally, what is less obvious here is the effect that better transparency and wider communication of the internal workings of these mechanisms could have at the margins—the ameliorative effect our public "stock of wisdom" broadly communicated could have on the *next* iterative step toward our (immense) collective goals. In my view, the possibilities are impressive, but that argument must rest on three admittedly contestable premises. First, *most* imperiled species today depend on active landscape management either to mitigate threats originating beyond their current range(s) or to alter habitat conditions to allow further dispersal. This includes everything from ecological restoration meant to increase the effective range of imperiled taxa to the control of invasive species introduced or released within a taxon's range and an immense variety of biophysical manipulations in between. And, of course, the behavior, location, and needs of many species vary throughout the year, often substantially.[110] Thus, measuring overall habitat functionality can be extremely complex and is often both spatially and temporally vague by necessity. SHAs, for example, are designed to induce exactly the kind of advantageous manipulations that many species need—but they are done at spatial and temporal scales that ignore most of the variability involved.

Second, listed species represent but a fraction of nature's composition and functionality now in jeopardy.[111] In some sense, this is a testament to nature's immensity. But it is also a useful reminder of the character of our legal system and the principal dilemma it presents for conservation: law is promulgated within a particular jurisdiction, and therefore its force is bounded to that jurisdiction. And, while in the United States land use (and, thus, habitat disturbance) has traditionally been a matter only for state and local government, the challenges of regulating land use were compounded when the federal government asserted control over land use through the ESA.[112] For, until we can *execute* on that federal legislation's promise, the success of habitat conservation efforts inevitably hinges on what the federal government has to *spend* as it displaces local jurisdiction. And that has meant, thus far at least, tragic underinvestment in biological diversity and habitat planning.

Finally, as I have argued elsewhere, the principal barriers to better conservation are almost all cognitive and informational. The key insight in conservation over the last three decades has been the necessity of acting without knowing. On most decisions, usable information is imperfect, dispersed, and in need of costly and time-consuming improvement. For example, whole life-cycle analysis of a product or service is needed before we decide which mode of consumption is more "environmentally friendly." Yet it is exactly that rich a form of analysis where information and cognitive costs so often outstrip our capacities. For even where near-term outcomes are relatively certain, we still have reason to bracket what we know (or what we think we know) and make provision for a more uncertain future. Resigning oneself to the inevitability of imperfect information, of course, resolves nothing about the appropriate levels of certainty, probability, or ignorance. But with these three premises in mind, it should become clear why the Services' habitat permissions must better adapt to an environment of multimodal communication and learning.

Like most regulatory problems, habitat loss is complicated by the challenges of assigning prices to externalities, the existence of concurrent jurisdiction, the fact that assets are usually controlled by managers (not owners), and the reality that many flawed past efforts now constrain our future options. For now, there is nothing that promotes the coordination of partial or small-scale actions toward the end of effective and broad-scale habitat conservation. Building effective conservation networks entails just the sort of infrastructural investment and collective action that will not arise spontaneously.[113] Besides the tools needed to pool and share information,[114] this means a broad and deep commitment to "learning from difference."[115] Making information broadly available in order to reap the rewards of more sophisticated aggregation is not without risk, admittedly. But it would almost certainly improve the chances that we breach "information cocoons,"[116] that we offer greater rewards for cooperating and sharing experiences, and that we set aside whatever (correlated) biases have affected this generation of habitat mechanisms. This may require some deliberate moves by regulators and the courts discouraging (or at least confining) opportunistic challenges that so often reward the secrecy and nondisclosure surrounding deals like our ESA habitat permissions.[117] What incentive(s) do the regulators have to tack in this direction? The incentive is their own influence—or lack thereof. Network effects are a powerful reminder to regulators that "to the standardizer goes power to set the standard." If what we are truly seeking are effective conservation networks, the kinds of power and governance that *networks* entail are the issue.

Bear in mind, though, that most conservation practitioners already know the first law of ecology: everything is connected to everything else. When officials focus on particular jurisdictions and places, or particular conservation "baselines" and resident wildlife populations, it is not that they are ignorant of this interconnectedness but because there are necessary limits to human cognition.[118] We need "action areas," specific parcels of property, discrete timeframes, and other finite locational frames for the simple reason that we cannot cognitively process the more realistic expressions of environmental diversity which entail understanding total systems and distinguishing their perturbations from their overthrow. Thus, if there is any clear normative gain in "globalization," it is its tendency to free people from the "tyranny of the local."[119] Yet, even supposing unprecedented computational or coordinative breakthroughs were to make globally scaled cognition practicable, we will still face the normative frictions generated when political power is limited by a polity's democratic traditions and geographic boundaries. In truth, no one—least of all the Services—has yet realized the capacity to become panoptically aware of our landscapes or of our economy while at the same time functioning as situated citizens, consumers, laborers, and neighbors.

Still, we *can* allocate present efforts as we build and then use tools like the ESA habitat permissions *as if* a richer, more complex whole is possible. The Internet, open-source software, Wikipedia, Creative Commons, and other digital collaborations have proven as much.[120] The trajectory of these projects often departs substantially from what their progenitors imagined—but that describes the ESA itself. Like all cognitively gargantuan enterprises, habitat conservation will only succeed because the many minds working on it find new ways to inter-operate, produce and share knowledge, and employ it collectively as they constitute and shape their common agency. Whether out of optimism or desperation, thus, the Services must facilitate the emergence of new modes of deliberation involving conservation's disparate agents—agents that are, themselves, temporally and spatially indeterminate. A certain measure of standardization and modularity could go a long way in enabling exactly the kind of aggregation and synthesis (some of which seems at first blush generous or even altruistic[121]) that would be so instrumental to a broader-scale form of deliberate land management.

Transitioning ITPs, SHAs, or CCAAs into more standardized instruments that are more like property, however, will likely open them up to *more* external scrutiny and, thus, perhaps more filtering by "stakeholders."[122] This is where the principals must act—prompting their agents to accept that scrutiny—and affirmatively urge our transition away from a territorial, "transactional" focus on singular land use permissions and toward a more integrative, managerial focus, which makes better use of the deliberation producing them.[123] The central problem to be solved if these permits are to serve such ends is the faster, freer production and dissemination of information—timely information about ecological composition and function, about system resilience, and especially about the profitable uses of those systems and the interactions of these variables.[124] If our behavioral sciences have at least complicated the picture enough to reveal our collective (often correlated) biases and other departures from rationality, they have thus far failed to generate anything like a complete picture. Available information about real human motivations and desires will color choices to engage with some as "partners" and not others, certainly. But property is so recognizable and common across jurisdictional boundaries precisely because of its modularity and the informational advantages it offers in a diverse and fast-changing environment.[125] Property comes in a limited number of standardized bundles of rights; our ability to agree to transactions based on those rights enhances our formation of expectations regarding our tangible assets. However, real property is undeniably entrenched in deeper, ecosystemic relationships that support much of its value. Revealing the most efficient means of reconciling owner autonomy with the public's power to protect what it values can conserve the resources that conservation itself needs to evolve in a world of increasingly diverse owners and sovereigns.

Conclusion

Landscape-scale planning requires at least a rough understanding of the desired future conditions we seek. Unfortunately, the ESA established no such understanding, and the ESA's model of habitat conservation is obviously a legislative work-in-progress. It is worth recalling, thus, that the ESA itself was an *amendment* of legislation enacted in 1966[126] and 1969.[127] Over the years, we have struggled to give more definition to our desired future conditions, and have usually settled on landscape *resilience*—the capacity of our lands to absorb change without being fundamentally altered. The more we understand what this will entail, the more our basic systems of production, consumption, and governance have forced us to create hybrid institutions like private property tied to governance permissions. And as these processes have continued to scale up, it has grown more evident that *global* resilience is now the question.

Establishing a global conservation system will require us to reimagine our concepts of commons, property, and governance as distinct—though not necessarily conflicting—topologies that are contouring a single landscape.[128] Instead of being inhibited or morally conflicted by "endowment effects," for example, we will have to anticipate and commandeer them.[129] Instead of using the past as some fictionally static baseline by which we can call something "property," we will have to integrate its variations and jurisdictional specificity into a workable and durable notion of ownership rights.[130] All of this will require us to view "property" and "permits" as tokens of a type: legal rules that can and should be used to force the kinds of continuous improvement processes that take consistent advantage of always-improving information and cognitive capacities.

Looking back over the ESA's evolution, one truly resilient trope is all too evident: the political *fear* of prohibiting behaviors that owners prefer—or at least *allegedly* prefer. When fears of the sort terminate our experiments in deliberative problem-solving prematurely, our evolutionary possibilities have been at their lowest ebb. The rapid loss of natural diversity in the coming century will hopefully spur us (or our successors) to force the issues a little more persistently.

Notes

1. Courts have made clear that permission requirements are generally the norm in land use contexts. See, e.g., *Tahoe Sierra Preservation Council, Inc. v. Tahoe Regional Planning Agency*, 535 U.S. 302 (2002); *City of Monterey v. Del Monte Dunes*, 526 U.S. 687 (1999).

2. Yochai Benkler, *The Wealth of Networks: How Social Production Transforms Markets and Freedom* (New Haven: Yale University Press, 2006) 91–99, 361–69 (arguing that self- and profit-seeking motives represent only a small fraction of what moves people to cooperate, compete, and produce).

3. David S. Wilcove, David Rothstein, Jason Dubow, Ali Phillips, and Elizabeth Losos, "Quantifying Threats to Imperiled Species in the United States," *BioScience* 48, no. 8 (1998): 607–15. "Habitat," however, denotes everything comprising an organism's relationship to its environment. See Jamison E. Colburn, "The Indignity of Federal Wildlife Habitat Law," *Alabama Law Review* 57 (2005): 417, 431–36.

4. E. C. Pielou, *After The Ice Age: The Return of Life to Glaciated North America* (Chicago: University of Chicago Press, 1991), 366.

5. See generally Michael L. Morrison, *Wildlife Restoration: Techniques for Habitat Analysis and Animal Monitoring* (Washington, D.C.: Island Press, 2002), 209.

6. "The plain intent of Congress in enacting this statute was to halt and reverse the trend toward species extinction, whatever the cost." *Tennessee Valley Authority v. Hill*, 437 U.S. 153, 184 (1978).

7. See generally Thomas K. McCraw, *Prophets of Regulation* (Cambridge: Harvard University Press, 1984), 387 (tracing the historical shift in regulation toward an "economist's" paradigm).

8. Charles Krebs, *The Ecological World View* (Berkeley: University of California Press, 2009), 574.

9. Elizabeth Kolbert, "The Sixth Extinction?" *New Yorker*, May 25, 2009, 53, http://www.newyorker.com/reporting/2009/05/25/090525fa_fact_kolbert.

10. There is no shortage of published work purporting to "interpret" the ESA as implicitly or somehow indirectly excluding cost and/or feasibility from the choice factors the statute provides to the Services in other contexts. However, the Supreme Court has made clear repeatedly that without express Congressional intent to *exclude* such considerations from agency deliberations, the presumption remains

that they are legitimately a part of agency decisions. See e.g., *Entergy Corporation v. Riverkeeper, Inc.*, 129 S. Ct. 1498, 1508–10 (2009); *Whitman v. American Trucking*, 531 U.S. 457, 471 (2001).

11. Pub. L. No. 97–304, § 2(b), 96 Stat. 1411, 1411 (1982), codified at 16 U.S.C. § 1533(b).

12. Philip Shabecoff, *Earth Rising: American Environmentalism in the 21st Century* (Washington, D.C.: Island Press, 2000), 6–7, 224.

13. Colburn, "The Indignity of Federal Wildlife Habitat Law," 417.

14. Doug Peacock and Andrea Peacock, *In the Presence of Grizzlies: The Ancient Bond Between Men and Bears* (Guilford, Conn.: The Lyons Press, 2009), 241. This is certainly the narrative that motivates most strategies in conservation's non-profit sector.

15. Jared des Rosiers, "The Exemption Process Under the Endangered Species Act: How the 'God Squad' Works and Why," *Notre Dame Law Review* 66 (1991): 825.

16. It is generally agreed that Congress created incidental take permits in response to a "habitat conservation plan" developed for San Bruno Mountain. See Lawrence R. Liebesman and Rafe Peterson, *Endangered Species Deskbook* (Washington, D.C.: Environmental Law Institute, 2003), 46. An overview of the San Bruno Mountain saga and the 1982 amendments can be found in *Friends of Endangered Species, Inc. v. Jantzen*, 760 F.2d 976 (9th Cir. 1985); see also Michael J. Bean and Melanie Rowland, *The Evolution of National Wildlife Law* 235, 2nd ed. (Westport: Praegen Publishers, 1997), 544.

17. Section 7 requires all federal agencies to "insure that any action authorized, funded, or carried out by such agency…is not likely to jeopardize the continued existence of any [endangered or threatened] species or result in the destruction or adverse modification of [its critical habitat]." 16 U.S.C. § 1535(a)(2).

18. Eric T. Freyfogle and Dale D. Goble, *Wildlife Law: A Primer* (Washington, D.C.: Island Press, 2009), 275.

19. 437 U.S. 153 (1978) (holding that ESA Section 7 prohibits federal agencies from taking *any* actions jeopardizing the continued existence of threatened or endangered species). The Tellico and Grayrocks dam projects were specifically named and placed on the committee's agenda in the 1978 amendments. Ultimately, the so-called God squad rejected the petitions. See Charles C. Mann and Mark L. Plummer, *Noah's Choice: The Future of Endangered Species* (New York: Knopf, 1995) 147–75.

20. See, e.g., Ronald Dworkin, *Law's Empire* (Cambridge: Harvard University Press, 1986), 20–23, 313–54; William N. Eskridge, Jr., *Dynamic Statutory Interpretation* (Cambridge: Harvard University Press, 1994), 218–25; Zygmunt J. B. Plater, "In the Wake of the Snail Darter: An Environmental Law Paradigm and Its Consequences," *Michigan Law Review* 19 (1986): 805, 825–28.

21. *Portland Audubon Soc. v. Endangered Species Committee*, 984 F.2d 1534 (9th Cir. 1993).

22. The Act's "best available science" mandate is often spotlighted as a driving force in ESA decision making. Science and scientifically gathered data are extremely costly and contentious, however. See National Research Council, *Science and the Endangered Species Act* (Washington, D.C.: National Academy Press, 1995).

23. Pub. L. No. 95–632 § 11, 92 Stat.3751, at 3766 (1978), codified at 16 U.S.C. § 1533(f).

24. Pub. L. No. 97–304 § 2, 96 Stat. 1411, at 1415 (1982), codified at 16 U.S.C. § 1533(f)(1)(A).

25. Pub. L. No. 100–478 § 1012, 102 Stat. 2306, at 2314, codified at 16 U.S.C. § 1544. The 1988 amendments also further refined recovery planning by requiring that each plan include "a description of such site-specific management actions as may be necessary to achieve the plan's goal for the conservation and survival of the species" and "objective, measurable criteria which, when met, would result in a determination, in accordance with [ESA § 4] that the species be removed from the list." Id. at § 1002, 102 Stat. at 2307, codified at 16 U.S.C. § 1533(f)(2).

26. Though "consultation" had been required by ESA Section 7 since 1973, on the eve of the 1978 amendments, the agencies testified that, in over 4,500 consultations that had been conducted, no formal record had ever been compiled and no formal proceedings had ever been carried out. See S. Rep. 95–874, Legislative History of Pub. L. No. 95–632, Endangered Species Act Amendments of 1978, 124 *Cong. Rec.* 9453, 9461 (1978) (hereafter "S. Rep. 95–874").

27. Pub. L. No. 97–304, § 6(1)(4)(A), 96 Stat. 1422, 1423 (1982), codified at 16 U.S.C. § 1539(a)(1).

28. Edward L. Rubin, "Law and Legislation in the Administrative State," *Columbia Law Review* 89 (1989): 369, 380–85; and Edward H. Rubin, *Beyond Camelot: Rethinking Politics and Law for the Modern State* (Princeton: Princeton University Press, 2005), 210–21.

29. The 1978 amendments expressly required the presentation of a "written opinion" by the Services and prohibited the action agency and/or any affected parties from making "any irreversible or irretrievable commitment of resources which has the effect of foreclosing the formulation or implementation of any reasonable and prudent alternative measures." 92 Stat. at 3752–53, codified at 16 U.S.C. §§ 1536(b) & (d).

30. 16 U.S.C. § 1536(b)(4). Congress did not specify what alternatives to jeopardy would ordinarily be "reasonable and prudent." However, a Senate Report accompanying the amendments concluded that "in many instances good faith consultation...can resolve many endangered species conflicts." S. Rep. 95–874, supra note 38, at 9462.

31. See, e.g., *Pacific Coast Federation of Fishermen's Association v. National Marine Fisheries Service*, 265 F.3d 1028 (9th Cir. 2001); and Holly Doremus and A. Dan Tarlock, *Water War in the Klamath Basin: Macho Law, Combat Biology, and Dirty Politics* (Washington, D.C.: Island Press, 2008), 146–80.

32. 50 C.F.R. § 402.02.

33. 50 C.F.R. § 402.14(d).

34. David J. Hayes, "Integrating ESA Goals Into a Larger Context: The Lessons of Animas-La Plata," *Natural Resources Journal* 47 (2001): 627, 630 ("[T]here is no question that the Service must rely primarily on the agency that is proposing the project in question to help identify potential alternatives. The ESA's Section 7 consultation process puts the FWS in a reactive role. The Service does not shape projects; it responds to projects that have been proposed by other federal agencies.").

35. Pub. L. No. 97–304, § 6(1)(4)(A), 96 Stat. 1422, 1423 (1982), codified at 16 U.S.C. § 1539(a)(1).

36. Section 10 may state that the Services may "permit" "any taking otherwise prohibited by [ESA § 9] if such taking is incidental to, and not the purpose of, the carrying out of an otherwise lawful activity." 16 U.S.C. § 1539(a)(1)(B). But Section 7 still obligates the Services—as it does all federal agencies—to "insure" that any actions it takes, funds, or authorizes, do not "jeopardize the continued existence" of any listed taxa or "result in the destruction or adverse modification" of designated critical habitat. Id. at § 1536(a)(2).

37. Colin Diver, "The Judge as Political Powerbroker: Superintending Structural Change in Public Institutions," *Virginia Law Review* 65 (1979): 43.

38. 273 F.3d 1229 (9th Cir. 2001).

39. 476 F.3d 1031 (9th Cir. 2007).

40. 273 F.3d at 1242; 476 F.3d at 1036.

41. 476 F.3d at 1037 ("Congress indicated that it preferred the Incidental Take Statement to contain a numerical limitation on the Federal agency or permittee or licensee.") (quoting H.R. Rep. No. 97–567, at 27 (1982)).

42. 476 F.3d at 1038.

43. Keith W. Rizzardi, "The Everglades in Jeopardy: A Drama of Water Management and Endangered Species," *Florida State University Law Review* 27 (2000): 349.

44. See, e.g., *Center for Biological Diversity v. Rumsfeld*, 198 F. Supp.2d 1139 (D. Ariz. 2002) (invalidating decision by the FWS to conclude a "memorandum of agreement" with the Department of Defense in lieu of reinitiating consultation to update a stale Biological Opinion and RPAs).

45. This is a misperception the Services battle constantly. See, e.g., U.S. Fish & Wildlife Service, *Critical Habitat: What Is It?* (Fort Snelling: U.S. Fish & Wildlife Service Endangered Species Program, 2009).

46. 16 U.S.C. §§ 1533(a)(3)(A), (b)(2).

47. Pub. L. No. 95–632, 92 Stat. at 3764 (Section 11(4), codified at 16 U.S.C. § 1533(b)(5). This notice requirement was further enhanced in the 1979 amendments, requiring the Services to publish actual maps of designated critical habitat. See Pub. L. No. 96–159 at § 3, 93 Stat. 1225 et seq. (1979), codified at 16 U.S.C. § 1533((f)(2)(B)(i).

48. See, e.g., *Arizona Cattle Growers' Association v. Kempthorne*, 2008 U.S. Dist. LEXIS 12783 (D. Ariz. 2008); *Center for Biological Diversity v. Bureau of Land Management*, 422 F. Supp.2d 1115 (N.D. Cal. 2006); *Home Builders Association of Northern California. v. U.S. Fish & Wildlife Service*, 2006 U.S. Dist. LEXIS 80255 (E.D. Cal. 2006); *Center for Biological Diversity v. Norton*, 240 F. Supp.2d 1090 (D. Ariz. 2003); *New Mexico Cattle Growers' Association v. U.S. Fish & Wildlife Service*, 248 F.3d 1277 (10th Cir. 2001); *Natural Resources Defense Council v. U.S. Dept. of Interior*, 113 F.3d 1121 (9th Cir. 1997); *Douglas County v. Babbitt*, 48 F.3d 1495 (9th Cir. 1996); and *Trinity County Concerned Citizens v. Babbitt*, 1993 U.S. Dist. LEXIS 21378 (D.D.C. 1993).

49. The Services argued that "adverse modification"—which they had defined as a "direct or indirect alteration that appreciably diminishes the value of critical habitat for both the survival and recovery of a listed species," 50 C.F.R. § 402.02—only occurred if an action diminished an area's habitat values *both* as to the taxon's "survival" *and* its "recovery." This approach was rejected by the Fifth, Tenth, and Ninth Circuits. See, e.g., *Sierra Club v. U.S. Fish & Wildlife Service*, 245 F.3d 434 (5th Cir. 2001); *New Mexico Cattle Growers' Association. v. U.S. Fish & Wildlife Service*, 248 F.3d 1277 (10th Cir. 2001); and *Gifford Pinchot Task Force v. U.S. Fish & Wildlife Service*, 378 F.3d 1059 (9th Cir. 2004).

50. This is not necessarily to give quarter on the inaction. But because critical habitat cannot be designated without an affirmative finding of "constituent elements" within the designated geography, 50 C.F.R. § 424.12(b), designations are already tightly coupled to a taxon's known habitat needs. See, e.g., *Cape Hatteras Access Preservation Alliance v. U.S. Dept. of Interior*, 344 F. Supp. 2d 108, 122 (D.C. Cir. 2004).

51. See, e.g., *Loggerhead Sea Turtles v. Council of Volusia County*, 148 F.3d 1231 (11th Cir. 1998). If the permission is from one of the Services, an "internal" consultation would be held (the language of ESA § 7(a)(2) is without exception).

52. 16 U.S.C. § 1539(a)(2)(B)(iii) & (iv).

53. Even in 1995, Justice Scalia thought it "unmistakably clear" that the Endangered Species Act was (still) structured to *avoid* the regulation of real property and property owners. See *Babbitt v. Sweet Home Chapter of Communities for a Greater Oregon*, 515 U.S. 687, 714–15 (1995) (Scalia, J., dissenting). "The Court's holding that the hunting and killing prohibition incidentally preserves habitat on private lands imposes unfairness to the point of financial ruin—not just upon the rich, but upon the simplest farmer who finds his land conscripted to national zoological use." Id. This takes inadequate account of the 1982 amendments, however, and their injection of incidental take permissions and "conservation plans" into the Act. See 515 U.S. at 703–08.

54. 50 C.F.R. § 17.22(b); *Handbook for Habitat Conservation Planning and Incidental Take Permitting Process*, available at http://www.fws.gov/endangered/hcp/hcpbook.html.

55. 50 C.F.R. § 17.22(b)(2)(C). The statute requires an affirmative finding by the Services that (1) the taking will be incidental, (2) *the applicant* will, to the maximum

extent practicable, minimize and mitigate the impacts of the permitted takings, (3) the taking will not appreciably reduce the likelihood of the survival and recovery of the species in the wild, (4) *the applicant* will ensure that adequate funding for the plan will be provided, and (5) any supplemental measures imposed as conditions on the permit will be met. See 16 U.S.C. § 1539(a)(2)(B). These findings are separate and apart from the content of the plan as mandated by ESA § 9(a)(2)(A).

56. Cf. *Spirit of the Sage Council v. Kempthorne*, 511 F. Supp.2d 31, 43 (D.D.C. 2007) ("[T]he specific statutory provisions in ESA Section 10 demonstrate the Congress did not intend ITPs to have to promote or maintain the recovery of listed species.").

57. But cf. Matthew E. Rahn, *Species Coverage in Multispecies Habitat Conservation Plans: Where's the Science?* (Washington, D.C.: American Institute of Biological Sciences, 2006), 56, 613–19, http://www.bioone.org/doi/abs/10.1641/0006-3568 (2006)56[613:SCIMHC]2.0.co;2 (tracing data disparities and deficiencies in large HCPs and concluding that the program is not adequately supported by science).

58. 16 U.S.C. § 1539(a)(2)(A)-(B).

59. See, e.g., J. B. Ruhl, "How to Kill Endangered Species, Legally: The Nuts and Bolts of Endangered Species Act 'HCP' Permits for Real Estate Development," *Environmental Law* 5 (1999): 345; and Steven G. Davison, "The Aftermath of *Sweet Home Chapter*: Modification of Wildlife Habitat as a Prohibited Taking in Violation of the Endangered Species Act," *William & Mary Environmental Law and Policy Review* 27 (2003): 541.

60. See, e.g., *Sierra Club v. Babbitt*, 15 F.Supp.2d 1274 (S.D. Ala. 1998) (invalidating Service findings as arbitrary and capricious); *National Wildlife Federation v. Babbitt*, 128 F. Supp.2d 1274 (E.D. Cal. 2000) (invalidating Service findings as arbitrary and capricious); and *Southwest Center For Biological Diversity v. Bartel*, 470 F. Supp.2d 1118 (S.D. Cal. 2006) (invalidating Service findings as arbitrary and capricious).

61. Cf. John Copeland Nagle and J.B. Ruhl, *The Law of Biodiversity and Ecosystem Management* (West Group Publishing, 2d ed., 2006). ("Despite the enactment of section 10(a)(1)(B), only three HCPs were adopted between 1982 and 1989."). It may bear mentioning that it also takes the enforcement—or, at least the plausible *threat* of enforcement—of ESA Section 9 to make ITPs an attractive option for landowners and that the 1980s were hardly the high water mark of ESA enforcement.

62. NSP was the subject of protracted litigation over its procedural and substantive validity. It was eventually completed as a notice-and-comment amendment to the "Permit Revocation Rule," see 50 C.F.R. §§ 17.22(b), 17.32(b), and upheld against all challenges. See *Spirit of the Sage Council v. Kempthorne*, 511 F. Supp.2d 31 (D.D.C. 2007).

63. *Spirit of the Sage Council v. Norton*, 294 F. Supp.2d 67, 77 (D.D.C. 2003) ("The [NSP] required Services approving HCPs to provide landowners with 'assurances' that, once an ITP was approved, even if circumstances subsequently changed in such

a way as to render the HCP inadequate to conserve listed species, the Services would not impose additional conservation and mitigation requirements....").

64. Cf. *Spirit of the Sage Council v. Kempthorne*, 511 F. Supp.2d 31, 41 (D.D.C. 2007) ("[I]f activity under an ITP hinders the recovery of a species, but not its survival, then the Services are foreclosed from revoking the permit under [the no surprises policy].").

65. See, e.g., *National Wildlife Federation v. Norton*, 2005 WL 2175874 *4-5 (E.D. Cal. 2005) (describing this as the key finding in determination to grant ITP). This is of questionable effect as a backstop, however, given the reality that any ITP of great enough scope will also trigger a self-consultation within the issuing Service under ESA § 7 and perhaps trigger NEPA as well. See, e.g., *Environmental Protection Information Center, Inc. v. Pacific Lumber Company*, 67 F.Supp. 1090 (N.D. Cal. 1999); and *National Wildlife Federation v. Babbitt*, 128 F.Supp.2d 1274 (E.D. Cal. 2000).

66. 50 C.F.R. §§ 17.22(c)(5), 17.22(d)(5), 17.32(c)(5), 17.32(d)(5).

67. 50 C.F.R. § 17.22(c)(2)(ii). The Service must find that "[t]he probable direct and indirect effects of any authorized take will not appreciably reduce the likelihood of survival and recovery in the wild" before issuing SHAs, id. at § 17.22(c)(2)(iii), that the SHA "is consistent with applicable Federal, State, and Tribal laws" and that it "will not be in conflict with any ongoing conservation or recovery programs" and that the applicant has shown it is capable and committed to "all terms" of the SHA. Id. at § 17.22(c)(2)(iv)-(vi).

68. Department of Interior, Department of Commerce, "Announcement of Final Safe Harbor Policy," 64 *Fed. Reg.* 32717, 32717 (1999) ("Although property owners recognize the benefits of proactive habitat conservation activities to help listed species, some are still concerned that additional land, water, and/or natural resource use restrictions may result if listed species colonize their property or increase in numbers or distribution due to their conservation efforts."). The take definition and ESA Section 9 are thought to present this prospect: with enhancements, a listed taxon might come to occupy an area and then be a bar to subsequent alterations of that area as habitat. Id.

69. 50 C.F.R. §§ 17.22(c)(2)(ii), (c)(5); 64 *Fed. Reg.* at 32718. Determining and characterizing "baseline conditions" within an SHA are, quite obviously, critical to the integrity of any particular SHA. Cf. id. ("The intent of the Services in determining baseline conditions is to ensure that the protection provided to covered listed species is not eroded below current levels.").

70. Department of Interior, Department of Commerce, "Announcement of Final Policy for Candidate Conservation Agreements With Assurances," 64 *Fed. Reg.* 32726 (1999). Indeed, the CCAA Policy states that CCAAs are aimed at *avoiding* listings. See id. at 32735.

71. "Threatened" species often have "protective regulations" specifically tailored to their needs, abundance, etc., pursuant to ESA § 4(d). See 16 U.S.C. § 1533(d). Some of these rules relax the "take" prohibition and render otherwise regulable conduct unregulated.

72. Patrick Ryan, Galen Schuler, and Jennifer Bell, "ESA Compliance Options: Section 10 and Other Tools," in *Endangered Species Act: Law, Policy, and Perspectives*, ed. Donald C. Baur and William Robert Irvin (Chicago: ABA Publishing, 2002), 295.

73. ITPs may be issued, consistent with the regulations, for intervals "sufficient to provide adequate assurances to the permittee to commit funding necessary." 50 C.F.R. § 17.22(b)(4). Thirty to fifty years are not uncommon durations. "The duration of [SHAs] must be sufficient to provide a net conservation benefit to species covered in the . . . permit." Id. at § 17.22(c)(8). The permits entailed in CCAAs "become valid if and when covered, proposed, candidate or other unlisted species is listed as an endangered species." Id. at § 17.22(d)(1). The duration of such permits following listing—exactly the contingency the agreements are meant to foreclose—is unspecified.

74. The exact counts (65 SHAs and 34 CCAAs) are imprecise, as several of each were in development as I was collecting documents from the various field offices.

75. A decade ago, the principal question surrounding these mechanisms was whether the Services could forgo listing a species because it was being managed in a CCA or an SHA. See Francesca Ortiz, "Candidate Conservation Agreements as a Devolutionary Response to Extinction," *Georgia Law Review* 33 (1998): 413.

76. National Research Council, *Science and Decisions: Advancing Risk Assessment* (Washington, D.C.: The National Academics Press, 2009).

77. See, e.g., Dean Lueck and Jeffrey A. Michael, "Preemptive Habitat Destruction Under the Endangered Species Act," *Journal of Law and Economics* 46 (2003): 27, 29, and nn. 6–7 (collecting references); and Jonathan H. Adler, "Money or Nothing: The Adverse Environmental Consequences of Uncompensated Land Use Controls," *Boston College Law Review* 49 (2008).

78. See, e.g., Barton H. Thompson, Jr., "The Endangered Species Act: A Case Study in Takings & Incentives," *Stanford Law Review* 49 (1996): 305; and Daowei Zhang, "Endangered Species and Timber Harvesting: The Case of Red-Cockaded Woodpeckers," *Economic Inquiry* 42 (2004): 150.

79. Lueck and Michael, "Preemptive Habitat Destruction," supra note 77, at 51–53.

80. The costs could be to the landowner, certainly. But, "[i]n the case of the [RCW], the cost of premature commercial timber harvest may not be large.... [P]reemptive harvest is not likely to diminish the net present value of the timber by much." Lueck and Michael, supra note 77, at 52. Moreover, as Lueck and Michael admitted: "[M]any landowners...use longer rotations [than their study had to assume] because of their multiple use objectives." Id. Costs to the RCW, however, are still only partly understood.

81. Privately owned pine forest on North Carolina's southern coastal plain (the only area studied) ranged from "high" to "low" woodpecker densities. See id. at 56. But none of the data Lueck and Michael collected specified the "stem density" of the acres at issue—a variable that seasoned foresters know to be highly salient to

habitat analyses, especially for birds. See T. Bently Wigley et al., "Habitat Attributes and Reproduction of Red-Cockaded Woodpeckers in Intensively Managed Forests," *Wildlife Society Bulletin* 27 (1999): 801, 806–7 (reporting studies that link understory conditions to prey biomass and, thus, to red cockaded woodpecker population health).

82. The red cockaded woodpecker's habitat "needs," despite its being one of the most studied species in modern ornithology, are still open to serious doubts depending on the precise location and populations in question. See William M. Block and Leonard A. Brennan, "The Habitat Concept in Ornithology: Theory and Applications," *Current Ornithology* 11 (2003): 35, 47–55 (describing the slack inherent in identifying morphological and physiological constraints on range and abundance).

83. Drake and Jones suggest, in survey data collected in North Carolina at roughly the same time Lueck and Michael were at work, that forestland owners' plans for their timber—particularly, a shift toward loblolly pine and away from long-leaf pine species—had less to do with the presence or absence of RCW than with the relative profitability of loblolly pine. See David Drake and Edwin J. Jones, "Current and Future Red-Cockaded Woodpecker Habitat Availability on Non-Industrial Private Forestland in North Carolina," *Wildlife Society Bulletin* 31 (2003): 661, 665–66.

84. Lueck and Michael, like some others, likely overestimate the importance of "critical habitat designation" to the regulated community. If it did respond as uniformly as they suggest, we should probably expect to see more downward trending than upward trending from those species that have had a critical habitat designation—when just the opposite appears to be true. See Martin F.J. Taylor, Kieran F. Suckling, and Jeffrey J. Rachlinski, "The Effectiveness of the Endangered Species Act: A Quantitative Analysis," *Bioscience* 55 (2005): 360, 361–63. Moreover, the variance in motivations toward habitat conservation, even among profit-seekers, is obvious. See H. Cardskadden and D.J. Lober, "Environmental Stakeholder Management as Business Strategy: The Case of the Corporate Wildlife Habitat Enhancement Programme," *Journal of Environmental Management* 52 (1998): 183, 186–87 (describing the rise of the Wildlife Habitat Council, an industry-led nonprofit that sets best practices and benchmarks for private land stewardship).

85. Hong S. He, David J. Mladenoff, Volker C. Radeloff, and Thomas R. Crow, "Integration of GIS Data and Classified Satellite Imagery for Regional Forest Assessment," *Ecological Applications* 8 (1998): 1072, 1073 (noting the limitations of FIA data because they are based on 1-acre sampling plots, executed at a density of 1-2 plots per 10 km^2).

86. See generally Richard A. Posner, *Economic Analysis of Law*, 7th ed. (New York: Aspen Publishers, 2007).

87. See generally Ian Shapiro, *The Flight from Reality in the Human Sciences* (Princeton: Princeton University Press, 2005) (describing the tendencies toward

"method-driven" instead of "problem-driven" research in economics, sociology, political science, and other "human" sciences).

88. One categorical assumption is probably as faulty as the next. See, e.g., "U.S. Fish & Wildlife Service, Safe Harbor Agreements and Candidate Conservation Agreements With Assurances; Revision to the Regulations," 69 *Fed. Reg.* 24084, 24088 (Washington, D.C.: U.S. Fish and Wildlife Service, 2004) (rejecting a commenter's accusation that permit applicants are all seeking to "game" the process by stating that "[a]pplicants enter in SHAs and CCAAs in good faith").

89. This issue has avoided adjudication several times already. See, e.g., *Northwest Resource Information Center v. National Marine Fisheries Service*, 56 F.3d 1060, 1060–70 (9th Cir. 1995) (dismissing claim as moot because ESA § 10(a)(1)(A) permit being challenged had expired). One permit ostensibly granted under ESA § 10(a)(1)(A) was invalidated in court, but it was an obvious sham. See *Humane Society v. Kempthorne*, 481 F. Supp. 2d 53 (D.D.C. 2006) (invalidating "enhancement of survival" permit granted to state allowing it to engage in "depredation control" killing of wolves).

90. Julia D. Mahoney, "Perpetual Restrictions on Land and the Problem of the Future," *Virginia Law Review* 88 (2002): 739, 785.

91. The general impracticability of accurately pricing "ecosystem services" has long been a given. E.G. Farnsworth, T.H. Tidrick, C.F. Jordan, and W.M. Smathers, "The Value of Natural Ecosystems: An Economic and Ecological Framework," *Environmental Conservation* 8 (1981): 275. On sustaining the effort, nonetheless, see J. B. Ruhl, Steven E. Kraft, and Christopher L. Lant, *The Law and Policy of Ecosystem Services* (Washington, D.C.: Island Press, 2006).

92. Robert C. Ellickson, "Property in Land," *Yale Law Journal* 102 (1993): 1315, 1317.

93. See, e.g., Michael A. Heller, "The Boundaries of Private Property," 108 *Yale Law Journal* (1999): 1163, 1176–82; Thomas W. Merrill and Henry A. Smith, "Optimal Standardization in the Law of Property: The Numerus Clausus Principle," *Yale Law Journal* 110 (2000): 1; Thomas W. Merrill and Henry A. Smith, "The Property/Contract Interface," *Columbia Law Review* 101 (2001): 773; Henry Hansmann and Reiner Kraakman, "Property, Contract, and Verification: the Numerus Clausus Problem and the Divisibility of Rights," *Journal of Legal Studies* 31 (2002): S373; and Adam Mossoff, "What is Property? Putting the Pieces Back Together," *Arizona Law Review* 45 (2003): 371, 439 ("The fundamental possessory rights that define the essence of property…[are] the rights to acquire, use and dispose of one's possessions").

94. See Wesley Newcomb Hohfeld, "Fundamental Legal Conceptions as Applied in Judicial Reasoning," *Yale Law Journal* 26 (1917): 710. Merrill and Smith have lately revivified Hohfeld's insight with a vengeance. See, e.g., Merrill and Smith, "Property/Contract," supra note 93; and Thomas W. Merrill and Henry A. Smith, *Property: Principles and Policies* (New York: Foundation Press, 2007).

95. Government permissions are, in this respect, similar to "contract" rights as opposed to property rights.

96. Jerry L. Mashaw, *Bureaucratic Justice* (New Haven: Yale University Press, 1983), 172.

97. 50 C.F.R. §§ 13.28, 17.22(b)(7), 17.22(c)(7), 17.22(d)(7).

98. 50 C.F.R. § 13.24.

99. Paige A. Najvar, "Stepping Up Recovery for the Houston Toad," *Endangered Species Bulletin* 35 (Spring 2009): 34, 35.

100. See Thomas W. Merrill, "The Landscape of Constitutional Property," *Virginia Law Review* 86 (2000): 885, 916–42.

101. See, e.g., *Meadow Green-Wildcat Corp. v. Hathaway*, 936 F.2d 601 (1st Cir. 1991).

102. See *Mobil Oil Exploration and Producing Southeast, Inc. v. United States*, 530 U.S. 604, 624, 638–39 (2000) (Stevens, J., dissenting).

103. See Tim Wu, "Intellectual Property, Innovation, and Decentralized Decisions," *Virginia Law Review* 92 (2006): 123, 131–41.

104. Morrison, *Wildlife Restoration*, supra note 5 at 44–66.

105. Much as The Nature Conservancy and the Land Trust Alliance have evolved to serve an ever-expanding population of local land trusts, a new breed of conservation intermediary has emerged to facilitate the deliverance of ESA habitat permissions. Call them the "cooperative conservation agents." Many case studies ranging from the New England Forestry Foundation to the Sonoran Institute are collected on the Web at http://www.cooperativeconservationamerica.org/mcs.shtm.

106. The so-called "permit revocation rule" allows that *any* permit "may be revoked" for any of five listed grounds, including the "willful" violation of federal or state statute or regulation, Indian tribal law or regulation that "involves a violation of the conditions of the permit or of the laws or regulations governing permitted activity," 50 C.F.R. § 13.28(a)(1), and any instance where "the statute or regulation authorizing the permit" is changed to prohibit the continuation of that permit. Id. at § 13.28(a)(4).

107. The FWS maintains that it "reserves the right to amend any permit for just cause at any time during its term, upon written finding of necessity" subject to the exceptions set out in the "assurances" described in this chapter. 50 C.F.R. § 13.23(b). This "just cause" standard thus operates as a default allowing *any* revocation not barred by valid and applicable assurances.

108. In addition to the discretion to set durations ad hoc set forth in Part 17, the FWS maintains that permits are "void" whenever "a permittee, or any successor...discontinues activities authorized by a permit." 50 C.F.R. § 13.26. This continuity of activity requirement is very clearly a characteristic that can undermine any comparability or commensurability among permits.

109. With the exception of "enhancement of survival or propagation" permits, the ESA habitat permits are all, in theory, transferable. See 50 C.F.R. §§ 13.25(b)-(d).

The abundant pre-clearance requirements for transfer, however, make transfers highly contingent.

110. Morrison, *Wildlife Restoration*, supra note 5, at 49.

111. See, e.g., Martha J. Groom, Gary K. Meffe, and C. Ronald Carroll,, "Meeting Conservation Challenges in the Twenty-First Century," in *Principles of Conservation Biology*, 3rd ed. (Sunderland: Sinauer Associates, Inc., 2006), 661, 671 (reviewing forecasts and scenario planning from the Millennium Ecosystem Assessment and concluding that more than 20 percent of global biodiversity will probably be lost by 2050).

112. Jamison E. Colburn, "Localism's Ecology: Protecting and Restoring Habitat in the Suburban Nation," *Ecology Law Quarterly* 33 (2006): 945.

113. Cf. Andrew F. Bennett, *Linkages in the Landscape: The Role of Corridors and Connectivity in Wildlife Conservation*, 2nd ed. (Gland, Switzerland and Cambridge, United Kingdom: The World Conservation Union, 2003) (describing the need to use the patchwork of protected areas and conduct restrictions to assemble networks of interconnected habitats and habitat elements); and Jonathan S. Adams, *The Future of the Wild: Radical Conservation for a Crowded World* (Boston: Beacon Press, 2006).

114. The collection, integration, and dissemination of information about ESA habitat permissions, conservation easements, protected public lands, and other habitat protection tools are analogous both to conventional real property/conveyance registration in the digital age (see, e.g., Dale A. Whitman, "Digital Recording of Real Estate Conveyances," *John Marshall Law Review* 32 [1999]: 227), and to more affirmative (and familiar) public information campaigns (see Janet A. Weiss, *Public Information, in The Tools of Government: A Guide to the New Governance* 217 [New York: Oxford University Press, 2002], describing the passive motivational technique of pushing information out publicly).

115. The emergence of "framework" goals and the freedom to advance toward them by any available means—in exchange for a commitment to report evenly one's setbacks and advances—have been critical to the European Union's exploitation of its decentralized structure. See Charles F. Sabel and Jonathan Zeitlin, "Learning from Difference: The New Architecture of Experimentalist Governance in the EU," *European Law Journal* 14 (2008): 271.

116. An "information cocoon" is the result of cognitive errors that allow us to hear only what we choose to, i.e., only what "comforts and pleases us." Cass R. Sunstein, *Infotopia: How Many Minds Produce Knowledge* (New York: Oxford University Press, 2006), 9.

117. The FWS has already been caught at least once taking exactly the kind of hide-the-ball actions aimed at deterring external scrutiny which administrative law was designed to combat. See *Gerber v. Norton*, 294 F.3d 173 (D.C. Cir. 2002) (invalidating ITP based in part on the FWS's failure to disclose maps and other explicit information being sought by opponents).

118. Unfortunately, none of the ESA permissions currently requires a detailed enough "baseline" assessment—let alone the broad dissemination of such assessments—that would confirm the presence/absence of targeted taxa, their relative abundance(s), the "constituent elements" of required habitat, etc. See 50 C.F.R. §§ 17.22(b)(1)(ii) (requiring that the ITP application include "common and scientific names of the species sought to be covered by the permit, as well as the number, age, and sex of such species, *if known*") (emphasis added). SHAs and CCAAs, in fact (the whole utility of which turns on the integrity of the baseline conditions), need not spell out *any* baseline data in particular. See 50 C.F.R. §§ 17.22(c)(1)(iii) (requiring SHA application comply with SHA "Policy"); U.S. Fish & Wildlife Service, "Notice of Final Safe Harbor Policy," 64 *Fed. Reg.* 32717, 32723 (1999) (SHA permit applications must include a "full description" of baseline conditions wherein "[t]o the extent determinable, the parties to the Agreement...identify and agree on the degree to which the enrolled property is inhabited, permanently or seasonably, by the covered species" but allowing substantial departures where "appropriate"); 50 C.F.R. §§ 17.22(d)(1)(iii) (requiring CCAA application comply with CCAA "Policy"); and U.S. Fish & Wildlife Service, "Notice of Final Candidate Conservation Agreement with Assurances Policy," 64 *Fed. Reg.* 32726, 32734 (1999) (CCAA permit applications must include "population levels (if available or determinable)...and/or the existing characteristics of the property owners' lands or waters included in the Agreement." Finally, whatever *monitoring* data are being collected as a result of these deals, they are not being shared publicly.

119. Cf. Ursula K. Heise, *Sense of Place and Sense of Planet: The Environmental Imagination of the Global* (New York: Oxford University Press, 2008) (arguing that the most constructive portrayals of globalization have been those that have shown the possibilities in cosmopolitan consciousness rather than territorial or cultural conquests).

120. Sunstein, *Infotopia*, supra note 116; Cass R. Sunstein, *A Constitution of Many Minds* (Princeton: Princeton University Press, 2009).

121. Benkler, *Wealth of Networks*, supra note 2, at 465–67 (dubbing the unpaid labor that clickworkers, wikipedians, Slashdot members, and SETI@home participants contribute as "social production" and contrasting it with the modes of production directed by profit motives or statist hierarchy).

122. "Stakeholders," of course, need not be "rightsholders." Still, administrative law norms and the text of the ESA protect their participatory rights all the same. See, e.g., 16 U.S.C. §§ 1539(c).

123. Structural amendment without repeal in 1978 and 1982 left the Act's interpreters in perhaps the hardest of all interpretive quandaries: interpreting disparate ends that were only partly reconciled with one another. Short of more legislative guidance—which is extraordinarily hard to generate in our system—the political leaders of the Services need to start reworking the internal structure of these agencies to better adapt to the information environments in which they actually

operate. Streamlining and standardizing permissions are only one step to that end. I have elsewhere argued that reforming the Section 4 and 7 programs is also both necessary and feasible. See Jamison E. Colburn, "Qualitative, Quantitative, and Integrative Conservation," *Washington University Journal of Law and Policy* 32 (2009): 237.

124. Thus, for example, the Malpai Borderlands Group (MBG), a collective of about 100 families that own and manage over a million acres of desert scrub and tobosa grasslands in southwestern New Mexico and southeastern Arizona, established an innovative partnership that not only pools range resources among its owner-participants and pools its problem-solving capacities, but also manages needed permissions for the conservation/use activities within its territory. See Adams, *Future of the Wild*, supra note 113, at 116–30. Most recently, MBG took the work it had put into an SHA for the Chiricahua leopard frog and parlayed it into a multispecies HCP as well. See http://www.malpaiborderlandsgroup.org/endg.asp?Page=1.

125. "Protection of a large and indefinite class of uses by delineating a thing and giving the owner a right to exclude others from the thing is a strategy well suited to situations in which it is not economical to decide first-order questions of uses on a use-by-use basis. Instead, the right to exclude from a thing…is the result of a second-order delegation to the owner to choose among any uses, known or unknown, of the thing." Henry E. Smith, "Property and Property Rules," *New York University Law Review* 79 (2004): 1719, 1754.

126. The Endangered Species Preservation Act of 1966, Pub. L. No. 89–669, 80 Stat. 926 (1966).

127. The Endangered Species Conservation Act of 1969, Pub. L. No. 91–135, 83 Stat. 275 (1969).

128. "Topology," a branch of mathematics, is the study of qualitative properties of given objects that remain invariant under different kinds of change. See James Munkres, *Topology* (Upper Saddle River: Prentice Hall, Inc., 2d ed., 2000), 3.

129. There is reason to believe that only certain kinds of property rules serve as the psychological triggers that lead people to demand more to part with an asset than they would spend to acquire it. See Jeffrey J. Rachlinski and Forest Jourden, "Remedies and the Psychology of Ownership," *Vanderbilt Law Review* 51 (1998): 1541, 1559–66.

130. See Jamison E. Colburn, "Splitting the Atom of Property: Rights Experimentalism as Obligation to Future Generations," *George Washington Law Review* 77 (2009): 1411.

5

Mark to Ecosystem Service Market: Protecting Ecosystems through Revaluing Conservation Easements

Jonathan Remy Nash

Though the Endangered Species Act (ESA)[1] has the laudable goal of preserving threatened and endangered species, it has been heavily criticized for its failure to achieve its objective. The ESA has failed to achieve its objectives for at least three reasons. First, the ESA's approach to preserving endangered species puts too little emphasis on preserving habitats and ecosystems. Second, the ESA's command-and-control structure sometimes encourages landowners to act in ways that run counter to the goal of preserving species. Third, the perception that the ESA imposes draconian restrictions on landowners has led landowners to protest implementation of the ESA in specific instances and even to call for its repeal.

I argue that amendments to the ESA to recalibrate the tax deductions for conservation easements would address these three criticisms. Conservation easements are already used under the ESA to limit development on parcels of land and thus to protect endangered species and their habitats and ecosystems. When a taxpayer gives a conservation easement that will protect a threatened species, the tax code rewards the donor with income tax, gift tax, and estate tax deductions. At present, these deductions are based upon the fair market value of the donated easement, that is, upon the reduction in value in the underlying piece of property resulting from the donation of the easement. I propose recalibrating these tax deductions to reflect the value of the easement to a threatened ecosystem. This valuation

---

For helpful comments and discussions, I am grateful to Jonathan Adler, Lee Anne Fennell, Marjorie Kornhauser, Edward Lloyd, Lori Nash, and Alex Raskolnikov.

would apply whenever the government certified that the piece of land in question lay within a critical ecosystem.

This change in the law would enable the ESA better to preserve threatened and endangered species and would address the three criticisms of the ESA mentioned above. First, it would encourage greater attention to preserving habitats and ecosystems. Second, the change would implement a market-based mechanism that would induce landowners to cooperate in conservation efforts rather than to evade such efforts. Third, the change would reduce landowners' opposition to the ESA.

This chapter proceeds as follows. I first describe the burdens the ESA imposes on private landowners and the problematic ways it regulates use of private land.[2] I then describe conservation easements, including their use to aid in the preservation of threatened and endangered species. I also describe the current federal tax incentives associated with donation of a conservation easement. Finally, I present my proposal to amend the ESA and the federal tax laws to provide greater tax deductions to landowners who donate conservation easements on land located in critical ecosystems. I describe the benefits of recalibrated tax deductions for conservation easements and address some possible objections to this proposal.

The ESA and Its Problematic Regulation of Private Land

The ESA imposes considerable burdens on landowners: it precludes them from "tak[ing] any specimen of an endangered fish or wildlife species.[3] The ESA broadly defines "take" to mean "to harass, harm, pursue, hunt, shoot, wound, kill, trap, capture, or collect, or to attempt to engage in any such conduct."[4] It capaciously defines "harm" in the definition of "take" to include "significant habitat modification or degradation where it actually kills or injures wildlife by significantly impairing essential behavioral patterns, including breeding, feeding or sheltering."[5] In *Babbitt v. Sweet Home Chapter of Communities for a Greater Oregon,*[6] the U.S. Supreme Court upheld the validity of the regulatory definition and thus of broad restrictions on private landowners whose actions disrupt endangered species' habitat. The ESA allows limited exceptions to the proscription against "takings." Section 10 of the Act grants the government discretion to issue a permit that allows a taking that is "incidental to, and not the purpose of, the carrying out of an otherwise lawful activity."[7] To receive such a permit, an applicant must submit a "conservation plan."[8] However, these limited exceptions have not prevented the serious criticisms about how the ESA regulates private land outlined below.

Too Little Focus on Habitats and Ecosystems. The aim of the ESA is to preserve species, and so it is not surprising that the language of the ESA emphasizes preserving species. However, the objective of the ESA might be better achieved with a greater emphasis on preserving habitats and, more broadly, ecosystems. A habitat-centered approach is preferable to a species-based approach because considerable damage may befall a species' habitat before the species becomes threatened or endangered.[9] In addition, a species' natural habitat may not be sufficiently valued if the species exists in other areas, with the result that consistent with the ESA, a species could survive but solely outside of its natural habitat.[10]

However, a habitat-centered approach fails to consider that the endangered species may depend on another species, for example as prey. If the endangered species' prey requires a broader ecosystem for its survival, the endangered species' habitat may not support the prey species. Unless the prey species is also endangered, the ESA might not afford clear protection to that prey species' habitat—thereby undermining the survival of the prey species and the basis for the listed species' survival. Therefore, an ecosystem-centered approach furthers environmental goals even more than does a habitat-centered approach. Ecosystem preservation is more likely to ensure the preservation of endangered species than is a habitat preservation approach. Preservation of the ecosystem in which an endangered species lives guarantees the continuation of the entire system in which the species exists. Moreover, an approach that seeks to protect whole ecosystems is more likely to further the goal of preserving biodiversity than an approach focused on only a single species or habitat.

Perverse Incentives. The ESA's inflexibility creates perverse incentives for landowners, who may be induced to take actions that threaten the successful implementation of the ESA. Over the years, private landowners have become more aware of the restrictions the ESA may impose on the use of their land. The widespread knowledge of these restrictions has had several ramifications.

First, the ESA encourages landowners to destroy habitat that houses endangered species. When landowners discover an endangered species on their land and fear that use of the land is likely to be severely restricted, they are disinclined to report that finding to authorities. To the contrary, they may destroy its habitat in order to encourage the creatures to vacate their property and discourage them from returning.[11] Moreover, a landowner who knows that an endangered species is in the area but who has yet to discover a specimen on his land enjoys the less controversial, and more clearly legally justified, option of preemptively destroying habitat and thus ensuring that no specimen appears on his land.[12]

Second, the ESA encourages landowners to develop their land when they know that their land houses animals or plants that are not yet listed as threatened or endangered but when such listing looks like a real possibility in the near future. As Professor Richard Epstein has explained: "If there is a sense that private land will be subject to controls, then the best strategy for the private owner is to destroy the habitat before it becomes protected: 'shoot, shovel, and shut up' becomes the war cry."[13] Indeed, the looming listing of a species that will affect landowners' ability to develop in a given area also gives rise to a perverse "race to develop." As Professor David Dana has described, landowners may hurry to develop their properties while "they still can," before the listing comes into effect.[14] This race to develop is undesirable because development may occur before it is warranted by local demand for developed land and because as more landowners do develop their land, more habitat of the species in question will disappear. That destruction of habitat may make more likely, and hasten, the listing of the species. In this sense, the race to develop is not only a race against time; it is also a race to develop against other landowners, on the assumption that at some point existing development will sufficiently threaten the species such that further development will not be possible.

Third, fears that the listing of a species as threatened or endangered will reduce the value of their land lead landowners to attempt to block the listing even when a species is genuinely threatened or endangered. Landowners may devote considerable economic and temporal resources to defeat the listing.[15] These efforts may be inefficient—indeed, they may be deadweight losses to the extent that they do not change the outcome. On other occasions their efforts may be sufficient to thwart offering a threatened or endangered species the protection that comes with being listed as such.

Resistance to the ESA. The broad effects of the ESA—real, perceived, and threatened—make it a target for landowners and property rights advocates, especially in the western United States.[16] Consequently, there have been efforts to amend or repeal the ESA.[17] Although there are other federal environmental regulations that, like the ESA, rely on threatened punishments rather than attractive inducements to protect the environment,[18] the ESA garners more opposition than other environmental regulation because, unlike most other environmental statutes, it directly affects landowners and therefore a large number of individual actors.[19] Individuals may favor environmental regulation as a general matter, yet be more reticent to accept regulation that applies to themselves.[20] Political entrepreneurs may more successfully feed off popular opposition to a statute that is seen to affect individuals' property rights.[21] These efforts to resist and repeal the ESA jeopardize the ESA's aim of preserving species.

The Promise of Conservation Easements

Conservation easements are designed to achieve conservationist and preservationist goals, such as restricting development and maintaining existing structures. Conservation easements are modeled upon common law easements. Like common law easements, a conservation easement involves two parties: the landowner who sells or donates the easement on his land, and the easement holder who has the power to enforce the easement. In common law, an affirmative easement empowers its holder to engage in behavior with respect to a neighbor's land. A negative easement precludes a neighbor from engaging in particular behavior with respect to his or her land. Conservation easements resemble negative easements in that they empower the holder of the easement to stop the owner of the land subject to the easement from developing his or her property. However, conservation easements are not like common law easements in every respect; for example, the holder of a conservation easement need not be a neighbor of the land subject to the easement and, indeed, may not be a landowner at all. Most jurisdictions authorize the creation and enforcement of conservation easements.[22] Federal law encourages these easements through provisions in the federal income tax law (the "Internal Revenue Code" or IRC) and through the federal estate and gift tax laws.[23]

The IRC allows a tax deduction for the donation of a conservation easement.[24] The deduction for charitable contributions allowed is generally equal to the fair market value of the donation[25]; the donor is also sometimes allowed to forgo any unrealized gain in the donated property, which would ordinarily be subject to tax were the landowner to have engaged in the economically equivalent transaction of first selling the property for its fair market value and then donating the proceeds.[26] (To his detriment, the donor also loses any unrealized loss in the part of the property allocated to the conservation easement.[27]) The IRC and the regulations that implement the IRC authorize a deduction specifically for the contribution of a conservation easement to a charitable organization.[28] The amount of the deduction equals the value of the easement donated.[29]

Federal income tax law dictates that the tax basis in the remaining property (which affects how much gain or loss the landowner will realize upon subsequent sale of the property) is reduced by "that part of the total basis that is properly allocable to the qualified real property interest granted."[30] Put another way, donation of a conservation easement requires dividing the pre-existing basis between the easement and real property in proportion to the value of each asset. Thus, for example, if an owner has a $100 basis in a piece of property worth $1,000 and donates a conservation easement on that property that is worth $200, then $20 of the original basis is allocated to the conservation easement and $80 of basis remains with the underlying property. Together, the tax deduction for the donation of a conservation easement and the reduction in the tax basis for the property are considerable inducements to donate land as a conservation easement.

The federal estate and gift tax structure also offers benefits to donors of conservation easements. The gift tax law allows for gift tax deductions for charitable donations,[31] and in particular makes the deduction available for donations of conservation easements.[32] The charitable gift tax deduction is generally equal to the value of the easement.[33] Further, to the extent that the donor has not enjoyed the benefit of the deduction during his life, his executor may claim a deduction, proportionate to the value of the donated easement, upon his death.[34]

The provisions for charitable donations of conservation easements follow the general tax treatment of charitable donations of property,[35] with one important exception. For a charitable donation of a conservation easement to be valid, the conservation easement must be one that will persist "in perpetuity."[36] This means that the recipient of the easement must effectively retain the donated easement forever. In contrast, the general provisions governing charitable donations do not require charitable organizations that receive donated property to retain that property. Indeed, though it is perhaps not generally understood (and political and public pressure may constrain the choice), environmental organizations need not retain tradable pollutant emissions allowances that are donated to them; in theory, these organizations might retain donated allowances or sell them once their market value has risen substantially.[37] Some commentators argue that inefficiencies arise from conservation easements that are designed to last in perpetuity.[38] Nonetheless, governing law provides that a conservation easement will last in perpetuity unless the instrument that creates it states otherwise.[39]

To the extent that the Tax Code expects the donation—and the enforcement of the donated easement—to be permanent, the tax treatment of donated conservation easements focuses on the environmental value of the donated property. A similar understanding does not, by contrast, underlie the general tax treatment of other property that is donated to charitable organizations. This differentiation provides a justification for the different valuation method for donated conservation easements that I propose below.

Increasing the Power of Conservation Easements to Preserve Habitats and Ecosystems

Conservation easements already contribute to the preservation of habitats of threatened and endangered species. However, conservation easements would likely be even more frequently established if the value of the donation of a conservation easement were based not upon the economic value of the donated easement but rather upon the value of the easement to the ecosystem.[40] The effect of the proposal would be to enhance the tax incentives for owners of property within an ecosystem to donate conservation easements and thus to protect the ecosystem.

Availability of the increased deduction would be triggered by action of the federal agency, usually the Fish and Wildlife Service (FWS), responsible for the species in question.[41] The agency would be empowered to designate ecosystems—presumably, those that include species perhaps close to the brink of being designated as threatened—as worthy of protection.

Variants on the basic proposal are also possible and may be desirable depending upon the attendant circumstances. For example, the proposal might be implemented only in areas where habitat trading programs are in effect. (Such programs are occasionally used to further wetlands mitigation, for example.[42]) As I discuss below, valuation of the tracts for environmental purposes would be easier in such areas. In turn, application of the proposal in these areas would serve over time to facilitate the expansion of the proposal's reach beyond these areas.

Benefits of the Proposal. This change to the value of conservation easements would have the advantages that it would be relatively simple to enact and would address the criticisms of the ESA I outlined above.

Simplicity of enactment. The proposal's enactment should be relatively simple. Though it would entail amendment of both the ESA and the federal tax laws, the extent of the amendments should be relatively minor. In particular, enacting the proposal would not require altering any of the regulatory provisions of the ESA, which would presumably draw more political opposition.

Remedying shortcomings of the ESA. The proposal addresses to some degree the shortcomings of the ESA that I outlined above. First, increasing the role of conservation easements would shift the approach of the ESA from a species-centered approach to a habitat- and ecosystem-centered approach. Moreover, to the extent the ESA in its current form calls for the protection of critical habitats (and, implicitly, ecosystems),[43] the proposal would authorize earlier action.

Second, this proposal would eliminate the perverse incentives that private landowners currently face. Under the proposal, landowners would remain free to sell or donate conservation easements as they see fit. The tax benefits that accompany donation would serve merely as an inducement to engage in a voluntary transaction. Additionally, to the extent that enough landowners accepted the invitation to donate easements, it would be less often necessary to impose coercive restrictions on landowners in order to protect threatened and endangered species. Indeed, better preservation of ecosystems should have the consequence that fewer species will become threatened or endangered—in short, the objective of the ESA will be better achieved under this proposal than is presently the case.

Third, this proposal might ameliorate opposition to the ESA. First, to the extent that tax incentives provide a substantial motivation for donation of conservation easements,[44] the proposal should generate more voluntary, cooperative action to preserve ecosystems and species.[45] Second, the reduction in reliance on command-and-control sticks, as discussed just above, should reduce the number of conflicts between landowners and regulators. Finally, the proposal might be seen to blunt the adverse impact on individuals, which, if true, would reduce popular opposition to the Act.

Potential Objections to the Proposal. Of course, there are potential objections to any proposal. I consider the most important objections below.

Exacerbating the race to develop land. It is possible that the proposal would exacerbate the race to develop land. The public may interpret the announcement that an ecosystem is one with respect to which donors of conservation easements will receive an enhanced tax benefit as a signal that listing of a species in the area is forthcoming. That fear may prompt, or exacerbate, a race to develop the land.

This possibility turns on an empirical question. The increased number of conservation easements donated in response to increased tax benefits might reduce the need to list a species and to rely on the ESA's power to impose restrictions on landowners. Moreover, people *already* learn of anticipated listing actions; thus, the race to develop is already a problem, and the proposal would not exacerbate it, at least not substantially. Still, it is possible that the proposal would in effect simply migrate the start of the race to develop from the impending listing of a species to the impending announcement that an ecosystem will be associated with the enhanced tax benefit program. Were the proposal to be enacted, the FWS should monitor its effects on the pace of development.

Possibility that ecosystems will not be designated as critical ecosystems. Will the government actually designate ecosystems for special treatment? The dysfunctional dynamics that have hindered listing decisions might be replicated in dysfunctional dynamics that will hinder critical ecosystem designations. It may be hoped, however, that the present dysfunctional dynamics will be replaced with cooperative efforts between landowners and environmental organizations to get the government to act.[46] The proposal could even allow landowners and environmental organizations to petition for such designations. The promise of economic benefit should motivate landowners to seek designations in order to gain access to tax benefits for which they would otherwise be ineligible.

Problems with valuation. Valuation of land for environmental purposes is not easy, and calculating the amount of the proper tax incentive might prove too difficult. At the same time, the problem is not insurmountable: methods exist to conduct such calculations, and the proposal might be limited initially to areas where such valuations are easier to ascertain. Alternatively, a multiplier on fair market value might be used as a proxy for environmental valuations that are simply too difficult or costly to calculate. I explore each of these possibilities in turn.

First, though far from perfect, methods exist to estimate environmental valuations. "Willingness-to-pay" measures have been used to produce values for endangered and threatened species.[47] Methods have also been developed, for purposes of developing habitat trading programs,[48] for determining how different characteristics of a plot of land may contribute to the plot's value to the ecosystem in which it lies.[49] For example, the presence of water or a number of trees may increase a plot's value. So, too, may larger plots of land with greater contiguity and fewer corners be more valuable. This opens up the possibility of multiple landowners joining their land together for a single donation, with the increase in total land mass and increase in contiguity resulting in an increase in each plot's ecosystem value.

All of that said, it must be conceded that the calculation will not be easy and may sometimes be controversial. One solution might be to use, initially at least, a variant of the proposal that would allow its use only in areas where habitat trading programs are already in place. In these areas, environmental valuations can be far more readily attained. Moreover, limiting the proposal to these areas would allow for the development of environmental valuation techniques that might eventually allow the proposal to be applied in other areas as well. (Indeed, the increase in experience, and expertise, with environmental valuations might have salutary effects even beyond the issue of valuing conservation easements for tax purposes.[50])

To the complaint that environmental valuation is complicated and costly, it is important to note that existing tax law also calls for a complicated and costly valuation question: the valuation of the conservation easement as a stand-alone economic interest. This is generally accomplished, albeit imperfectly, through the retention of real estate experts who estimate the value of land with and without the applicable conservation easement. In any event, to the extent that the valuation for ecosystem services proved unworkable, one could, as a proxy, simply value the tax benefit at a multiple of the economic value of the plot—e.g., if the donation of a conservation easement on plot X would result in a tax deduction of y under ordinary circumstances, the tax benefit could be set as 150 percent of y to the extent that the plot lies within a designated ecosystem.[51]

Problems in allocating tax basis. Another difficulty is with allocating the tax basis between the conservation easement and the remainder of the property. As noted above, the current system calls for the taxpayer's original basis in the property to be allocated between the underlying plot and the conservation easement in proportion to the fair market value of the two constituent properties (with the result that any unrealized gain or loss effectively allocated to the easement is dissipated).[52] How would such allocations be conducted to the extent that valuation of one of the properties is conducted at fair market value and the other based upon ecosystem value? Indeed, if the ecosystem value of the plot is large, virtually all the basis would be allocated to the easement.

One answer to this question is simply to use economic valuation for the conservation easement for allocation purposes and ecosystem valuation otherwise. That solution, however, requires two different valuation methods to be used for the same property, thus increasing costs and litigation risk. Another solution calls for the reexamination of the basis allocation rules in any event: as I have argued elsewhere, as things now stand, the basis allocation rules wipe out both unrealized gain and loss. That encourages the donation of easements on appreciated land but discourages it on depreciated land. There is no reason, however, to think that the environmental value of a plot of land is related to whether it has appreciated or depreciated in economic terms,[53] as a piece of land may be of substantial (and growing) environmental value, yet, because of independent market forces, now be worth less than what the owner paid for it. And, conversely, a piece of land that has appreciated in market value may be of comparatively little environmental value.

The proposal's tax incentives are unnecessarily large. The increased tax benefits generated by the proposal offer too great of an incentive to donate conservation easements, and so perhaps too many people would donate easements. Alternatively, perhaps the same environmental objective could be achieved with less of an incentive to donate conservation easements. To the extent this is the case, the tax benefit could be made proportionate to the ecosystem value of the plot, but at a rate less than 100 percent.[54]

The proposal might be too costly in terms of tax revenues. Some might say that the proposal's benefits do not merit the tax expenditures it would entail or that the tax expenditures would better be used elsewhere. It is difficult to respond to this objection. Note, however, that the current system already uses tax expenditures, and the current tax structure is not clearly tied to environmental goals. The proposal would involve a marginal increase in tax expenditures, but perhaps the marginal environmental benefits would outweigh that cost. Moreover, if anything, the federal government has historically *spent too little*, not too much, on species conservation.[55] Thus, even if there is a net cost in tax revenues, that result might be normatively desirable in order to supplement suboptimally low spending on species conservation.

The propriety of compensating for ecosystem services. Others might say that the proposal improperly seeks to compensate landowners for "ecosystem services." The proposal would effectuate in some way payment to landowners for the ecosystem services—that is, for the benefits to the ecosystem—that their land provides. While paying property owners for ecosystem services has been lauded in the literature in recent years,[56] the notion is also the subject of criticism. It can be argued that paying for environmentally friendly behavior should be the exception rather than the rule.[57] Indeed, the notion that some are being paid (through a tax benefit) for ecosystem services may make others who do not receive that payment less likely to voluntarily perform those services at less or no cost. It may also have a broader effect on societal norms: if a person (not a landowner) learns that landowners are receiving a benefit for performing ecosystem services, he or she may decline to behave in environmentally friendly ways absent some payment.[58]

Conclusion

The best response to these concerns is to note that, whatever their merit, the proposal does not itself give rise to tax benefits for conservation easement donation. Those rules already exist. The proposal's goal is simply to amplify the beneficial impact of those rules. To the extent that one objects to the notion of using tax benefits to create incentives for environmentally friendly behavior, one should take issue not with the proposal but with the underlying, existing tax rules on which the proposal is based. The proposal is designed to work in complementary fashion with the other provisions of the ESA. If the proposal works as anticipated, then the need to rely upon the more stringent provisions of the ESA should be reduced.

Notes

1. 16 U.S.C. §§ 1531–1544.

2. Although I focus on how the ESA affects landowners' use of their property, the ESA also substantially limits government actions that may affect threatened or endangered species. See, e.g., Endangered Species Act § 7(a)(2), 16 U.S.C. § 1536(a)(2) (directing the federal government generally to act in ways that are "not likely to jeopardize the continued existence of any endangered species or threatened species" and that will not "result in the destruction or adverse modification of habitat of such species"); *Tennessee Valley Authority v. Hill*, 437 U.S. 151 (1978) (ESA precluded completion of dam).

3. Endangered Species Act § 9(a)(1)(B), 16 U.S.C. § 1538(a)(1)(B). The government has extended section 9's "take" prohibition to threatened species as well. See Barton H. Thompson, Jr., "The Endangered Species Act: A Case Study in Takings & Incentives," *Stanford Law Review* 49 (1997): 305, 314.

4. Endangered Species Act § 3(19), 16 U.S.C. § 1532(19).

5. 50 C.F.R. § 17.3.

6. 515 U.S. 687 (1995).

7. Endangered Species Act § 10(a)(1)(B), 16 U.S.C. § 1539(a)(1)(B).

8. Ibid., § 10(a)(2)(A), 16 U.S.C. § 1539(a)(2)(A).

9. See Jonathan Remy Nash, "Trading Species: A New Direction for Habitat Trading Programs," *Columbia Journal of Environmental Law* 32 (2007): 1, 8, reprinted in *Environmental Reporter News & Analysis* 38 (2008): 10539.

10. Ibid.

11. See ibid., 10.

12. See ibid.

13. Richard A. Epstein, "*Babbitt v. Sweet Home Chapters of Oregon*: The Law and Economics of Habitat Preservation," *Supreme Court Economic Review* 5 (1997): 1, 33.

14. See David A. Dana, "Natural Preservation and the Race to Develop," *University of Pennsylvania Law Review* 143 (1995): 655.

15. See, e.g., Thompson, "The Endangered Species Act," 312nn32–33 and the authorities cited therein. See also ibid., 312 ("Faced with political opposition and threats of lawsuits from property owners and other economically interested parties, the [government] sometimes finds that the simplest course is to avoid making the listing decision altogether.").

16. Widespread public opposition does not in itself imply that the ESA is a bad law. Public opposition may be fomented by political entrepreneurs; these entrepreneurs may even have agendas unrelated to the views of the public. Still, the fact that the ESA has, it seems, garnered greater public opposition than other environmental laws cannot be dismissed. Sustained opposition to a law weakens the law's perceived legitimacy. And political entrepreneurs, wily though they may be, cannot generally generate public opposition out of whole cloth; an underlying sentiment against the law must already have taken root.

It should be noted that the frame through which a law is viewed may affect the extent to which it is accepted. See generally Jonathan Remy Nash, "Framing Effects and Regulatory Choice," *Notre Dame Law Review* 82 (2006): 313, 324; Jonathan Remy Nash and Stephanie M. Stern, "Property Frames," *Washington University Law Review* 87 (2010): 449. In the case of the ESA, the "natural frame"—that is, the frame which most people spontaneously adopt—seems to engender negative responses to the ESA. Ibid., 492–93; Jonathan Remy Nash, "Packaging Property: The Effect of Paradigmatic Framing of Property Rights," *Tulane Law Review* 83 (2009): 691, 725.

17. See, e.g., J.B. Ruhl, "Section 7(a)(1) of the 'New' Endangered Species Act: Rediscovering and Redefining the Untapped Power of Federal Agencies' Duty to Conserve Species," *Environmental Law* 25 (1995): 1107, 1153–59 (discussing some bills from the early 1990s that would have weakened the Act).

18. See Nash, "Framing Effects," 324.

19. Wetlands regulation under the Clean Water Act also can apply to individual actors. To the extent that wetlands regulation engenders less general opposition than the ESA (and it is not clear that it has), this may be because of two reasons. First, the Act affects (or at least is perceived to affect) a broader cross-section of the population. Second, wetlands regulation can be understood to be justified on traditional nuisance-avoidance grounds. Actions by individuals that result in others being subjected to flooding and harm to the water system are perhaps more readily accepted as properly subject to regulation. In contrast, the Act secures little direct, tangible benefits to others; the notion that developing one's land—which is the type of action that the Act subjects to regulation—constitutes a "nuisance" is, traditionally at least, a stretch. Cf. *Lucas v. S.C. Coastal Council*, 505 U.S. 1003, 1031 (1992) ("It seems unlikely that common-law principles would have prevented the erection of any habitable or productive improvements on petitioner's land; they rarely support prohibition of the 'essential use' of land...." [citation omitted]).

20. See Jonathan Remy Nash, "Environmental Regulation Through the Looking Glass: The Curious Political Economy of Conservation Easements and Tradable Degradation Permits," working paper, presented at the Annual Meeting of the Canadian Law and Economics Association, Toronto, Canada, October 1–2, 2010.

21. See, e.g., Dale B. Thompson, "Political Obstacles to the Implementation of Emissions Markets: Lessons from RECLAIM," *Natural Resources Journal* 40 (2000): 645, 686–87 (describing how a local, elected air quality management district board decided not to include the public in local emissions trading program where the public objected to the idea).

22. For example, the Uniform Conservation Easement Act (UCEA), 12 U.L.A. 163 (1996), has been adopted in several states and in the District of Columbia.

23. Commentators divide over what motivates landowners to donate conservation easements. Some believe that altruistic environmental goals provide the primary motivation. See, e.g., Peter M. Morrisette, "Conservation Easements and the Public Good: Preserving the Environment on Private Lands," *Natural Resources Journal* 41 (2001): 373, 404. Others believe that incentives offered by the tax laws to induce donations of conservation easements play a larger role. See, e.g., Federico Cheever, "Public Good and the Private Magic in the Law of Land Trusts and Conservation Easements: A Happy Present and a Troubled Future," *Denver University Law Review* 73 (1996): 1077, 1087-91. For further discussion, see Jonathan Remy Nash, "Taxes and the Success of Non-Tax Market-Based Environmental Regulatory Regimes," in *5 Critical Issues in Environmental Taxation* 735, 754 n. 68 (Oxford: Oxford University Press, 2008), and the authorities cited therein.

24. See generally IRC § 170.

25. But see ibid., § 170(b)(e) (explicating restrictions).

26. For discussion, see generally Daniel Halperin, "A Charitable Contribution of Appreciated Property and the Realization of Built-In-Gain," *Tax Law Review* 56 (2002): 1.

27. See Nash, "Taxes and the Success of Non-Tax Market-Based Environmental Regulatory Regimes," 741.

28. See IRC § 170(f)(3)(B)(iii), (h); Treas. Reg. § 1.170A-14. Code section 170(f)(3)(A) seems at first to preclude deductions for donating conservation easements by limiting the availability of the deduction for a charitable contribution of "an interest in property which consists of less than the taxpayer's entire interest in such property." However, Code section 170(f)(3)(B) authorizes a charitable deduction for the contribution of, inter alia, a "qualified conservation contribution." IRC § 170(f)(3)(B)(iii). Subsection (h) of section 170 then elucidates the term "qualified conservation contribution" as a "contribution—(A) of a qualified real property interest, (B) to a qualified organization, (C) exclusively for conservation purposes." Ibid. § 170(h)(1). Subsection (h) also defines "qualified real property interest" to include "a restriction (granted in perpetuity) on the use which may be made of real property." Ibid. § 170(h)(2)(C).

29. See Treas. Reg. § 1.170A-14(h)(3)(i) ("The value of the contribution under section 170 in the case of a charitable contribution of a perpetual conservation restriction is the fair market value of the perpetual conservation restriction at the time of the contribution.").

Professor Nancy McLaughlin explains how the federal income tax deduction for donations of conservation easements offers far more upside for wealthier taxpayers than for poorer ones. *See* Nancy A. McLaughlin, "Increasing the Tax Incentives for Conservation Easement Donations—A Responsible Approach," *Ecology Law Quarterly* 31 (2004): 1, 29-36.

30. Treas. Reg. § 1.170A-14H)(3)(iii) ("The amount of the basis that is allocable to the qualified real property interest shall bear the same ratio to the total basis of the property as the fair market value of the property before the granting of the qualified real property interest.").

31. See generally IRC § 2522.

32. Ibid., § 2522(d).

33. See ibid., § 2522(a).

34. See ibid., § 2031(c). Professor McLaughlin explains how the structure of the Code rewards wealthier taxpayers far more than poorer ones with respect to the estate and gift tax deductions for conservation easements. See McLaughlin, "Increasing the Tax Incentives," 36–38. State and local tax laws often also offer tax benefits based upon the economic value of the donated conservation easement. See ibid., 39–40, n. 134.

35. See generally IRC § 170.

36. Ibid., § 170(h)(2)(C). Note that state law may also render conservation easements largely permanent by severely limiting the circumstances under which they may be lifted. See supra note 25.

37. For discussion and the argument that such sales might benefit the environment more than retaining the allowances—to the extent that the proceeds from the sales could be used to achieve other, more pressing environmental goals—see Nash, "Taxes and the Success of Non-Tax Market-Based Environmental Regulatory Regimes," 750–51.

38. See, e.g., Julia B. Mahoney, "Perpetual Restrictions on Land and the Problem of the Future," *Virginia Law Review* 88 (2002): 739; Nancy A. McLaughlin, "Rethinking the Perpetual Nature of Conservation Easements," *Harvard Environmental Law Review* 29 (2005): 421 (2005).

39. E.g., UCEA § 2(c), 12 U.L.A. at 173. As I discuss below, favorable tax treatment also generally turns on the easement with respect to which a deduction or credit being sought is perpetual in nature. See infra text accompanying notes 35–36 and note 43 and accompanying text.

40. Cf. Rodney B. W. Smith and Jason F. Shogren, "Voluntary Incentive Design for Endangered Species Protection," *Journal of Environmental Economics and Management* 43 (2002): 169, 181-82 (explaining benefit of incentive-based systems for land conservation that take into account greater value often inherent in larger, contiguous blocks of land).

The proposal thus correctly recognizes that it is *not* the case that the current tax deduction (based on economic valuation) "makes sense since, disregarding tax consequences, the donation of an easement is economically equivalent to selling the easement and then donating the proceeds to charity." Nash, "Taxes and the Success of Non-Tax Market-Based Environmental Regulatory Regimes," 740n11. The property itself may be of greater environmental value than it can fetch on the open market.

41. I present the proposal in terms of amendment of the federal Endangered Species Act and the federal tax laws. That said, it would be easy for state and local governments that offer incentives for donated conservation easements to piggyback on the proposal. Alternatively, or in addition, state and local governments could allow appropriate state agencies to render designations that would trigger increased state and local tax benefits.

42. For discussion, see David Sohn and Madeline Cohn, "From Smokestacks to Species: Extending the Tradable Permit Approach from Air Pollution to Habitat Conservation," *Stanford Environmental Law Journal* 15 (1996): 405.

43. See Endangered Species Act § 3(5), 16 U.S.C. § 1532(5) (defining "critical habitat" for threatened and endangered species to include areas, both occupied by the species and not currently occupied by the species, that are "essential to the conservation of the species"); but see Thompson, "The Endangered Species Act," 315 ("[T]he FWS has specified the critical habitat for less than 15 percent of listed species.").

44. See supra text accompanying notes 28–29.

45. It is possible, however, that the increased financial incentive to donate conservation easements might "crowd out" altruistic donations. See, e.g., Steven P. Kelman, *What Price Incentives? Economists and the Environment* (Westport: Auburn House, 1981), 62-69 (discussing how financial incentive might undermine altruism and spontaneity). Insofar as the existing tax code structure already offers a financial incentive for such donations, the "crowding out" problem might already exist. The question, thus, is the extent to which "crowding out" would increase by virtue of the increase in financial incentives that the proposal would create.

46. Cf. Todd J. Zywicki, "Environmental Externalities and Political Externalities: The Political Economy of Environmental Regulation and Reform," *Tulane Law Review* 73 (1999): 845 (arguing that, much as Prohibition resulted from a confluence of interests of Baptists and bootleggers, most environmental legislation can be seen to result from support from both environmentalists—the "Baptists" in the analogy—and existing industrial actors—the "bootleggers").

47. See generally Jason J. Czarnezki and Adrianne K. Zahner, "The Utility of Non-Use Values in Natural Resource Damage Assessments," *Boston College Environmental Affairs Law Review* 32 (2005): 509.

48. See supra the text accompanying note 43.

49. See Nash, "Trading Species," 20–23.

50. See Nash, "Framing Effects," 331n66 ("Sometimes…commodification actually might make people realize how valuable something really is—either because

the market value is higher than what people might have anticipated, or because of the realization that the market value does not in fact capture the item's true worth.).

51. Bonus payments above fair market value have been used to compensate for government takings. See, e.g., Richard A. Epstein, *Takings: Private Property and the Power of Eminent Domain* (Cambridge: Harvard University Press, 1985), 174, 184 (discussing historical examples).

52. See supra the text accompanying notes 28–29.

53. See Nash, "Taxes and the Success of Non-Tax Market-Based Environmental Regulatory Regimes," 743.

54. To the extent that, as some have argued, it is inefficient to create numerous presumptively perpetual conservation easements (see supra note 24 and accompanying text) one could imagine another modification to the current tax laws that would retain favorable tax treatment even where a conservation easement is not granted in perpetuity. Assuming the current valuation rules remain in effect, however, this would have the effect of reducing the tax benefits received by donating a non-perpetual conservation easement. In some sense, this reduction in value might be countered by *increasing* the tax benefits by a rate greater than 100 percent. Conceivably, the factor by which tax benefits are reduced might be offset (at least roughly) by the extent to which one needs to augment the tax benefits for non-perpetual, but more desirable, conservation easements, such that in the end one would simply retain the rule of basing the tax benefit on 100 percent of the value of the non-perpetual easement donated.

55. See, e.g., Karin P. Sheldon, "Habitat Conservation Planning: Addressing the Achilles Heel of the Endangered Species Act," *New York University Environmental Law Journal* 6 (1998): 279, 305nn160–162. I am grateful to Jonathan Adler for this point.

56. See, e.g., James Salzman, "Creating Markets for Ecosystem Services: Notes from the Field," *New York University Law Review* 80 (2005): 870; J.B. Ruhl and James Salzman, "The Law and Policy Beginnings of Ecosystem Services," *Journal of Land Use and Environmental Law* 22 (2007): 157.

57. Jonathan Baert Wiener, "Global Environmental Regulation: Instrument Choice in Legal Context," *Yale Law Journal* 108 (1999): 677, 781–82 (arguing that payments to actors to reduce pollution may be expected where actors' participation in pollution reduction scheme is purely voluntary). But see Salzman, "Creating Markets," 927-28 (arguing that Professor Wiener's argument that cross-subsidies may be expected at the international level has application to the setting of establishing markets for ecosystem services for nonpoint water pollution sources).

58. For discussion, see Nash, "Framing Effects," 326–27 (discussing how perception that "right to pollute" has been given to some societal actors may affect other societal actors' views toward undertaking environmentally friendly actions).

6

Protecting Species through the Protection of Water Rights

James L. Huffman

Whenever a threatened or endangered species' habitat includes surface waters, groundwater, or riparian zones, private water rights are likely impacted. For example, a government mandate that water of a certain quantity, flow, or temperature remain in a stream to preserve an endangered fish may require farmers to forgo using water to which they have a right under state law. Similarly, water users may be prohibited from withdrawing water from a reservoir that serves as breeding habitat for an endangered waterfowl. These and a multitude of other conflicts between species protection and water use raise two fundamental questions: (1) Do the endangered species or the possessor of the water right have first claim to the water? (2) How does the resolution of this conflict affect the protection of species, on the one hand, and the socially optimum use of water, on the other hand?

Heretofore, species-protection advocates and government regulators have presumed the answer to the first question to be obvious and beyond debate—the species have first claim on whatever water is necessary. This presumption is often founded in a moral claim that nature trumps mere human claims to nature's bounty but also is said to be implicit in the mandatory, nondiscretionary responsibilities of the government under the Endangered Species Act (ESA). The answer to the second question follows from this presumption—species protection is, on principle and by Congressional declaration, the socially optimum use of water.

Property rights advocates and possessors of water rights object that the presumptive preference for species protection over other water uses is in conflict with constitutional protection of property rights. The point of the Fifth Amendment takings clause, they argue, is that, no matter what Congress determines to be in the public interest and no matter how important it is thought to be, there must be compensation for property rights taken as a result of government action. From this perspective, the wisdom of species protection is entirely independent from the government's responsibilities under the takings clause. That clause in no way prohibits government from taking property to protect species; it only requires that compensation be paid.

As a practical matter, species protection and compensation of affected property owners are unavoidably linked. Resources devoted to compensating property owners cannot be devoted to species protection or other public purposes. This does not mean, however, that compensation for losses resulting from ESA-based regulations will necessarily undermine or lessen species protection. To the contrary, as I argue in this chapter, the constitutional protection of property rights in general and water rights in particular can provide the foundation for greater conservation of water-dependent species. The relationship between species protection and the exercise of water rights is not a zero-sum game: by reducing the perverse incentives inherent in regulation and in property rights made contingent by that regulation and other legal factors, it is possible to create new value that can be devoted to both species protection and other productive uses of water.

The ESA is sometimes said to allow for no compromise of its objective of preserving species. However, this cannot be an acceptable or viable public policy: attempting to prevent all impact on endangered species is like attempting to eliminate pollution, in that at some point the marginal benefits of additional gains in species protection will be less than the opportunity costs of achieving those gains.[1] Usually, whether explicitly or implicitly, species protection is compromised to competing values when those values exceed the benefits of species protection.[2] When such accommodation does not occur, net social welfare is diminished. The pretense of species protection being only about science leads us to obscure these value choices and leave them to government scientists. It also leads us to view private property as a threat to species protection rather than as an institution that can contribute to the overarching goal of species survival.

Thus, the public policy objectives must be: (1) to achieve a level of species protection consistent with other public values dependent on scarce water resources, and (2) to maximize the net social benefit (including species protection) derived from water resources by establishing institutional arrangements that get the incentives right. Contrary to the prevailing view among both advocates for species protection and defenders of private property, getting the incentives right requires a combination of private rights, public rights, and government regulation.

In this chapter I explore the current framing of the species protection–water rights debate, which I later describe as the "species protection-takings dance," and argue that reframing that discussion can lead to mutually reinforcing measures to protect endangered species and to uphold secure, well-defined property rights.

I begin by summarizing the state law bases of private water rights, the relationship between the ESA and private water rights, and the sources of federal authority to adopt and implement the ESA. I then examine the apparent conflict between species protection and water rights and provide several illustrative examples. I describe and critique the current framing of the issues by discussing two federal court cases in which ESA-based regulations have been found to result in unconstitutional takings, I suggest a general framework for understanding the relationship between ESA-based regulations and the takings clause, and I then consider several theories, based on existing law, for avoiding future takings holdings. Next I examine legal innovations intended to avoid takings claims in the event existing alternatives prove ineffective. I propose a better way to think about the relationship between species protection and private rights in water by explaining how greater reliance on property rights can create positive incentives and eliminate perverse incentives arising from regulation and resultant threats to property interests. Finally, I discuss the positive role for property rights and markets in species protection and recommend several measures for achieving that objective.

State Water Law and the ESA

As a consequence of deeply rooted historical practice and express federal deference, state law provides the foundation for water allocation in the United States. In the colonial and early postindependence periods the common law riparian doctrine recognized the right of all riparian landowners to the reasonable use of adjacent waters, subject only to public rights to navigate, fish, and bathe in navigable waterways. As a general rule, that approach remains the law in states on, and east of, the 100th meridian. During the second half of the nineteenth century, many territories and states of the arid American West developed an appropriation doctrine, according to which the right to use water was acquired by appropriating water to a beneficial use. A few of those states retained aspects of the riparian doctrine, resulting in mixed (and mixed-up) systems. Under the riparian doctrine rights are correlative, meaning that riparian landowners may use water for purposes and in amounts that are reasonable in relation to the uses of other riparians and to the capacity of the water source. The volume or flow of a riparian right thus varies with the available supply and the demands of other riparian landowners. Under the appropriation doctrine, water rights are fixed with respect to quantity (or flow) and priority. This means that each user has an exclusive right to the full amount of his water right unless the supply is insufficient to satisfy the rights of all senior rights holders drawing from the same source. Rights to groundwater are allocated on the basis either of overlying surface ownership or capture. Most states have superimposed permitting processes on their common law rights systems, originally as a means of establishing better records of established rights and more recently as an opening for government control of water allocation through the police power.

In the ESA, Congress took special notice of these state water laws, declaring "the policy of Congress [to be] that Federal agencies shall cooperate with State and local agencies to resolve water resource issues in concert with conservation of endangered species."[3] Although this expression of cooperative intent contrasts with Congress' total deference to state water authority in prior laws,[4] the mere reference to water, but not land, as requiring cooperation with the states underscores Congress' recognition of the states' longstanding, leading role in water allocation. On the other hand, one might read Section 1(c)(2) as evidencing a Congressional intent to break with the total deference of earlier legislation. However the declaration with respect to state water authority is understood, there should have been no doubt that the mandatory prescriptions of the ESA and state-recognized water rights would be in frequent conflict, particularly in the appropriation doctrine states. A water rights system allowing total depletion of stream flows inevitably will conflict with the mandatory protection of species dependent on some minimum quantity and condition of water in the stream.

One solution to such conflicts, anticipated in the ESA, is the acquisition of water rights where species protection requires restriction of those rights. Section 4(a) authorizes the federal government "to acquire by purchase, donation, or otherwise, lands, waters, or interest therein."[5] Not surprisingly, this section is seldom mentioned in discussions of the ESA and seldom has been used in the implementation of the Act. Rarely does any government exercise authority to purchase property if it can accomplish its purposes by regulating the use of property without judicially mandated compensation to the affected owners.

The ESA is not the only federal law affecting private water rights. Although Section 1 of the Act suggests that one of its central purposes is to facilitate U.S. compliance with several referenced treaties and international agreements, the constitutional authority for the Act, like the authority for most other federal regulation of water rights, derives from the commerce clause of Article I, Section 8.[6] The commerce clause has been firmly linked to navigable waters at least since the Supreme Court's 1824 decision in *Gibbons v. Ogden*.[7] Since then, the power of the federal government to regulate commerce has had few limitations, so there is little doubt that Congress has significant authority to regulate private rights in water.[8] Central among those commerce clause powers, but also rooted in preexisting public rights of navigation on navigable waters, is the federal navigational servitude pursuant to which the federal government assures that the navigable waters of the United States remain unobstructed.[9]

The foregoing summaries of state water law, the ESA, and the sources of federal power over water suggest the following conclusions: (1) to the extent Congress' power to enact the ESA derives from the commerce clause, claims by affected private water-rights owners should be analyzed as regulatory takings absent facts establishing a categorical taking,[10] and (2) where the ESA, either by design or in effect, serves to protect public rights established prior to the vesting of affected private water rights, there can be no taking because nothing is taken under those circumstances. Considered together, these conclusions lead the government and most species-protection advocates to assert that the ESA serves to enforce a preexisting public right in species protection and therefore is an effective trump on any takings claim put forward by a private water-right owner.

Species Protection versus Water Rights

Ever since the famous snail darter case in which the Supreme Court held that the ESA forbade the continued construction of a large dam in order to protect an endangered and obscure fish,[11] the statute has led to conflict between species protection and human enterprise. Although the Tellico Dam was ultimately completed after Congress exempted it from the ESA's constraints,[12] the very public controversy surrounding the dispute set the stage for four decades of continuous political and legal battle over the impact of the ESA on private property rights. More than a few of these conflicts have pitted water use against species preservation. A few recent examples are illustrative.[13]

- For most of a century farmers in southern Oregon and northern California have relied on irrigation water from a Bureau of Reclamation project on the Klamath River. A severe drought in 2001 led the Bureau to curtail water delivery to the farmers in order to sustain three ESA-protected fish species. For some farmers the loss of a season's crops was economically devastating, so they sued seeking compensation under the takings clause. After a trial court decision against the farmers, appeal to the Federal Circuit Court of Appeals and certification to the Oregon Supreme Court of questions relating to Oregon property law, the case has been remanded to the trial court for a final resolution of the takings claim in light of the Oregon court's finding that the farmers do have a property right under Oregon law.[14]

- Farmers in the Carson-Truckee Basin engaged in a decades-long dispute with the Pyramid Lake Paiute Tribe (PLPT) over federal project water drawn from Pyramid Lake located on the Tribe's reservation. Upstream diversions, especially the Newlands Project operated by the Truckee-Carson Irrigation district, caused the lake to fall below the minimum levels needed to support populations of endangered Cui-Ui and Lahontan Cutthroat trout. In 1989, the PLPT sued the Secretary of Interior to block the release of water for agricultural purposes.[15] In 1990, Congress passed the Truckee-Carson-Pyramid Lake Water Rights Settlement Act mandating development of a process for revision of the operating criteria for the Truckee River including the federal dams. These processes are meant to take account of agricultural, urban, and species protection water needs.

- The Central Valley Project (CVP) is the largest federal water management project in the United States and provides water to users under contracts with the Bureau of Reclamation. The Westlands Water District draws Project water pursuant to a 1963 contract. In 1990 and 1993, after the Sacramento River winter-run Chinook salmon and the Delta smelt of the Sacramento-San Joaquin Delta were designated threatened species, water allocated to Westlands from the CVP was cut by 50 percent.[16]

- In Eastern Washington's Methow Valley, irrigators' rights to transport water across federal lands were restricted by the Forest Service in an effort to assure adequate water for endangered salmon and steelhead. The irrigators and local governments challenged the federal government's authority to impose such restrictions. The court ruled the Forest Service had the power to restrict the use of water transported over federal lands because "the permits, from their inception, provided government with unqualified discretion to restrict or terminate the rights-of-way" under 16 U.S.C.A. § 475.[17]

- Irrigators, the City of Albuquerque, and the State of New Mexico all challenged the federal government's decision to curtail withdrawals from the Middle Rio Grande River to protect the endangered Rio Grande silvery minnow. Advocates for the minnows prevailed in court, but Congress intervened to overturn, in effect, the court's decision. As the court in *Rio Grande Silvery Minnow v. Keys* stated, the litigation was the convergence of two issues, "one targeting the survival of the silvery minnow in its critical habitat under the ESA, the other challenging the impact of that designation on New Mexico's agricultural communities and burgeoning urban centers under the National Environmental Policy Act, 42 U.S.C. § 4321, which requires all federal agencies to examine the environmental impact of "major Federal actions significantly affecting the quality of the human environment." 42 U.S.C. § 4332(2)(C).[18]

In the context of these and many other disputes, objectors to ESA-based restrictions on water use have relied upon four different theories, only one of which has been successful thus far. Courts have rejected the argument that species protection, despite the historically dominant role of the states in wildlife management and regulation, falls outside the reach of Congress' commerce clause powers.[19] This is not surprising, given the almost unlimited reach of the commerce power since the New Deal. The courts have also rejected claims made on behalf of water users holding contractual rights to water delivery from federal projects, although that argument is raised again in the Klamath litigation.[20] A third line of argument has been that the combination of state sovereignty over and ownership of waters within a state exempts states and those holding water rights under state authority from ESA regulations. Although courts have not passed judgment on this theory, it is very unlikely to succeed, given the Supreme Court's upholding of federal reserved rights[21] and its conclusion that the concept of state ownership of water, like state ownership of wildlife,[22] is only an expression of the importance these resources have for the public.[23]

Thus, the only chink in the considerable armor of the ESA may prove to be the takings clause. But, as I argue in this chapter, a strong takings clause does not necessarily obstruct achievement of the species protection objectives of the ESA. To the contrary, enforcement of the takings clause can benefit species protection by reducing the perverse incentives of the existing regime, by creating positive incentives for species and habitat preservation, and by imposing the discipline of market pricing on government decision making.

Taking Property versus Taking Species

Where ESA regulations restrict the exercise of state-recognized water rights and the federal government fails to exercise its acquisition authority under Section 4(a), the takings clause of the Fifth Amendment to the United States Constitution may be implicated. When, if ever, do ESA-based regulations of private water rights result in the unconstitutional taking of private property? That question has never been addressed by the United States Supreme Court, but two federal courts have found that takings can result from ESA-based regulations.

California's Central Valley is home to endangered Chinook salmon and Delta smelt. During the summers of 1992 to 1994, Central Valley irrigators were required to reduce water withdrawals below the levels authorized pursuant to their rights under California law. Takings claims were filed in the United States Court of Federal Claims, and for the first time an enforcement action under the ESA was held to result in an unconstitutional taking in *Tulare Lake Water Basin Storage District v. United States*.[24] The court concluded that the mandated withdrawal reductions, measurable in acre-feet, constituted physical appropriations of the water and thus per se takings consistent with the Supreme Court's ruling in *Loretto v. Teleprompter Manhattan CATV Corp*.[25] The decision was celebrated by property rights advocates but widely criticized by environmentalists as based on a misunderstanding of the nature of water rights under California law and for applying the per se takings test where regulatory takings analysis was argued to be appropriate.[26]

In 1956, Casitas Municipal Water District agreed with the United States to repay, over forty years, the construction costs of the Ventura River Project in return for "the perpetual right to use all water that becomes available through the construction and operation of the Project." In the same year, California issued permits allowing Casitas Municipal Water District to appropriate the Project water. Thirty-eight years later, Casitas was ordered to construct a fish ladder and provide water sufficient for the survival of the endangered West Coast steelhead trout.[27] Casitas Municipal Water District sued for compensation in the Court of Federal Claims. The Court granted the government's motion for summary judgment,[28] but a divided United States Court of Appeals for the Federal Circuit reversed and remanded for the trial court to consider the takings claim.[29] The majority agreed with the *Tulare* court that there was a physical taking of water constituting a categorical taking. The dissent echoed the view of *Tulare* critics that regulatory takings analysis should apply. The government petitioned for rehearing and rehearing en banc, both of which petitions were denied.[30]

A third controversy, also noted above, is currently before the Federal Circuit Court of Appeals. When the Bureau of Reclamation terminated water deliveries to Klamath Basin irrigators to protect three species of endangered fish in 2001, the irrigators sought compensation in the Court of Federal Claims for alleged taking of private property and deprivation of contractual rights. The Court of Claims found against the irrigators on both claims.[31] The case was appealed to the Federal Circuit, and that court determined that the resolution of the takings question turned on issues of Oregon law that the court certified to the Oregon Supreme Court for resolution.[32] The Oregon Court concluded that the irrigators did have property rights under Oregon law unless those rights had been altered by contract with the United States. The Federal Circuit then remanded to the Court of Claims for a decision on the takings claim in light of the Oregon Court's answers to the certified questions.[33] Failing proof by the United States that the irrigators' property rights have been altered by contract, the irrigators should prevail on remand. This will be an important precedent for the 140,000 farmers receiving Bureau water nationwide.

However, an Oregon Supreme Court conclusion that Bureau of Reclamation water users do not have a property right will not conclude the issue in any other state. Furthermore, even if Bureau water users have no protected property interest, other Oregon water-rights holders may still have viable takings claims. Based on the two federal cases discussed above, the critical issue will continue to be whether ESA-based limitations on water rights should be analyzed as categorical or regulatory takings. Under the categorical takings analysis of *Loretto*, water rights holders will prevail as in *Tulare* and *Casitas*. But if the regulatory takings analysis of *Penn Central Transportation Co. v. New York City*[34] applies, water-rights owners are almost certain to go uncompensated when ESA-based regulations limit their use of water.

Stepping back from the particulars of these cases and from the Supreme Court's strained takings jurisprudence, it is useful to frame the takings question with reference to the purported source of authority relied upon by Congress in enacting the ESA. When Congressional enforcement of the federal navigation servitude affects the exercise of private water rights, there is no infringement of those rights because the navigation servitude is a public right that predates the vesting of any private rights. For example, federal regulation of navigation-obstructing structures in and over the Mississippi River or other waterways that are navigable in fact cannot infringe the rights of riparian property owners whose titles have never included authority to obstruct navigation. In enforcing the navigation servitude Congress does not take private rights; rather it prevents the private taking of public rights.

Similarly, where Congress asserts that federal reserved water rights justify constraints on private water rights, there also may be no basis for takings claims. Reserved water rights are proprietary interests existing within each state's water rights regime and subject to enforcement on the same terms as any private proprietary claim.[35] Under the Supreme Court's reserved rights doctrine, for example, the National Park Service has rights to the water necessary for achieving Yellowstone's purposes, dating from the park's creation in 1872. Thus a federal reserved water right will exempt the federal government from takings claims brought by any appropriator with a later priority.[36] Given the early date of Yellowstone's creation, this excludes claims by all private water users. The theory for this federal reserved rights "exemption" from takings claims is straightforward. However, application of the doctrine has created extensive uncertainty for private water users because the federal rights are almost always implied and there is pervasive uncertainty about the quantity of water reserved to the federal government.

The federal navigation servitude and federal reserved water rights (like any federal property right) have in common that they help to define the boundaries of private water rights in the same way as do other private rights. The nature and scope of one property right are bounded by the nature and scope of other property rights, whether public or private. Where a takings claim fails because of the navigation servitude or a federal reserved right, it is because there is no private right to be taken. A private claimant never possessed the right to obstruct navigation or to interfere with a federal right reserved prior to the private appropriation.

The same relationship exists between private claims and public rights asserted pursuant to what Justice Scalia labeled "background principles" of state property law.[37] Background principles include common law nuisance and the public trust doctrine pursuant to which the public has rights that predate and therefore function as limits on the scope of private water rights. Private water rights affected by public action taken to protect these public rights never included the right to be free from such effects. Thus the navigation servitude and federal reserved rights enforced by Congress and background principles of common law enforced by the states help to define the nature and scope of private rights in water. In the context of a takings claim, they help answer the question of whether the claimed property right exists, not whether an existing property right has been taken.

But where federal action under the ESA is not rooted in enforcement of the navigation servitude or exercise of federal reserved or other property rights—where it is effectively an exercise of delegated state police powers—the *Tulare* and *Casitas* cases underscore that it is not a foregone conclusion that affected water-rights owners have no takings claim against the federal government. With respect to water supplied from federal projects under contract between the water user and the United States, the threat of takings claims might easily be eliminated through a contract provision allowing for nondelivery when necessary to comply with the ESA. But because virtually all of these contracts date back several decades to the time of project construction, the opportunities for such contractual protection of the federal government must await contract expiration and renewal. Even then, it appears that the government has been slow to revise contracts with an eye to limiting its potential liability for ESA-based water delivery restrictions.[38] But where existing contracts include no such provision and where ESA-based restrictions apply directly to state-recognized water rights, the prospect of more cases like *Tulare* and *Casitas* is thought by most species-protection advocates to undercut the effectiveness of the ESA.[39]

The usual explanation for this pessimism is that governments cannot afford to pay the price of compensating affected water-rights owners. While this claim seldom reflects a serious assessment of the actual costs of compensation, the objection is rooted more in disagreement with the core principle of the takings clause than in a concern for the public purse. Most species-protection advocates, like most mainstream environmentalists, view the protection of property rights as a lesser good, if a good at all, than the protection of species and the environment. But belief in a higher good does not carry the argument in a rule-of-law regime. Absent acceptance of the proposition that secure and well-defined property rights can serve rather than obstruct the objective of species protection, the reality of the takings clause requires that species-protection advocates propose legal rationales for avoidance of the constitutional requirement of compensation.

Avoiding the Takings Clause

An obvious way for the government to avoid future takings claims is to provide for compensation to affected property owners when ESA-based constraints are imposed. But when such compensation was proposed in the 2000 Farm Bill, most water-rights owners were adamantly opposed. Farmers objected that federal acquisition of water rights for endangered species protection could lead to forced sales at prices set by the government, but earlier opposition to states allowing for the purchase and sale of instream flows suggests that many farmers would object to federal acquisition of water rights even if only from willing sellers. There is a widespread fear among defenders of the family farm that any loss of water rights will be another nail in the coffin of already struggling Western agriculture. But this to-the-barricades view on the part of farmers may leave them with nothing. In light of the Supreme Court's expansive interpretation of the public use language of the Fifth Amendment,[40] there is little doubt that water rights can be taken by eminent domain for ESA purposes.

History evidences, however, that governments will virtually always prefer uncompensated regulation over purchase by eminent domain. Absent a Supreme Court affirmation of the holdings in *Tulare* and *Casitas*, few governments would resort to eminent domain, even if Congress or state legislatures managed to appropriate the necessary funds. Governments are always loath to pay for their impacts on private property absent clear physical takings for government facilities or a court order. Invariably it is argued that compensation will deplete governments' limited resources, making it impossible to pursue important public purposes like species protection. "Government hardly could go on," wrote Justice Holmes in oft-quoted language, "if to some extent values incident to property could not be diminished without paying for every such change in the general law."[41]

Drawing on other language from the Holmes opinion quoted above, one approach is to engage in a balancing of public and private interests to determine whether a particular regulation goes "too far" in impacting on private property.[42] Such balancing is the central feature of the Supreme Court's regulatory takings doctrine. Absent physical invasions or total loss of value, the "too far" balancing approach applies in all takings cases.[43] The problem with this approach in any regulatory context, including those resulting in conflicts between water rights and endangered species protection under the ESA, is that property rights are made necessarily contingent. They are contingent on the perceived importance of the conflicting public purposes, and those public purposes will almost always be found to justify limits on property. Property rights become mere interests, and water-rights owners become mere stakeholders among the many who will collaborate in water management.[44]

Property rights in water are also made contingent, and thereby less protected under the takings clause, by liberal interpretation of the beneficial use, waste, and public interest standards of appropriation doctrine. Western water law has long limited appropriators to beneficial uses, a concept originally intended to preclude speculation and waste and later relied upon by established users like irrigators and miners to exclude newer desired uses like instream flow and habitat maintenance. Some now urge that the doctrine be applied by courts and water administrators to pick and choose among vested water uses based upon changing perceptions of the public interest. It is also suggested that the traditional prohibition on waste gives judges and administrators similar discretion to adjust existing water uses without regard to established priorities and quantities. Liberally construed, the statutory public interest standard that generally applies to permit grants and transfer approvals also allows for discretion contributing to the evermore contingent nature of water rights.

Another theory used to evade claims made under the takings clause is that the ESA preempts state law, including state water laws pursuant to which water users claim a right to use water that has been determined necessary to species protection.[45] But the takings clause as applied to the federal government would be eviscerated if, in the preemption of state law, property rights established under that state law become null and void. To the contrary, the act of preemption would result in the taking of any property rights existing under the preempted state law. If the federal government cannot take the property of individuals, all of which exists under state law, surely it cannot take the property rights of everyone by pre-empting state law. By its very existence, the takings clause contradicts the argument that federal law can preempt state property laws. Or, alternatively, one might conclude that if and when federal law preempts state property laws, the federal government is required to compensate for property taken as a result.

In the context of federal laws relating directly to water use and allocation, there has never been any doubt that the federal government must defer to vested property rights under state law. In the 1866 and 1870 Mining Acts, Congress acknowledged the validity of water rights under state law.[46] The 1877 Desert Land Act explicitly affirmed that the right to use water on lands acquired under the Act "shall depend upon bona fide prior appropriation," and that any unappropriated waters on such lands would be subject to private appropriation under state law.[47] The previously mentioned Reclamation Act similarly deferred to state authority over water.[48] In 1952 Congress reaffirmed the central role of the states in defining and enforcing water rights by waiving its sovereign immunity, explicitly allowing the United States to be "joined as a defendant in any suit [in state court] for the adjudication of rights to the use of water of a river system or other source."[49]

At least some of the foregoing theories for avoiding the takings clause might hold water, so to speak, if water users have nothing more than a permitted privilege that the state is free to withdraw or limit. But that cannot be the nature of private water rights if those rights are to provide the stability and security necessary to wise and efficient water utilization. State and federal courts have repeatedly ruled, as did the Court of Claims in *Tulare* and *Casitas*, that water rights are property. Much is sometimes made of the fact that water rights are usufructuary, meaning that they are rights of use and not of physical possession, but this is a distinction without a difference for purposes of the takings clause. The prospect of use (including non-consumptive use) is what gives all property value. To suggest that use rights can be taken without infringing the Fifth Amendment would, again, eviscerate the takings clause. That clause requires just compensation when property is taken. The measure of just compensation is use value as reflected in the market.

Taking Water Rights by Other Means

If *Tulare* and *Casitas* are the law of the land, government will have to compensate where a water right owner is precluded from using specific quantities of water so that endangered species' requirements may be met. The only way government can avoid compensating, short of revoking or waiving the regulatory constraint, is to prove the existence of superior government or public rights like those founded in the public trust and navigation servitude. One such source of public rights, suggested by Professor Dan Tarlock, is what he labels "federal regulatory rights."[50] The concept is that at least some regulations effectively create federal or public rights that insulate the government from takings claims by affected property owners.

If all federal regulations create rights superior to regulated private rights there can be no takings and the takings clause is a nullity, at least with respect to the federal government. This cannot be the case, not least because for over a century the takings clause had application only to the federal government, and no provision of the Constitution can be understood to have no practical consequence. The argument might be salvaged if only some federal regulations affecting property create federal regulatory rights. But there is no rational basis for finding some, but not all, regulations to be the source of federal rights. Congress could declare that certain regulations create federal rights, but if the consequence of such a declaration is to insulate the government from takings claims, Congress will have every incentive to make such a declaration in every regulation affecting private property. Thus the idea of federal regulatory rights is nothing more than a poorly disguised effort to shield government from legitimate compensation claims.

Any regulatory constraint on water use can be measured in concrete volume or flow terms, and thus qualify as a categorical physical taking. But because flows vary with the time of day and season of the year, meaning that particular water rights may or may not be affected by particular regulations, some courts are sure to conclude that there is no physical taking when regulations impose variable restraints. In such cases courts will be left to apply the regulatory takings analysis of *Penn Central*, pursuant to which property rights are balanced against public purposes. The case law since *Penn Central* makes clear that property rights are seldom found to outweigh the public's purposes, so it is safe to assume that ESA-based regulations that are found not to result in a physical taking will not require compensation unless there is a total loss of economic value in the affected property. Governments can be counted upon, therefore, to insist that ESA-based regulations do not result in physical takings or total loss of economic value, and to design regulations to make those claims plausible.

Another approach to limiting the federal government's exposure to takings claims could be the reform of state water law with an eye to making water rights more contingent and therefore less secure. The federal government can encourage changes in state law through unfunded mandates or subsidies conditioned on desired changes. Particularly when states are strapped for revenue, they show little resistance to federal carrots. Most state water administrators also are predisposed to making water rights more contingent, thereby expanding their own powers to manage water resources. Absent the sort of appreciation for the incentive benefits of secure property rights advocated in this chapter, the only downside to greater contingency of water rights that will be recognized by the states is the unlikely prospect that courts would require compensation for piecemeal curtailment of property rights in water. With rare exceptions,[51] courts have held that, in calculating the extent of property taken, the denominator is the whole legal parcel, not some portion of that interest, even if severable.[52]

For most states, an effective path to greater contingency in water rights is expansion of the traditional public trust doctrine and related common law doctrines including public nuisance. In the name of an evolving common law, many state courts and some state legislatures have reinterpreted historic common law doctrines that have long been the "background principles" helping to define the nature and extent of property rights. For example, the public trust doctrine which from early common law has guaranteed public rights to fishing and navigation in tidal and other navigable waters has been reinterpreted to guarantee public rights of beach access across private uplands[53] and public access to all waters that can be used for any form of recreation.[54] Michael Blumm and many others have urged that courts should similarly reinterpret historic common law doctrines to limit land and water uses that were once clearly an attribute of private property rights.[55] Such changes in common law doctrine are claimed to be in the long tradition of common law evolution and therefore within the reasonable expectations of property owners. Because property owners should anticipate such changes in the common law rules, it is argued, there is no unconstitutional taking of affected property rights.

Shifting the Focus to Incentives for Species Protection

Much energy, emotion, and resources are expended by all parties to this species protection-takings dance. Water-rights owners see their livelihoods threatened by uncompensated species protection regulations, and environmentalists see their species protection objectives threatened by cases like *Tulare* and *Casitas*. The environmentalist worries are encouraged by government insistence that it cannot afford to compensate affected property owners. While agricultural water users claim they should be compensated for losses resulting from species protection, they oppose the occasional proposal to provide for such compensation. Clearly they are relying on the courts to follow *Tulare* and *Casitas* and the government's plea of impecuniosity to lessen ESA-based restraints on their use of water. The ESA-takings dance is more about rent seeking through the legislative and administrative processes than it is about protecting species or property rights. Environmentalists seek species protection benefits at the expense of private property owners, and property owners seek insulation from the market power of environmentalists. The incentives are wrong, and it will be difficult to get them right because the solution requires that species-protection advocates embrace property rights and water-rights holders accept a water market to which all potential water users have equal access.

Although water-rights owners are generally pleased with the holdings in *Tulare* and *Casitas*, takings law in general and their personal experience in particular give them little reason for optimism about future protection of their water rights. The same is true for owners of riparian and submerged land. Thus their incentive is to avoid having ESA-based regulations apply to them.[56] The incentive to eliminate endangered species on one's property or to destroy habitat that might attract such species is powerful if one believes the alternative is a prohibition on the use of one's water or land. Perhaps more important, in light of the extensive habitat destruction that has already taken place throughout the country, is the lack of incentive in the existing regime for habitat restoration. A recent Montana case in which the Montana Supreme Court found a public right of access to the waters and private submerged lands of Mitchell Slough that had been privately restored as fish and wildlife habitat illustrates the problem. The owners had invested over a million dollars in the restoration work on the assumption that they could control access. When the court held that there was public access to the restored habitat, the owners announced that they would not invest in maintenance of the restored habitat.[57] This is not a surprising reaction, given the almost certain resource destruction that results from open access.

The ESA, like most regulatory regimes, also creates perverse incentives for what have come to be called "stakeholders." A mere assertion of interest in species protection entitles any individual or interest group to seek influence in the process, including for purposes incidental or unrelated to species preservation. Those seeking to stop a development, for example, normally can participate in the ordinary permitting process, but chances for success are much greater if an endangered species can be found. Absent the restraint of a compensation requirement, regulators have little incentive to resist such rent-seeking behavior. An illustration of such rent seeking was the successful campaign to curtail logging over vast areas of the Pacific Northwest in the name of protecting spotted owls. While many who argued for owl protection were genuinely concerned for the owl, at least a few acknowledged that protecting owls was the means to the larger objective of curtailing logging. The ESA provided a trump card over those concerned for the timber industry and the jobs it provided. Similar examples exist in every region of the country.

Even if the search for threatened or endangered species does not succeed, the high costs of participation in the administrative process can induce settlement by resource users and developers, including compromise of vested property rights. Administrative challenge and litigation are familiar strategies for inducing settlement and compromise. Developers faced with the all or nothing consequence of an endangerment determination will be forced to settle even if they believe there is a high probability of prevailing when the process is finally concluded. The trumping nature of a determination of endangerment thus distorts the weighing of costs and benefits. Although it is widely asserted that the ESA does not allow for cost-benefit analysis, Dale Goble's previously mentioned work demonstrates that something resembling balancing of competing interests is inherent in the ESA.[58]

Property Rights, Markets, and Species Protection

The length and intensity of the species protection versus water rights debate launched by the ESA will lead most advocates on both sides to conclude that there is no middle ground. The assumption on both sides seems to be that for water-dependent species to survive, water rights must give way. Implicit in this assumption is that there will be no compensation to affected water-rights owners, both because the government cannot afford it and because, by one theory or another, private water rights are legally inferior to the public's interest in species protection. But there is some middle ground that would provide greater security to water-rights owners and incentives for private species protection while lessening the existing perverse incentives for species and habitat destruction.

As the example of Montana's Mitchell Slough illustrates, private individuals will invest in habitat restoration and wildlife protection, but only if their property rights are reasonably well defined and secure against trespass. As Garrett Hardin noted in his seminal essay years ago, property rights are a sure way to avoid the tragedy of the commons.[59] While it may offend the egalitarian sensibilities of some who are excluded, there is no reason to believe that the tragedy of the commons is less likely to occur where water or wildlife, rather than any other resource, is effectively a commons. Private actors, both individual and collective, will invest in species protection where their rights are secure, and will make other investments to conserve privately owned resources upon which species depend, including water. But private actors cannot be expected to take such steps voluntarily if there is reason to expect that their property rights will be found to be contingent and their investment will be for naught. This is not to suggest that all species protection will be accomplished privately. That is obviously not the case due to public-goods-related market failures. But the public goods nature of much species protection should not lead us to abandon the significant powers of private initiative and markets where they do serve the objectives of the ESA.

Traditionally, Western water law imposed a "use it or lose it" requirement on rights owners. Water-rights owners were required to make "productive use" of their water rights to retain them. This frustrated conservation efforts as rights owners who left their water in the stream for the benefit of fish or other species could lose their rights. More recently, however, states have begun to modify their water law to allow the acquisition of water rights for instream use and other environmental purposes. Under Oregon law, for example, individuals may sell, purchase, lease, and donate water rights for instream use, allowing groups like the Oregon Water Trust to acquire water rights and devote them to fish conservation.[60] This creates a market-based avenue for conservation efforts that do not require environmentalists to lobby for increased government restrictions on land and water use, and greater opportunities for voluntary exchange. For this avenue to be effective, however, the underlying water rights must be secure.

Clarifying and protecting water rights can also encourage agricultural users to make more efficient use of their water rights, and help lessen political resistance to species conservation efforts. If a water user knows that he has a secure right in unused water, and that this water has economic value, he is more likely to invest in efficiency improvements, making more water available for other uses in the process, and potentially reducing the level of conflict between agricultural users and environmental conservation. Such efficiency improvements, combined with voluntary acquisition of instream rights, will not eliminate conflicts over species preservation, but they are significant steps toward a more effective and equitable species conservation approach.

To encourage private investment in species and habitat protection, several things will have to happen:

- Water rights must be clearly defined and strictly enforced. The same is true of associated private rights in riparian and submerged lands. As this chapter makes clear, much in existing law and policy leads water rights in particular to be contingent. Principal sources of contingency include the "too far" test for regulatory takings, the various and variable claims of public rights in water, and the significant discretion inherent in the identification of endangered species and the enforcement of ESA-based and other police power restrictions on water rights.

- The contingencies arising from the "too far" takings standard will be remedied only by clearer definition of what constitutes a taking of private property and an understanding that restrictions on use have at least as much impact on investment and management incentives as do physical occupations of property. Recognition that market value is rooted in use value, rather than possession, is particularly important in the context of water. The fact that water rights are usufructuary should make no difference in the determination of whether or not a taking has occurred.

Elimination or reduction of the contingencies arising from takings jurisprudence is necessary but not sufficient to unleashing the powers of the market for both efficient water use and species protection. In addition, state water law regimes must be reformed to encourage water markets and to facilitate investment in species and habitat protection and restoration. Critical reforms include:

- Beneficial and reasonable use standards must encompass all water uses, including instream flow maintenance and habitat for fish and wildlife.

- Restraints on water rights transfers must be eliminated except to the extent they are necessary to protect other vested water rights. The vague public interest discretion granted to state water administrators in many water transfer statutes contributes to the contingent nature of water rights and should be made far less discretionary, if not eliminated.

- State water laws should permit and facilitate commodity sales of water. Although temporary water use transfers have long taken place on an informal basis, state laws have generally discouraged or prohibited formal commodity markets in water. In light of the seasonal and annual variability of water supplies, commodity transfers will often make sense where permanent rights transfers do not. Greater flexibility in water use can only facilitate species and habitat protection.

- Water use by individuals and organizations without water rights under state or federal law must be policed and curtailed. The level of illegal water use, particularly in the West, is significant and thus contributes to the contingent nature of property interests in water.[61]

Due to the public goods nature of species protection in some circumstances, government regulation of and ownership of water rights are important and necessary parts of species protection, even with recognition that private investment can play a much more significant role than it does presently. Such a mixed system of public and private action requires that public actions respect private rights and that compensation be provided when private rights are taken, whether or not compensation is constitutionally required. As noted above, the ESA anticipates the acquisition of private rights in Section 5.

Conclusion

Conflict between species protection and water rights will never be eliminated. But the magnitude of the conflict can be much reduced—from all-out warfare to isolated skirmishes—if both sides take a more practical and less principled approach. One difficulty is that advocates for species protection have to give up more on principle than do the defenders of property rights. They have to abandon the claim that constitutional protections of property have no relevance for water rights. That difficulty should be overcome, however, by a realization that species protection and other environmental values can and do benefit from more secure rights in water. A second difficulty is that water rights claimants have to accept a water market open to all wishing to bid. That difficulty should be overcome by a recognition that voluntary sale at a mutually agreeable price is preferable to the forced sale of eminent domain. A third difficulty is that government will have to pay market value when species protection requires regulation resulting in the taking of private water rights. This may prove to be the biggest challenge of all, unless the law as set forth in *Tulare* and *Casitas* becomes the law of the land.

Notes

1. See William Baxter, *People or Penguins: The Case for Optimal Pollution* (New York: Columbia University Press, 1974).

2. Professor Dale Goble of the University of Idaho argues persuasively that "a decision that a species is endangered or threatened (or jeopardized under the section 7 consultation standard) is not a purely scientific determination because it requires an ethical/policy decision that the risk the species faces is unacceptably large. While this decision is based on science (or legally is required to be), the acceptability question is not science." Thesis presented to faculty colloquium, Lewis & Clark Law School, April 21, 2009, and confirmed in email message from Professor Goble to James Huffman, June 4, 2009.

3. 16 U.S.C. § 1531(c)(2) (2000).

4. For example, Congress declared in the Reclamation Act no intent "to affect or to in any way interfere with the laws of any State or Territory relating to the control, appropriation, use, or distribution of water used in irrigation, or any vested right acquired thereunder." 43 U.S.C. § 383 (2000).

5. 16 U.S.C.A. § 1534(a)(2).

6. "Congress shall have the Power…To regulate Commerce with foreign Nations, and among the several States, and with the Indian tribes."

7. 9 Wheat. (22 U.S.) 1, 190 (1824). "All America understands, and has uniformly understood, the word 'commerce,' to comprehend navigation."

8. The only federal laws held not to fall within the commerce regulating power since the New Deal were the Gun Free School Zone Act (*United States v. Lopez*, 514 U.S. 549 [1995]) and the Violence Against Women Act (*United States v. Morrison*, 529 U.S. 598 [2000]).

9. See *United States v. Gerlach Live Stock Co.*, 339 U.S. 725 (1950).

10. The general rule under current Supreme Court takings law is that, absent a physical occupation (*Loretto v. Teleprompter Manhattan CATV Corp*, 458 U.S. 419 [1982]) or total loss of economic value (*Lucas v. South Carolina Coastal Commission*, 505 U.S. 1003 [1992]), the existence of an unconstitutional taking depends on an ad hoc assessment of (1) the economic impact of the regulation, (2) the owner's reasonable investment-backed expectations, and (3) the character of the regulatory action. *Penn Central Transportation Co. v. New York City*, 438 U.S. 104 (1978).

11. *Tennessee Valley Authority v. Hill*, 437 U.S. 153 (1978).

12. See Zygmunt J.B. Plater, Robert H. Abrams, and William Goldfard, *Environmental Law and Policy: Nature, Law, and Society*, 2nd ed. (New York: Aspen, 1998), 684.

13. All of these examples are discussed in greater detail with citations to the relevant authorities in Reed D. Benson, "So Much Conflict, Yet So Much in Common: Considering the Similarities between Western Water Law and the Endangered Species Act," *Natural Resources Journal* 44 (2004): 29, 30–32.

14. *Klamath Irrigation District v. United States*, 67 Fed. Cl. 504, 526–27 (2005), 75 Fed. Cl. 677 (2007), *Klamath Irrigation Dist. v. United States*, 348 Or. 15, 227 P.3d 1145 (Or. 2010) (en banc), *Klamath Irrigation District v. United States* (2011). For a not-entirely-objective account of the *Klamath* litigation, see Dan Tarlock and Holly Doremu, *Water War in the Klamath Basin: Macho Law, Combat Biology, and Dirty Politics* (Washington, D.C.: Island Press, 2008).

15. *Pyramid Lake Paiute Tribe of Indians v. Hodel*, 882 F.2d 364 (Ninth Circuit 1989).

16. *Orff v. United States*, 545 US 596 (2005).

17. *Okanagan County v. National Marine Fisheries Service*, 347 F.3d 1081 (Ninth Circuit 2003).

18. *Rio Grande Silvery Minnow v. Keys* 333 F.3d 1109 (Tenth Circuit 2003) (vacated on appeal).

19. See, e.g., *GDF Realty Investments v. Norton*, 326 F.3d 622 (Fifth Circuit 2003) and *Gibbs v. Babbitt*, 214 F.3d 483 (Fourth Circuit 2000).

20. Most federal water contracts shield the government from liability for failure to deliver a full supply of water. These provisions have been held to apply to water delivery reductions made necessary by the ESA. See, e.g., *O'Neill v. United States*, 50 F.3d 677, 681–84 (Ninth Circuit 1995); and *Rio Grande Silvery Minnow v. Keys*, 333 F.3d 1109, 1138 (10th Cir. 2003). In the Klamath case, this issue was certified by the Federal Circuit Court of Appeals to the Oregon Supreme Court, where it is pending. *Klamath Irrigation District v. United States*, 2009 Ore. LEXIS 4.

21. *Cappaert v. United States*, 426 U.S. 128 (1976).

22. *Hughes v. Oklahoma*, 441 U.S. 322 (1979)

23. *Sporhase v. Nebraska ex rel. Douglas*, 458 U.S. 941, 951 (1982).

24. 49 Fed. Cl. 313 (2001).

25. Supra note 10.

26. See, e.g., Melinda Harm Benson, "The Tulare Case: Water Rights, the Endangered Species Act, and the Fifth Amendment," *Environmental Law* 32 (2002): 551, 555–56 (2002).

27. *Casitas Municipal Water District v. United States*, 543 F.3d 1276, 1280–82 (2008).

28. *Casitas Municipal Water District v. United States*, 72 Fed.Cl. 746 (2006); and *Casitas Municipal Water District v. United States*, 76 Fed.Cl. 100 (2007).

29. *Casitas Municipal Water District v. United States*, 543 F.3d. at 1279.

30. *Casitas Municipal Water District v. United States*, 556 F.3d 1329 (2009).

31. *Klamath Irrigation District v. United States*, 67 Fed. Cl. 504, 526–27 (2005) (holding that the irrigators had no property rights or equitable interests under Oregon law); and *Klamath Irrigation District v. United States*, 75 Fed. Cl. 677 (2007) (holding that the sovereign acts doctrine gave the United States a complete defense against breach of contract claim).

32. *Klamath Irrigation District v. United States*, 532 F.3d 1376 (2008).

33. *Klamath Irrigation District v. United States*, 348 Or. 15, 227 P.3d 1145 (Or. 2010) (en banc), *Klamath Irrigation District v. United States*, WL 537853, C.A.Fed., February 17, 2011 (NO. 2007-5115).

34. *Penn Central Transportation Co. v. New York City*, 438 U.S. 104 (1978).

35. The concept of reserved water rights is rooted in the understanding that the United States held the original right to use water arising and flowing on lands owned by the federal government. The Supreme Court has concluded that when those lands were reserved from private acquisition under the Homestead Act and other land disposal acts of Congress, sufficient water to satisfy the purposes of the reservations was impliedly reserved as well. The concept was first applied to Indian reservations in *Winters v. United States*, 207 U.S. 564 (1908) and later to reservations for particular federal purposes in *Arizona v. California*, 373 U.S. 546, 597–598 (1963).

36. When the reserved rights doctrine was first conceived in *Winters*, Id., private rights holders reasonably thought that their prior appropriative rights had been taken. But a century of precedent and expansion of the doctrine to apply to federal reservations has buried such claims under the weight of stare decisis.

37. Lucas v. South Carolina Coastal Council, 505 U.S. 1003, 1030 (1992).

38. A 1991 General Accounting Office report on the renewal of Central Valley Project water delivery contracts urged consideration of the government's ESA responsibilities and noted that the eleven contracts renewed to date were subject to modifications to assure compliance with federal environmental laws including the ESA. But the report went on to conclude, nevertheless, that "the Bureau must deliver the full volume of water specified in the contracts…unless drought conditions or other unavoidable causes prevent this." General Accounting Office, *Report to the Chairman, Subcommittee on Water, Committee on Energy and Natural Resources, U.S. Senate: Reclamation Law—Changes Needed before Water Service Contracts are Renewed* (GAO/RCED 91–175), (Washington, D.C., 1991), 11.

39. The 10th Circuit Court of Appeals ruled in *Rio Grande Silvery Minnow v. Keys* that even lacking specific reference to ESA-based restrictions on delivery of contract water, the Bureau of Reclamation could curtail delivery of water pursuant to contract language precluding liability where there is a water shortage "due to drought *or other causes.*"

40. See *Kelo v. City of New London*, 545 U.S. 469 (2005).

41. *Pennsylvania Coal v. Mahon*, 260 U.S. 393, 413 (1922).

42. Id. at 415.

43. See note 10 supra.

44. One such effort undertaken by the Western Governors' Association and the Western States Water Council led to what become known as the Park City Principles. See D. Craig Bell, Jo S. Clark, Julia Doermann, and Norman K. Johnson., "Retooling Western Water Management: The Park City Principles," *Land and Water Law Review* 31 (1996): 303, 303–4.

45. See, e.g. Melissa K. Estes, "The Effect of the Federal Endangered Species Act on State Water Rights," *Environmental Law* 22 (1992): 1027, 1044 (arguing that failure of an ESA amendment mandating federal deference to state water law could only mean that Congress intended for the ESA to trump state allocation in the face of direct conflict).

46. Mining Act ch. 262, §9, 14 Stat. 251, 253 (1866); and Act of July 9, 1870, ch. 235, §17, 16 Stat. 217, 218 (1870)

47. Desert Land Act, ch. 107, §1, 19 Stat. 377, 377 (1877).

48. Supra note 4.

49. McCarran Amendment, 66 Stat. 560, 43 U.S.C. §666(a).

50. A. Dan Tarlock, "Western Water Rights and the Act," in *Balancing on the Brink of Extinction: The Endangered Species Act and Lessons for the Future*, ed. Kathryn A. Kohm (Washington, D.C.: Island Press, 1991).

51. *Loveladies Harbor v. United States*, 28 F.3d 1171, 1180 (Fed. Cir. 1994).

52. *Penn Central Transportation Co. v. New York City*, 438 U.S. 104, 130 (1978).

53. *Raleigh Avenue Beach Association v. Atlantis Beach Club*, 879 A.2d 112 (N.J. 2005).

54. Montana Coalition for Stream Access v. Curran, 682 P.2d 163 (Mt. 1984).

55. See Michael C. Blumm and Lucas Ritchie, "Lucas's Unlikely Legacy: The Rise of Background Principles in Categorical Takings Defenses," *Harvard Environmental Law Review* 29 (2005): 321.

56. See Adler; Wilkins (this volume).

57. See Jeff Hull, "For the Love of a Ditch," *Montana Quarterly* 5 (2009): 21.

58. Supra note 2.

59. Garrett Hardin, "The Tragedy of the Commons," *Science* 162 (1968): 1243, 1245.

60. See Bishop Grewell and Clay Landry, *Ecological Agrarian: Agriculture's First Evolution in 10,000 Years* (Purdue: Purdue University Press, 2003), 107–13 (discussing activities of Oregon Water Trust and other groups); and Janet C. Neuman, "The Good, The Bad, and the Ugly: The First Ten Years of the Oregon Water Trust," *Nebraska Law Review* 83 (2004): 432.

61. See David E. Filippi, "The Impact of the Endangered Species Act on Water Rights and Water Use," in *Proceedings of the 48th Annual Rocky Mountain Mineral Law Foundation Institute* (Westminster, Colo.: Rocky Mountain Mineral Law Foundation, 2002), chapter 22 at footnote 42.

7

Dumb Queues and Not-So-Bright Lines: The Use and Abuse of Science in the Endangered Species Act

Brian F. Mannix

Laws written to protect health, safety, and the environment will often have a provision calling for the best available science.[1] This is uncontroversial; few people explicitly advocate inferior science, unavailable science, or an altogether unscientific approach. Typically the implementation of such laws is accompanied by vehement technical and legal arguments about what, exactly, the best available science tells us. Reform proposals abound for improving science. But the intense focus on the quality of science can be a red herring. The greater difficulty lies not in improving science but in figuring out how to apply science in the service of a statutory objective. Laws are not scientific instruments or studies; rather, they govern the behavior of humans by setting forth rules, penalties, rights, and instructions to agencies. Which rules will produce what results? It is not an easy question, even if we have a good idea of what results we desire and what the applicable science is.

The Endangered Species Act (ESA), as interpreted by the federal courts and the agencies that implement it, has caused dramatic changes in human behavior. Some of these changes have protected particular species and biodiversity in general. Some of them have been counterproductive.[2] But both its biological successes and failures appear to be second-order effects; the primary effect of the ESA has been controversy, litigation, large and arbitrarily distributed economic losses, and staggering administrative inefficiency.

It would not be fair to attribute this dismal record to the state of ecological science; nor would proposals for improving the science be likely to effect a significantly different outcome. Rather, the problem lies in the way federal agencies are compelled to apply science to administrative decisions under the ESA, and only a fundamental change in the law will allow agencies to deliver better performance.

In this chapter I explore the obstacles that prevent federal agencies from improving their use of science in the service of species protection. First, I illustrate the difficulties with the ESA's consultation process (ESA Section 7) by looking at the experience of the Environmental Protection Agency (EPA) with the process as it applies to the EPA's pesticide registration program. Second, I extrapolate from the EPA's pesticide experience in order to explain why both the Bush and the Obama administrations have expressed a preference for new legislation to address climate change rather than rely on the Clean Air Act and the ESA. Finally, I suggest some directions for ESA reform in order to improve the way that science is used to inform decisions about endangered species.

Hard Lessons at the EPA

The EPA registers pesticides under the Federal Insecticide, Fungicide, and Rodenticide Act (FIFRA), and must review registered pesticides every fifteen years to ensure that they continue to meet applicable statutory requirements.[3] In the course of that review, if there is any risk that the pesticide may affect endangered or threatened species or their designated critical habitat, the EPA must consult with the Fish and Wildlife Service (FWS) at the Department of the Interior or with the National Marine Fisheries Service (NMFS) at the Department of Commerce (collectively, the Services). The Services' biological opinions are binding on the EPA.[4]

The EPA has considerable expertise on the ecological effects of pesticides, which, along with human health risks, are a central focus of its review function.[5] In addition to effects on listed species, the agency examines potential risks to other vulnerable species, including economically important species—both privately owned bees and wild pollinators, for example. It investigates a number of broader risks, such as those from the chronic exposure of aquatic species to a mixture of chemicals that are found at low levels in surface waters, and it gives priority to pest-control strategies and chemistries that will reduce overall risks to human health and the environment. The EPA's review of pesticides is not a binary yes-or-no process; in order to avoid unreasonable risks, the agency can approve a pesticide but disallow particular uses, modify application rates or methods, or require that only a licensed applicator use the product. All of its decisions are subject to scientific peer review.

To comply with the ESA, the EPA must ensure that its decisions on pesticides will not adversely modify critical habitat or jeopardize the continued existence of listed species. The agency has expressed confidence in its own ability to render expert biological opinions. Moreover, in other contexts, the agency has enjoyed considerable deference on such matters. For example, several statutory provisions exempt certain EPA actions from review under the National Environmental Policy Act (NEPA), on the theory that federal actions intended to protect the environment will not be made in ignorance of their environmental effects. Even when statutes are silent, courts have granted the EPA similar exemptions under a doctrine of "NEPA equivalence." No other agency, including the FWS,[6] has received such deference from the courts on its environmental decisions.

The ESA provides no exception for EPA actions, however, and courts have found that only the designated Services (FWS and NMFS) can render an authoritative biological opinion under the ESA. Defenders of this exclusive arrangement under Section 7 typically argue that action agencies—the agencies whose actions trigger ESA consultation—often have a "development mandate" that conflicts with the ESA mandate, or that action agencies may not have the resources or the expertise to render biological opinions on their own. These arguments sound hollow when applied to the EPA's pesticide program, which exists for the express purpose of preventing harm to human health and the environment and which has all of the requisite expertise.

The determination that a species is threatened or endangered—and therefore "listed"—is made by the Services and is strictly a scientific determination. Yet it has two consequences for the EPA's review of pesticides. The first is a substantive policy change: effectively, it requires the EPA to be more protective of listed species than it is of unlisted species. This is something that the agency can easily do on its own. The second is a procedural change to incorporate Section 7 consultations with the Services. Complying with the consultation requirement has presented a serious challenge for the EPA. If the agency believes that a pesticide presents a threat to human health or the environment, including a threat to a listed species, it has the authority under FIFRA to address the threat. It can do so at any time, regardless of the status of a pesticide's registration review. On the other hand, to complete a pesticide registration review the EPA must obtain a final, authoritative, and timely opinion from the cognizant Service that such a threat does not exist; if the opinion is challenged, the EPA must get a court to accept that opinion. This is another matter entirely. Indeed, until very recently it had never happened. Despite many attempts to come up with a workable process, the pesticide office's consultations with the Services typically take many years, and even then do not reach a legally robust conclusion.

While the ESA sets a time limit for formal consultations, the Services generally will not begin the formal process without what they regard as a complete record (a common practice among regulators, including the EPA's pesticide office); in the absence of adequate information the Services will, with some support in the ESA legislative history, "give the benefit of the doubt to the species."[7] An informal consultation process therefore precedes the formal consultation, so that all of the involved agencies are confident they have the information they need. The result is an administrative process that is protracted but still not conclusive.[8]

The EPA maintains active registrations for more than 1,000 active ingredients (grouped into about 675 categories) and 20,000 pesticide formulations. Another 100,000 registrations are inactive. Its registration review process makes about 1,600 discrete decisions per year with respect to these products, any of which, in theory, could trigger consultation with one or both of the Services on one or more listed species in one or more geographic areas. In this respect pesticide registration differs from most federal actions in that its effects are national rather than limited in geographic scope. A pesticide—particularly a "home and garden" formulation—can typically be sold anywhere, so each pesticide potentially encounters, not one or a handful of listed species, but all 1,320 of them.

It is not possible for the EPA to solve this problem working with the Services. It has been widely reported that the process of listing endangered and threatened species, and of designating their critical habitat, has been so beset by litigation that the Services are paralyzed. Department of the Interior officials have testified that their priorities are not driven by their own estimates of what is important but by the need to respond to litigation:

> Simply put, the listing and critical habitat program is now operated in a "first to the courthouse" mode, with each new court order or settlement taking its place at the end of an ever-lengthening line. We are no longer operating under a rational system that allows us to prioritize resources to address the most significant biological needs.[9]

The Section 7 consultation program has similarly been burdened by court-ordered mandates that exceed the Services' ability to fulfill these mandates. What is distinctive about the Section 7 consultation program is that the judicial mandates are causing administrative gridlock not only within the Services but also within the action agencies. After decades of trying, the EPA has never been able to conclude even one consultation with the Fish and Wildlife Service. The record of the National Marine Fisheries Service is only slightly better: on September 11, 2009, it concluded its first such consultation. The press release by the EPA noted the exceptional fact that the NMFS and the EPA were able to conclude their consultations for three pesticides:

> EPA has announced plans to place additional limitations on the use of three organophosphate pesticides—chlorpyrifos, diazinon, and malathion—to protect endangered and threatened salmon and steelhead in California, Idaho, Oregon, and Washington.... These new limits are especially significant because they mark the first time that EPA and National Marine Fisheries Service (NMFS) have completed the consultation process under the Endangered Species Act in more than 20 years....The new use limitations are the result of consultations that EPA initiated with the National Marine Fisheries Service in 2002, 2003, and 2004.[10]

From the EPA's perspective, the fifteen-year cycle of mandatory pesticide registration reviews will provide *millions* of potential obligations to consult with the Services—each, based on experience, taking as much as ten years. That is not a remotely feasible enterprise, nor is it one that promises anything tangible in the way of ecological benefit. As matters now stand, EPA biologists are unable to focus on the systematic reviews that Congress has called for because judges have set a different agenda. Agency managers describe it as a daunting challenge.[11]

There have been a number of legislative and administrative attempts to fix this problem, none of them successful. In 2008, the Interior and Commerce departments conducted a rulemaking to streamline the consultation process and clarify different agencies' responsibilities. The new rule became effective on January 15, 2009, and then was promptly repealed by the incoming administration. The prospect for renewed administrative reform is poor, given the sheer weight of litigation under the ESA: so many court opinions have interpreted the key words of the statute that there is little room left for the implementing agencies to issue any regulation that is interpretive in character. As a result, any significant reforms must be effected in legislation.

Clean Air, Endangered Species, and Climate

The EPA's experience with pesticide reregistration undoubtedly has colored the agency's view about the likely effect of using the Clean Air Act (CAA) and the Endangered Species Act to address climate change. Both the Bush Administration and the Obama Administration have taken the position that the Congress should pass new legislation to regulate greenhouse gas (GHG) emissions rather than rely on the CAA. Both administrations also took the position that the listing of polar bears as threatened under the ESA required only those actions that were already underway under the Marine Mammal Protection Act and that the ESA should not be regarded as a primary vehicle for managing climate change.

The reluctance to rely on these two laws is understandable because each law, by itself, is poorly suited to managing climate, and together they form a toxic combination. Yet, in the absence of Congressional action, regulation by litigation will force both of these statutes to the forefront of climate policy. The Supreme Court held that greenhouse gas emissions are pollutants under the Clean Air Act[12] subject to regulation if they endanger human health or the environment, and the EPA Administrator has now made "the endangerment finding."[13] The regulatory regime that will emerge from this is still uncertain, but we know that it will inevitably involve, among other things, a dramatic expansion in the number of permit decisions that will be required.

The CAA sets fixed thresholds for sources of pollution that require a Prevention of Significant Deterioration (PSD) permit: 100 tons annually of a single pollutant or 250 tons of a combination. When these statutory thresholds are applied to a minor and unintentional byproduct of combustion, like carbon *mono*xide, it means that the largest facilities must have permits adjudicated by the EPA. When applied to a major and necessary product of combustion, like carbon *di*oxide, the same statutory thresholds capture facilities that are two orders of magnitude smaller. As the EPA itself explained:

> Currently, EPA estimates that EPA, state, and local permitting authorities issue approximately 200–300 PSD permits nationally each year for construction of new major sources and major modifications at existing major sources. Under existing major source thresholds, we estimate that if CO_2 becomes a regulated NSR pollutant (either as an individual GHG or as a group of GHGs), the number of PSD permits required to be issued each year would increase by more than a factor of 10 (i.e., more than 2,000–3,000 permits per year), unless action were taken to limit the scope of the PSD program under one or more of the legal theories described below. The additional permits would generally be issued to smaller industrial sources, as well as large office and residential buildings, hotels, large retail establishments, and similar facilities.[14]

Combine (1) that dramatic expansion of the CAA's permitting domain with (2) the potential requirement to consult with (probably both) Services in each of these permitting decisions, under (3) the theory that climate change itself may present a threat to an increasing number of listed species, and (4) the argument that any greenhouse gas emission at all contributes to the overall threat, while (5) the courts have recognized no *de minimis* exemptions in the ESA. Shake well. The result is that the absurd general-ization of NIMBYism, BANANA (Build Absolutely Nothing Anywhere Near Anybody), will quickly be truncated to just BAN. With global climate change, proximity ceases to be relevant.

It will do no good to argue that some endangered species, somewhere, will be helped by climate change (or by permitted facilities that contribute to it); the ESA recognizes only harm. Neither will it help to point out that the effect of a particular facility on climate, let alone on listed species, is not detectable by any method known to science. Any individual facility emit-ting greenhouse gases will have an incredibly small effect on climate, but one that can be estimated and calculated, and it will not be zero.

The EPA made an effort in 2008 to outline a workable regulatory system for greenhouse gases under the CAA; other agencies expressed grave reser-vations about the feasibility and legality of the proposal and its effect on the economy. In an extraordinary preface to the notice, the EPA Administrator noted: "I believe the ANPR [Advance Notice of Proposed Rulemaking] demonstrates the Clean Air Act, an outdated law originally enacted to control regional pollutants that cause direct health effects, is ill-suited for the task of regulating global greenhouse gases."[15] In any event, given the rigidity with which courts have read the CAA,[16] creative administrative solutions stand little chance of success, and the actual regulatory regime is more likely to emerge from future litigation than from thoughtful planning. Similarly, although the Department of the Interior has attempted to circumscribe the requirements of listing of polar bears as threatened, courts have historically been unsympathetic to administrative attempts to stay the most onerous provisions of the ESA. It is unfortunate that, as Congress debates the merits of climate legislation, the existing regulatory regime will be holding the U.S. economy hostage—shackled by the combination of the CAA and the ESA.[17]

What's the Problem?

Administrative controversy and litigation have placed a paralyzing burden on all agencies charged with implementing the ESA. But why? Is it because the science is not up to the task? Or have we given it the wrong task?

I suspect most scientists would agree, at least in the abstract, that they can determine which species are thriving and which are in jeopardy, as well as what the causes of species decline are and what measures might be taken to reverse species decline. Disagreements would not be trivial, but they would mostly be a matter of degree. In a legal context, however, particularly the way the ESA is drafted, matters of degree become Maginot lines. One observer described the Act as having become "weaponized."[18]

Take the definition of a species. Both the legal rule and the scientific rule are similar: roughly, distinct populations that do not interbreed. But science finds interesting exceptions, such as "ring species." In Britain, herring gulls and lesser black-backed gulls are easily distinguished and do not interbreed. Yet the morphology of the herring gull changes gradually as one follows a line of latitude around the Pole, to North America, across Asia, and back to Western Europe. By the time you arrive back at the starting point, the herring gull has changed by degrees into a lesser black-backed gull! Richard Dawkins describes the paradox:

> At every stage around the ring, the birds are sufficiently similar to their immediate neighbors in the ring to interbreed with them. Until, that is, the ends of the continuum are reached, and the ring bites itself in the tail. The herring gull and the lesser black backed gull in Europe never interbreed, although they are linked by a continuous series of interbreeding colleagues all the way round the other side of the world.[19]

He describes another example of a ring species, a salamander, in the mountains surrounding California's central valley. "I shall not bend over backwards to avoid using discontinuous names for species in this book. But the Salamander's Tale explains why this is a human imposition rather than something deeply built into the natural world."[20]

Fuzzy definitions do not present a problem for science, which can easily deal with genetic gradations, shifting probabilities, and more or less arbitrary classifications. They can present a serious problem for administrative law, however. It is commonplace for the law to set thresholds along a continuous spectrum: the Constitution establishes age thresholds for holding elective office; state courts routinely decide closely argued cases disputing whether a speed limit was, or was not, exceeded. Under the ESA, however, unimportant scientific distinctions become the fulcrum on which large policies—and large penalties—are made to hinge.

By "unimportant distinctions," I mean those that would not, on their own, have important implications for conservation management in the absence of a legally created need for different parties to advance their policy preferences by arguing about them. If three populations of rare sparrows inhabited a range that was entirely on federal land, for example, and no incompatible uses of the land were contemplated, then studying the distinctions among the three would be an academic exercise. Are they three varieties or three species? Do they interbreed? Are they threatened individually? Or collectively? Scientists might want to know the answers to these questions, but the answers might be ambiguous, and that might be perfectly acceptable.

Federal land managers concerned about the survival of the sparrows might not be troubled by such ambiguities, either, as they considered what restrictions might be enacted, or what resources might be made available, to help protect the birds. Under the ESA decision framework, however, neither scientists nor land managers ever have the luxury of weighing facts dispassionately. The question of whether a population is distinct and threatened ceases to be a matter of degree, and becomes a legal finding of profound consequence. As a result the interested parties, the agencies, and the courts will ask scientists to draw bright lines, even where bright lines do not exist in the real world. Scientists will do their best, but the lines they draw will inevitably be arbitrary. So, for example, a northern spotted owl becomes a California spotted owl—and vice versa—when it flies across the Pit River.

When distinctions are arbitrary, they are contestable; yet the resources expended in settling such contests may be wasted. As a state official, I once reviewed a request for a permit to recover a shipwreck, discovered with sand-penetrating sonar beneath state waters, that might include as much as $500 million in gold. According to the Attorney General's Office, if any part of the wreck was protruding above the sand, then state law treated the find as an abandoned shipwreck and allowed for a discretionary state royalty in cash or in kind; a plurality of coastal states set such a royalty at 25 percent. On the other hand, if no part of the wreck was protruding above the sand, then the applicant would need a sand-and-gravel mining permit—the precise composition of the gravel was not germane—for which the royalty was again discretionary, but traditionally had been set at 5 percent. I notified the applicant that the state would require a royalty of 25 percent, regardless of which statute turned out to be applicable. There was nothing to be gained by putting the parties in a position of having a $100 million argument about the meaning of "part," "shipwreck," "was," and "protruding." Undoubtedly a great deal of technology, evidence, and expert scientific and legal testimony could have been brought to bear on these questions. But the answers were of no real interest to any party, and setting an invariant royalty made the answers legally immaterial as well.[21] Fortunately, the applicable laws in this case afforded sufficient discretion to avoid getting entangled in unproductive arguments about trivial points of fact. No such discretion exists in the ESA, so that contentious disputes about values masquerade as intractable scientific disputes.

Directions for Reform

The profound controversies surrounding the Endangered Species Act are not a reflection of profound differences about science; neither do they reflect profound differences about the objective of preserving endangered species, which enjoys widespread support. Rather, the controversies arise from disagreements about the details of policies and priorities—ultimately political questions that Congress would do well to tackle head on, rather than embed them artificially in scientific findings of fact. In other words, politicians should not try to do the science, but neither should they try to force scientists to do the politics. I offer three suggestions for moving in that direction.

Distinguish between Science and Policy. In reviewing EPA decisions about protecting human health under a range of statutes, the National Academy of Sciences has, for decades, recommended that risk assessment and risk management decisions should be carefully separated.[22] While this is easier said than done, the principle has enjoyed widespread support. If that makes sense for humans, why not for other species? Such a separation would free scientists to render objective scientific advice and would allow policymakers to take the responsibility for making policy.[23] Congress can set whatever criteria it likes for making those policy decisions—or it can reserve to itself the final say—without hiding behind the fiction that science will provide all of the answers. The ESA should be amended so that scientific findings can be made objectively, with no automatic policy consequences.

Assign Responsibility for Making Policy Decisions. Whatever scientific expertise the Services may have to offer, it is inconceivable that they could assemble in one place all of the information and all of the expertise needed to render final decisions on the vast array of federal actions that are touched by the ESA. It is not possible to have an effective, responsible government unless action agencies are held accountable for their own actions, and that is where responsibility for policy decisions should lie. Congress's goal should be to ensure that the decision making agency has access to the best available science, and that it has clear direction about legislative intent. The most venerable of environmental statutes, the National Environmental Policy Act, certainly has had a profound influence on federal decisions, and it has certainly been responsible for its share of litigation. Ultimately, however, NEPA has become an effective, workable statute because it puts information and assigns accountability to the decision making agency. The ESA is unlikely ever to become an effective statute until it does something similar.

Stop Wasting Effort on Trivial Distinctions. A primary goal of ESA reform should be to rewrite the law so that government agencies and affected parties can stop wasting time and resources arguing about things that substantively are, and legally ought to be, immaterial. Are two adjacent populations of salmon sufficiently distinct to be treated as separate species? It may not matter biologically, but such questions get inordinate attention because Congress wrote a law that dramatically alters public policy, contingent upon such subtle scientific distinctions. The protection of endangered species should be treated less as a merely adversarial process, and more as a complex and cooperative endeavor in which science is meant to be informative, not dispositive.

Among the distinctions that scientists should not be forced to waste their time on, the most prominent is the distinction between zero and practically zero. We emit carbon dioxide, for example, every time we exhale. As long as breathing does not require a federal permit, we are unlikely to get caught up in ESA consultations. Shockingly, however, the sheer tininess of the contribution would not necessarily be considered exculpatory. To date, the courts have not recognized any *de minimis* limitation to the reach of the ESA; the Congress should provide one. If the ESA is going to become a successful statute, the responsible agencies must have the ability to focus on what is important and must be released from the tyranny of trivia.

Notes

1. These are sometimes called "science mandates." Holly Doremus and A. Dan Tarlock, "Science, Judgment, and Controversy in Natural Resource Regulation" (Paper No. 50, UC Davis Legal Studies Research Paper Series, University of California, Davis, August 2005).

2. "We find some evidence that the expenditure of substantial government funds on the recovery of a species can be effective, but listing, by itself, is not effective and can even be detrimental." Paul J. Ferraro, Craig McIntosh, and Monica Ospina, "The effectiveness of the US endangered species act: An econometric analysis using matching methods," *Journal of Environmental Economics and Management* 54 (2007): 245–61. See also Joe Kerkvliet and Christian Langpap, "Learning from Endangered and Threatened Species Recovery Programs: A Case Study Using U.S. Endangered Species Act Recovery Scores," *Ecological Economics* 63 (2007): 499–510.

3. The Pesticide Registration Improvement Act, as amended, imposes the "registration review" requirement, which is a successor to the "reregistration" program required under an earlier statute. See www.epa.gov/pesticides for a full description of the multifaceted pesticide program and its governing laws.

4. ESA Section 7(a)(2).

5. See "Overview of the Ecological Risk Assessment Process in the Office of Pesticide Programs, U.S. EPA: Endangered and Threatened Species Effects Determinations," EPA, January 23, 2004, http://www.epa.gov/oppfead1/endanger/consultation/ecorisk-overview.pdf.

6. Charles H. Eccleston, *NEPA and Environmental Planning, Tools Techniques, and Approaches for Practitioners* (Boca Raton: CRC Press, 2008), 136–7.

7. Congressional Research Service, *The Endangered Species Act and "Sound Science,"* updated January 8, 2007, 20.

8. One involved official summarized it as follows: "The problem with informal consultation is that it never ends; the problem with formal consultation is that it never begins." Personal communication.

9. Testimony of Craig Manson, Assistant Secretary for Fish, Wildlife, and Parks, Department of the Interior, before the Subcommittee on Fisheries, Wildlife, and Water of the Senate Committee on Environment and Public Works, April 10, 2003

(http://www.fws.gov/laws/Testimony/108th/2003/2003april10.html); the same text appears in the testimony of his successor, Julie MacDonald, eighteen months later in field hearings of the full Senate Committee on Environment and Public Works, August 23, 2004, http://www.fws.gov/laws/Testimony/108th/2004/Macdonald ESAWY.htm.

10. U.S. Environmental Protection Agency, "New Limits on Pesticide Uses Will Protect Salmon," press release, September 11, 2009, http://yosemite.epa.gov/opa/admpress.nsf/a543211f64e4d1998525735900404442/cd1f6f9dbe3db7d6852576 2e004f693a!OpenDocument.

11. Andy Beer, "US endangered species assessments challenge EPA's workload," *Agrow World Crop Protection News*, April 18, 2008 (http://www.agrow.com/news 215.shtml).

12. *Massachusetts v. Environmental Protection Agency*, 549 U.S. 497 (2007). 13.74 FR 66495, December 15, 2009.

14. EPA Advance Notice of Proposed Rulemaking, 73 FR 44354, July 30, 2008.

15. Ibid.

16. See, for example, the District of Columbia Circuit Court of Appeals rulings on EPA's Clean Air Interstate Rule and its Clean Air Mercury Rule.

17. See J. B. Ruhl, chapter 8 in this volume.

18. Thanks to Rafe Petersen of Holland & Knight LLP for this colorful term.

19. Richard Dawkins, *The Ancestor's Tale* (New York: Houghton Mifflin, 2004), 303.

20. Ibid, 310.

21. See *Sea Hunt, Inc. v. Unidentified, Shipwrecked Vessel or Vessels*, 22 F. Supp. 2d 521, 526 (E.D. Va. 1998) and related cases. Federal and international legal issues in this case proved to be far more difficult than state legal issues; the sought-after gold so far has not been recovered. Unless the U.S. Supreme Court grants certiorari, the King of Spain (who, until a federal judge forbade it, was represented in court by the U.S. Justice Department!) now holds the shipwreck recovery rights. For a narrative of the legal twists and turns in this case, see www.thehidden galleon.com/treasurehunter.

22. See, e.g., "The History of Risk at EPA," at www.epa.gov/risk/history.htm.

23. Katrina Wyman gives a rationale for decoupling the listing of species from the regulatory decisions about what protections to afford them. "Rethinking the ESA to Reflect Human Dominion Over Nature," *NYU Environmental Law Journal* 17 (2008): 490–527.

8

Pit Bulls Can't Fly:
Adapting the Endangered Species Act
to the Reality of Climate Change

J.B. Ruhl

Notwithstanding its reputation as the "pit bull" of American environmental laws, the Endangered Species Act (ESA) has its limits. It has helped stem the decline of endangered species in terrestrial, freshwater, and marine ecosystems largely because of its suitability to regulating discrete land and resource development uses. A new subdivision consumes habitat of an endangered lizard; a dam blocks passage of an endangered fish; seine nets threaten an endangered sea turtle—these fit easily within the ESA's reach because they present straightforward causal scenarios with easily identified causal agents. But when cause and effect become attenuated by spatial and temporal discontinuities, or when causal agents are dispersed, numerous, and difficult to identify, the ESA has proven unwieldy and ineffective in application. There is no better example of these limiting factors than the ill fit between the ESA and the challenges of addressing climate change. In short, asking the ESA to take on the causes of climate change is like asking pit bulls to fly. They can't.

This chapter explores the poor fit between the ESA and climate change and recommends reforms designed to avoid ineffective applications of the ESA while enhancing ways to employ the statute to assist climate-threatened species. The great divide in this respect is between using the ESA to force reductions in greenhouse gas emissions (known as climate change *mitigation*), which is a path to folly, and using it to help species

179

through the massive transformations climate change will inflict on ecosystems (known as climate change *adaptation*), which is a much more promising role for the ESA. In the first section of the chapter I summarize the ecological consequences of climate change in terms relevant to ESA policy. In the next section I provide a brief review of the legal context that has formed thus far with respect to the ESA and climate change, focusing in particular on greenhouse gas emissions. In the final section I propose reforms designed around the concept of transition—that is, focusing first on getting species through the ecological consequences of climate change and worrying later about how to recover them from their imperiled status.

Climate Change and the ESA

Three metrics drive much of the discussion of climate change as a *global* phenomenon: rising tropospheric carbon dioxide levels, escalating mean *global* surface temperatures, and rising sea levels.[1] The cause and effect relationships at this level are fairly well understood: carbon dioxide and other greenhouse gases trap heat radiating from the earth's surface, which causes surface level temperatures to rise, which in turn causes polar and glacial ice to melt and ocean water volume to expand, which causes sea levels to rise.[2]

Of course, what matters for most regulatory agencies is not how well we predict global trends such as mean surface temperature and sea levels but what happens in the subglobal regions and locales in which agencies act. This will be the vexing problem for the agencies that will implement the ESA through the era of climate change, the U.S. Fish & Wildlife Service (FWS) and National Marine Fisheries Service (NMFS).[3] The issues for these agencies are not going to be limited to the temperature and the high tide line, but will encompass matters of rainfall, snowmelt, vegetative transition, migrating species, fire regimes, drought, flooding, and much more. The FWS and NMFS will be concerned with these local ecological transitions and their effects on imperiled species. The agencies, in other words, must find models that reliably predict the effects of global climate warming on a wide range of physical and biological cycles, "downscale" those effects to local ecological conditions, and then evaluate the effects of those local changes on the species of concern.

The FWS and NMFS have no models of this sort at their disposal, however, because nobody has the experience or knowledge at present to develop them. Ultimately, moreover, such models may simply be beyond our capacity. Although all ecosystems undergo disturbance regimes such as flood, fire, and drought, ecologists understand that these forms of disturbance are part of the stable disequilibrium of resilient, dynamic ecosystems.[4] Climate change is not an instance of a mere disturbance regime, the operations of which we can extrapolate from current ecological knowledge; rather, it will be the undoing of ecosystems as we know them. As one comprehensive study concluded: "The resilience of many ecosystems is likely to be exceeded this century by an unprecedented combination of climate change, associated disturbances (e.g., flooding, drought, wildfire, insects, ocean acidification), and other global change drivers (e.g., land-use change, pollution, over-exploitation of resources)."[5] Of course, there will always be ecosystems; rather, their physical and biological conditions, in particular the assembly of species in any locale, will undergo transition for many decades to come.

Although accurate prediction of climate change effects on local ecological conditions is for now (and perhaps always will be) beyond the capacity of ecological models, a taxonomy of effects can be constructed and may be useful for evaluating where the ESA can be employed most effectively when climate change threatens the continued existence of a species:[6]

- *Primary Ecological Effects.* Species with specific ecological needs and limited migration capacity are likely to face significant threats from first-order changes in ecological conditions such as altered water regimes, rising temperature, and vegetative transitions. Some species will be unable to tolerate these changes but also unable to do anything about it given limited migratory capacity.[7] The polar bear, for example, has limited options as the ice melts below its feet. Some species that are able to migrate may not be able to find the critical habitat attributes needed to sustain them anywhere on the planet.[8] Other species will suffer when life-sustaining links with other species are broken. For example, consider an insect that hatches when soil temperature reaches a certain level, which will change with climate change, and a bird that times breeding based on the hours of daylight, which will not change. If the latter depends on the former to feed its young, the new timing mismatch may disrupt both species.[9]

- *Secondary Ecological Effects.* Not all species will find it necessary and possible to adapt to climate change by migrating from their current ecosystems to find new homes, but many will. Others will stay to fight it out. While humans might cheer species on as they fight to adapt or fight to stay put, the aggregate effects of ecological disruption and species reshuffling are likely to lead to several secondary threats, including increased stress from the first-order changes in the ecosystem,[10] competition between species that have successfully migrated to survive and those that have stayed put,[11] and opportunistic invasion through expansion of range by other species into the ecosystem once previous limiting barriers are diminished.[12] Consider, for example, rising water temperatures in a marine ecosystem. One species of fish may find the higher temperature tolerable, but just so, the stress of which may make it more susceptible to disease and parasites. Another species of fish which formerly could not inhabit the area because the temperature was too low may now find it just right, in which case the former species may have a new competitor or, worse, a new predator.

- *Human Adaptation Impacts.* Just as the primary threats to species before climate change centered on human-induced ecological change, it is likely that human adaptation to climate change will play a leading role in threatening species. Human adaptation impacts will come in the form of direct habitat conversion as human populations migrate,[13] degraded ecological conditions as people fortify their communities from the effects of climate change,[14] and species invasions induced as people move themselves, their belongings, and their infrastructure to new places.[15]

The question for the ESA, of course, is what to do about these three categories of threats induced by climate change. The central purpose of the

ESA is to "provide a means whereby the ecosystems upon which endangered species and threatened species depend may be conserved."[16] The FWS and NMFS have authority over several core programs aimed toward that objective:

- *The Listing Programs.* Section 4 authorizes the FWS (for terrestrial and freshwater species) and NMFS (for marine and anadromous species) to identify "endangered" and "threatened" species, under what is known as the listing function,[17] and then to designate "critical habitat"[18] and develop "recovery plans"[19] for the species.

- *Interagency Consultation and the Jeopardy Prohibition.* Section 7 requires all federal agencies to "consult" with the FWS or NMFS (depending on the species) to ensure that actions they carry out, fund, or authorize do not "jeopardize" the continued existence of listed species or "adversely modify" their critical habitat.[20]

- *The Take Prohibition.* Section 9 requires that all persons, including all private and public entities subject to federal jurisdiction, avoid committing "takes" of species of fish and wildlife listed as endangered or, if the listing agency decides pursuant to section 4(d), as threatened.[21] Take is defined to include any act that causes actual death or injury to the listed species, including habitat modification.

- *Incidental Take Permits.* Sections 7 (for federal agency actions)[22] and 10 (for actions not subject to Section 7)[23] establish a procedure and criteria for the FWS and NMFS to approve "incidental take" of listed species.

While preserving ecosystems is clearly the statute's primary goal, precisely how to use the agency's regulatory weaponry to "provide a means" of achieving that goal in the face of climate change threats is not self-evident from the text of the statute. No provision of the ESA addresses pollutants, emissions, or climate in any specific, regulatory sense. Climate change thus creates several policy quagmires for the FWS and NMFS:

- *Identifying Climate-Threatened Species.* As no regulatory authorities of the ESA operate until a species is listed as endangered or threatened under section 4 of the ESA, the initial issue is how the agencies use available science to evaluate the effects of climate change on particular species and which are threatened by the primary or secondary effects of climate change.

- *Regulating Greenhouse Gas Emissions.* If the FWS or NMFS identifies climate change as a basis for designating a species for protection under the ESA, the agency inevitably will face the questions of whether federal actions that cause, fund, or authorize greenhouse gas emissions jeopardize the species under section 7 and whether any person emitting greenhouse gases is taking the species in violation of section 9.

- *Regulating Non-Climate Effects to Protect Climate-Threatened Species.* Regardless of how aggressively the ESA is used in attempts to regulate greenhouse gas emissions, the FWS and NMFS will continue to face the problem of how aggressively to regulate other actions that injure a climate-threatened species but do not contribute to climate change, such as habitat conversion, water diversion, and pollution.

- *Designing Conservation and Recovery Initiatives.* As the FWS and NMFS regulate more activities associated with climate-threatened species, the agencies inevitably will face the need to design conservation measures as conditions for approval of incidental take under sections 7 and 10, as well as the need to formulate recovery measures for the species under section 4.

- *Species Trade-Offs.* As noted above, the ESA depends on an overriding purpose of conserving ecosystems. Yet the reshuffling of species under climate change conditions will make it difficult to identify "the ecosystems" to be conserved and is likely to pit species against species in a manner unprecedented under the ESA.[24]

- *Dealing with the Doomed.* Perhaps the most confounding question for the FWS and NMFS will be how to respond with respect to species that appear doomed because of lack of migratory and adaptive capacity to withstand climate change effects in their natural habitat range.

These questions are hardly the usual policy fodder for the FWS and NMFS. To be sure, the ESA has been dragged into scenarios that cover vast expanses of land, such as the spotted owl in the Northwest forests, and that involve complex issues of dispersed and indirect causation, such as water usage in Western states. But never before have the FWS and NMFS been asked to respond to a phenomenon as dynamic, complex, and global as climate change. It seems reasonable that the agencies might ask for time for serious thought about how to pull it off. Yet, as the next section discusses, some interest groups, in their zeal to wrangle control of greenhouse gas emissions, have attempted to rush the ESA into the fray in ways that are unlikely to prove useful in the long run.

Asking Too Much of the ESA

A wave of "mitigation litigation"—litigation designed to force agencies into regulating greenhouse gas emissions under existing laws—is rising in full force.[25] For example, with over $6 million of funding already committed, the Center for Biological Diversity recently formed the Climate Law Institute to, among other things, "establish legal precedents requiring existing environmental laws such as the Clean Air Act, Endangered Species Act, National Environmental Policy Act, Clean Water Act, and the California Environmental Quality Act to be fully implemented to regulate greenhouse gas emissions."[26] While it has pushed a few agencies into examining the role of existing authorities, this kind of mitigation litigation in the long run is unlikely to produce a coherent and effective national climate change policy.[27] Existing legislation, if creatively applied within the bounds of permissible agency statutory interpretation, offers many opportunities for agencies to pursue mitigation and adaptation policies, but not all such opportunities necessarily should be employed to the maximum that an agency's policy discretion might allow. Mitigation litigation against federal agencies has been undertaken to push them into emissions mitigation regulation because litigation is an easily available strategy. However, such litigation proceeds with no clear vision of how to regulate emissions at the agency level and no plan for how to coordinate a government-wide climate change policy initiative that includes both mitigation and adaptation.

Nowhere is this more evident than in the debate over how to integrate the ESA into climate change policy. Like most other existing environmental laws, the ESA does not mention climate change but is riddled with provisions that offer varying ranges of discretion to agencies to formulate climate change mitigation and adaptation policies,[28] making it a prime object of mitigation litigation. In particular, section 7(a)(2) of the ESA provides:

> Each Federal agency shall, in consultation with and with the assistance of the Secretary, insure that any action authorized, funded, or carried out by such agency…is not likely to jeopardize the continued existence of any endangered species or threatened species or result in the destruction or adverse modification of habitat of such species which is determined…to be critical.…[29]

The statute builds an elaborate procedure for carrying out these consultations under which the agency proposing the action (known as the "action agency") must consult with, depending on the species, either the FWS or NMFS through a series of steps designed to predict the impact of the action on listed species, with the ultimate product being a "biological opinion" from the FWS or NMFS "setting forth the [agency's] opinion, and a summary of the information on which the opinion is based, detailing how the agency action affects the species or its critical habitat."[30]

The substantive content for conducting the consultation analysis is defined primarily in joint FWS–NMFS regulations.[31] "Jeopardize" is defined there as "to engage in an action that reasonably would be expected, directly or indirectly, to reduce appreciably the likelihood of both the survival and recovery of a listed species in the wild by reducing the reproduction, numbers, or distribution of that species." "Action" is defined as "all activities or programs of any kind authorized, funded, or carried out, in whole or in part, by Federal agencies in the United States or upon the high seas." "Effects of the action" include "the direct and indirect effects of an action on the species or critical habitat, together with the effects of other activities that are interrelated or interdependent with that action, that will be added to the environmental baseline." The "indirect effects" are "those that are caused by the proposed action and are later in time, but still are reasonably certain to occur."

On the one hand, greenhouse gas emissions and their climate change consequences arguably fit in this framework. Greenhouse gas emissions from actions carried out, funded, or authorized by federal agencies contribute to tropospheric warming, the indirect effects of which could at some later time adversely affect a protected species. Although determining reliably whether these effects actually do occur may be difficult in particular scenarios, the point is that they could occur.

On the other hand, there are considerable legal, scientific, and practical difficulties with fitting climate change into the consultation framework at the level of detail necessary to evaluate particular federal agency actions (all of which would apply equally to claims that emissions lead to a "take" of climate-threatened species in violation of ESA section 9). Consider, for example, a proposed coal-fired power plant in Florida and its effects on the polar bear in the Arctic.[32] The argument for applying the ESA goes as follows: the power plant emits greenhouse gases (a direct effect of the action), greenhouse gases are reasonably certain to warm the troposphere (an indirect effect of the action), a warming troposphere is reasonably certain to adversely alter ecological conditions for the polar bear, and it is reasonably expected that such ecological changes will bring an end to the polar bear as a species.

While that chain of events makes for an easy A leads to B story, in fact any effort to link the individual plant's emissions as the jeopardizing agent for the polar bear species would meet obvious objections stemming from the fact that all greenhouse gas emissions worldwide are subject to the same causal analysis. All greenhouse gas molecules are equally to blame for whatever impact climate change has on a species. It is not possible, therefore, to "upscale" emissions from a particular source and "downscale" them to a particular impact on the ground, which is precisely what the section 7 consultation process would require the FWS and NMFS to do for every action funded, carried out, or authorized by federal agencies. Every source of greenhouse gas emissions funded, carried out, or authorized by a federal agency, therefore, would in theory be a causal source of jeopardization for a climate-threatened species. In other words, going down the mitigation road with section 7 would subject a vast segment of our nation's economy to greenhouse gas regulation *under* the ESA, with no principled way of distinguishing between emission sources for purposes of assigning "jeopardizing" causal status. Either all federal actions involving greenhouse gas emissions would trigger jeopardy status and be subject to regulation by the FWS and NMFS,[33] or the FWS and NMFS would have to adopt arbitrary thresholds for assigning jeopardy status, such as quantity or efficiency of emissions.

Either scenario is disastrous for the agencies and the ESA. The comprehensive regulation approach, besides being politically unacceptable, would be beyond the resources and expertise of the FWS and NMFS. Proponents of this use of the ESA have yet to explain how the FWS and NMFS would establish emission caps for different sources. Neither agency is equipped to function in an EPA-like role of emissions regulator across a multitude of industries, and neither has the resources to do so even if the expertise could be acquired. The selective regulation approach would face difficult legal challenges. Moritz et al. argue, for example, that "the Services could set a threshold level for consultation, as long as it was reasonable and sufficiently protective of listed species."[34] But they do not point to authority in section 7 or elsewhere in the ESA for differentiation between sources in terms of legal status if there is no scientific basis for causal differentiation. Why would greenhouse gas emissions from, say, a farm not cross the jeopardy threshold but emissions from a large power plant would? If a species is put in jeopardy by the incremental molecule of carbon dioxide, how will the agency know which source was the causal agent? Questions like these, for which there simply is no good answer under the ESA, are bound to become routine litigation fodder in response to any such regulatory push.

Nevertheless, many interest groups, with the Center for Biological Diversity in the lead, are pursuing mitigation litigation to force the agencies to build section 7 of the ESA into a greenhouse gas regulation regime. The George W. Bush Administration launched a counteroffensive against the pressure to employ the ESA in this way. In May 2008, the FWS promulgated a final rule listing the polar bear as threatened based on factors that included the impacts of climate change on Arctic sea ice.[35] Secretary of the

Interior Dirk Kempthorne stressed at the time that the listing would not provide a basis for using the ESA to regulate greenhouse gas emission sources.[36] The FWS also issued interim and final section 4(d) rules for the polar bear, exempting from section 9 take prohibitions any activity already exempt or authorized under the Marine Mammal Protection Act and, for any activity outside of Alaska, also exempting all takes incidental to a lawful purpose.[37] The unspoken purpose of the latter approach undoubtedly was to cut off claims that greenhouse gas emissions sources outside of Alaska are causing unauthorized takes of the polar bear. In tandem with that, the Department of the Interior also issued a memorandum explaining it would not consider greenhouse gas emissions in consultations about the polar bear or other species listed due to climate threats.[38]

The FWS and NMFS later followed up on that position by promulgating new section 7(a)(2) consultation regulations designed to, among other things, preclude consideration of greenhouse emissions in consultations. Culminating one of the most controversial rulemakings in the history of ESA implementation, in December 2008, the FWS and NMFS promulgated a final rule revising various features of the section 7 consultation regulations. The changes, too extensive to assess in detail here, fell into three categories: (1) revised and new definitions for causation and effects analyses; (2) revisions to applicability designed to preclude consideration of greenhouse gas emissions in consultations; and (3) streamlined consultations through a shift in decision authority to action agencies. Some of the changes merely codify existing conditions, such as a new provision limiting consultations to discretionary actions. But some provisions had the potential to alter radically consultation practice substantially. Some significant changes included:

- Indirect effects are limited to those effects that occur later in time for which the proposed action is an "essential cause."[39]

- If an effect will occur whether or not the proposed action takes place, it is not an indirect effect.[40]

- Indirect effects must be reasonably likely to occur based on "clear and substantial information."[41]

- For actions not anticipated to cause take, no consultation is necessary if the effects are manifested through "global processes" that cannot be reliably predicted or measured, have an insignificant impact, or pose only a remote risk.[42]

- For actions not anticipated to cause take, no consultation is necessary if the effects are not capable of being measured in a way that permits "meaningful evaluation."[43]

- Action agencies will determine for themselves whether, under these new standards, formal consultation is necessary.

The rule attracted considerable controversy, with tens of thousands of comments filed on the proposed rule, and litigation was filed immediately to challenge the final rule. Many environmental strategists outlined ways the Obama Administration could, through executive action or in concert with Congress, swiftly nullify the rule. In March 2009 President Obama ordered FWS and NMFS to review the rules and authorized other federal agencies "to follow the prior longstanding consultation and concurrence practices."[44] Soon thereafter Congress passed legislation allowing the agencies to withdraw the polar bear section 4(d) rule and the consultation rule with no notice and comment procedures,[45] which the agencies did for the consultation rule effective May 4, 2009.[46]

Other than raise a fuss about the Bush Administration consultation rule, however, neither Congress nor the Obama Administration has shown any interest in dragging the ESA into the war on greenhouse gas emissions. Nothing in the legislation allowing the agencies to overturn the rules or in the agencies' statement accompanying the decision to overturn the consultation rule so much as mentions climate change or greenhouse gas emissions. Indeed, all indications suggest environmental groups will not like the Obama Administration's position much more than the Bush Administration's: David Hayes, the Deputy Secretary of the Department of the Interior, told senators during his confirmation hearing that the endangered species law is ill-suited for addressing greenhouse gas emissions; Tom Strickland, the Assistant Secretary for Fish, Wildlife and Parks overseeing the ESA, said the same at his hearing; and, more directly to the point, FWS spokesman Josh Winchell said in February 2009 that "we have zero legislative authority to regulate carbon emissions. That's just not what we do. With the polar bear, the science definitely pointed to climate change, but that doesn't all of a sudden give us the authority to address the underlying cause, which is carbon emissions."[47] Putting those words into action, on May 8, 2009, Interior Secretary Ken Salazar announced the agency's decision not to rescind the polar section bear section 4(d) rule, proclaiming that "the Endangered Species Act is not the proper mechanism for controlling our nation's carbon emissions."[48] In other words, the Obama Administration understands pit bulls can't fly.

Adapting the ESA for the Future

In its quest to regulate coal-fired power plants and other industrial sources of greenhouse gases, the mitigation litigation charge is leading the ESA away from its central mission of conserving ecosystems. The most effective applications of the statute maintain its original concern with what is happening on the ground and in the water in specific locales rather than being concerned with what is happening in the troposphere. A decisive measure thus must be adopted to prevent the ESA from being used to police greenhouse gas emission sources. To forge an integrated climate change policy, however, emission sources should not simply be comprehensively excluded from ESA jurisdiction. Rather, the statute should be amended to exclude from its provisions emissions of greenhouse gases subject to other federal, state, or local controls, including any cap-and-trade program, carbon taxes, direct emissions regulation, or other code or regulation designed to reduce emissions without directly regulating them, such as a "green" building code. This exclusion of "covered greenhouse gas emissions" would extend to all ESA regulatory provisions, including section 7 consultations and the section 9 take prohibition, but would not extend to any other feature of an emission source that could pose risks to protected species, such as habitat modification or water diversion. Because emission sources not subject to other controls are likely to become insignificant in scope, they would be at no risk of being deemed a cause of jeopardy or take of climate-threatened species on the basis of their emissions.

Turning to what can be done proactively for species on the ground, I propose the following interrelated reforms, all of which can easily be engrafted onto the existing ESA structure, designed to replace the goal of *recovery* with that of *transition* through climate change for species listed primarily due to threats associated with climate change.

Listing of Climate-Threatened Species. Indeed, the first reform proposal would create a new category of listing, "climate-threatened species," to identify species that should be managed for adaptation to climate change over a fifty-year period rather than with the unrealistic goal of recovery. The ESA currently has two listing categories: an "endangered species" is one "in danger of extinction throughout all or a significant portion of its range,"[49] and a "threatened species" is one "likely to become an endangered species within the foreseeable future throughout all or a significant portion of its range."[50] Climate-threatened species would be defined as "any endangered or threatened species the threats to which are attributable substantially to climate change and its impacts on the ecological conditions upon which the species depends for its survival." Climate-threatened species would hold the same status as threatened species for purposes of the take prohibition— i.e., allowing the FWS and NMFS to craft specialized rules under ESA section 4(d) regarding what actions constitute take under Section 9[51]—but in addition would be tracked into a transition program designed to maintain their chances of survival through the fifty-year climate change period, at which time their status would be reevaluated.

Replacing Recovery with Transition. Whereas the recovery goal applied to other species is activated through conservation measures designed "to bring any endangered species or threatened species to the point at which the measures provided pursuant to this chapter are no longer necessary," climate-threatened species would benefit from "transition measures" designed to maintain their chances of survival as a species at the conclusion of the fifty-year transition period. In other words, the ESA plan for the species should address transition first so as to keep recovery a viable goal for the more distant future. The existing provision for recovery plans in section 4(f) of the ESA thus will be amended to include "transition plans," which will apply only to climate-threatened species. Transition plans will specify transition measures, defined as "the methods and procedures which are necessary to maintain the survival of any climate-threatened species." The transition plan, which should be prepared within one year of the listing (otherwise, what's the point?), would (1) develop and employ the best available model of how climate change will affect the species over the fifty-year time frame to identify changes in the species' home ecosystem; (2) identify likely areas in which suitable habitat will emerge and to which the species could adaptively migrate or be relocated, to be identified in the transition plan as "transition habitat;" and (3) identify likely conflicts with other species. The plan would then outline practicable cost-effective strategies for assisting the survival of the species through the fifty-year period. This may involve anything from reducing stress in its current ecosystem to improving conditions in transition habitat areas.

Transition Consultations. A new "transition consultation" procedure should be added to the Section 7 consultation provisions, requiring federal agencies to consult with the FWS or NMFS to determine the impact of their actions on climate-threatened species. The transition consultation should ensure that a federal agency action does not substantially interfere with the goals of the relevant transition plans, and to identify transition measures the federal agency can reasonably incorporate into its action. Thus, in parallel with the consultation procedure used for endangered and threatened species, the transition consultation provision will require that "each Federal agency shall, in consultation with and with the assistance of the Secretary, insure that any action authorized, funded, or carried out by such agency is not likely to substantially reduce the likelihood of survival of any climate-threatened species or to substantially impair the value to such species of the transition habitat identified in the transition plan prepared for such species." Importantly, however, the transition consultation provision will specifically exclude evaluation or regulation of "covered greenhouse gas emissions" from the scope of the consultation. In all other respects the consultation procedure used for climate-threatened species will track the procedure currently used for endangered and threatened species.

Incentives for Non-Federal Actions. Using the playbook Interior Secretary Bruce Babbitt developed in the Clinton Administration, an incentive-based series of reforms should be installed to enlist nonfederal actors in the transition plans for climate-threatened species. For example, nothing in the ESA prevents a landowner from passively allowing ecological conditions to deteriorate, and nothing requires a landowner actively to improve ecological conditions. In other words, unless a landowner affirmatively proposes to develop or otherwise use the land, the ESA sits on the sidelines. Areas identified in a species' transition plan as deteriorating habitat or potentially emerging transition habitat thus may receive little assistance without an incentive to prompt landowners into taking conservation measures consistent with the plan. Landowners voluntarily reducing climate change stresses in an ecosystem or improving the chances of emerging transition habitat in another ecosystem—for example, by controlling invasive species, improving groundwater recharge, or introducing controlled fires—could be awarded transition measures "credits" for sale or transfer to other landowners or agencies whose proposed land uses or other actions are subject to ESA regulation, and who thus are required to support transition measures, because of regulated impacts on the species. As Neal Wilkins explains in chapter 3 in this volume, this kind of approach already is used in the agencies' habitat conservation banking and recovery crediting programs, and could prove useful in particular for protecting the value of transition habitat that is outside the scope of federal public lands.

Biodiversity Priority. Finally, it is likely that as climate change grips more and more species, prompting many to migrate and putting many others in stressed conditions, there will be conflicts between different species' recovery and transition plans as one species' adaptive migration imposes stress on another species' fight to stay put, or as measures to reduce stress for one species in an ecosystem may increase stress for other species in that or other ecosystems. In those situations the FWS and NMFS should be authorized to suspend their species-specific mission and manage conditions in the relevant ecosystems with the goal of maximizing overall species biodiversity through the transition period. In other words, the Services should be able to do what is best for the transition of ecosystems as whole systems rather than on behalf of particular species in the ecosystems. This would require suspension of the transition plans developed for each of the protected species in the relevant ecosystems and, in their place, development of an "integrated ecosystem transition plan" employing adaptive management measures to conserve overall species biodiversity to the extent practicable.

The new provision thus should require that "where the Secretary determines that the recovery goals for endangered and threatened species and the transition goals for climate-threatened species in the same ecological region are in conflict and incompatible due to the effects of climate change on ecological conditions, the Secretary shall prepare an integrated ecosystem transition plan for the region." The plan would have the goal of "maintaining the level of ecosystem, species, and genetic diversity the Secretary deems reasonable and appropriate for the region to remain ecologically resilient in response to climate change." The ecosystem-based plan "shall replace the recovery plans and transition plans for all affected species in that region for all purposes under the Act." Consultations under section 7 would also shift from a species-specific focus to consultation as to whether the federal action "substantially impairs the ecosystem, species, and genetic diversity of the region covered by the integrated ecosystem transition plan."

This and the other measures outlined above recognize that the ESA, as tough as it is on the ground, is no match for climate change. The focus must be not on a futile quest to use the ESA to stop climate change, but rather on responding to the ecological transition conditions species are likely to face.

I recognize, to be sure, that my proposals are incremental and work within the existing structure of the ESA to respond to a focused question— what to do about climate change? One could envision some form of comprehensive federal climate change regulation integrating greenhouse gas emission controls, renewable energy production, green building codes, and including species protection measures to supplant the ESA entirely. Or, more modestly, but no less a pipe dream, one could envision a comprehensive overhaul of the ESA that would, among other things, take care of the climate change question in some integrated manner. I chose the tinkering approach because, once one opens the door to comprehensive climate change legislation or ESA reform, the range of possibilities is simply too wide to anticipate how the climate change issue would be resolved. It is also, I believe, far more likely that anything Congress does with respect to climate change and the ESA will be incremental and will not disrupt the basic structure of the statute, which has attained third-rail status politically.

Conclusion

The ESA is both noble and arrogant. It commits humans to protect the species our actions threaten, but it assumes we can do so while still having our way. The reality is that the ESA has worked out as a pragmatic compromise—few species actually recover, but few slide into extinction, and people don't always get to do whatever they want. It will be difficult to keep that pact intact in the face of climate change. Some species are doomed; we just don't know which yet. Some species can make it through climate change without a scratch; we just don't know which yet. Most species, however, will hobble through it, but some will need our help. My proposals are designed to respond to those species' needs by focusing on transition over the next fifty years. Attempting to use the ESA to regulate greenhouse gas emissions would waste resources and ultimately fail legally, politically, and practically. Taking greenhouse gas emissions out of the picture allows the FWS and NMFS to focus on employing the ESA where it works best—managing local challenges to species' survival. Emphasizing transition planning rather than recovery as the goal, at least for the next fifty years, responds to the reality of climate change as a prolonged event of massive ecological reshuffling. In short, the ESA must become noble and humble if it is to have any chance of helping species through the era of climate change.

Notes

1. Stefan Rahmstorf, Anny Cazenave, John A. Church, James E. Hansen, Ralph F. Keeling, David E. Parker, and Richard C. Somerville, "Recent Climate Observations Compared to Projections," *Science* 316 (2007): 709.

2. Intergovernmental Panel on Climate Change, *Summary for Policymakers, Climate Change 2007: The Physical Science Basis, Contribution of Working Group I to the Fourth Assessment Report of the Intergovernmental Panel on Climate Change* (2007), 10–17, http://www.ipcc.ch/pdf/assessment-report/ar4/wg1/ar4-wg1-spm.pdf.

3. The discussion of climate change and ESA policy in this section is drawn with permission from J.B. Ruhl, "Climate Change and the Endangered Species Act: Building Bridges to the No-Analog Future," *Boston University Law Review* 88, no. 1 (2008): 1–62.

4. Lance H. Gunderson and C.S. Holling, eds., *Panarchy: Understanding Transformation in Human and Natural Systems* (Washington, D.C.: Island Press, 2002), 3–22.

5. Intergovernmental Panel on Climate Change, *Summary for Policymakers, Climate Change 2007: Impacts, Adaptation and Vulnerability, Contribution of Working Group II to the Fourth Assessment Report of the Intergovernmental Panel on Climate Change* (2007), 8, http://www.ipcc.ch/pdf/assessment-report/ar4/wg2/ar4-wg2-spm.pdf.

6. Intergovernmental Panel on Climate Change, *Climate Change and Biodiversity, IPCC Technical Paper V* (2002), 16–23, http://www.ipcc.ch/pdf/technical-papers/climate-changes-biodiversity-en.pdf.

7. Ibid., 22.

8. Ibid., 17-18.

9. Ibid., 12.

10. Ibid., 13–14.

11. Ibid., 17.

12. Ibid., 16–17.

13. Many human communities are likely to find it necessary and possible to migrate to avoid rising sea levels along coastal areas, to relocate agricultural land uses, and to obtain secure water supplies. These migrations will necessarily involve some conversion of land uses in areas that presently provide suitable ecological

conditions for particular species, in some cases at scales sufficient to pose a threat to the species. Ibid., 3–4 (discussing some environmental effects of climate-motivated human migration).

14. Ibid., 43.

15. Human adaptation to climate change is likely to involve spatial relocations, as well as increased flow of goods to new settlement areas, which as in the past are likely to introduce non-native species to local ecosystems, some of which will establish themselves. The EPA has suggested that "important progress has been made in identifying climate change effects on invasive species, but…our understanding of effects on specific species and interactions of other stressors needs to be improved." "Effects of Climate Change on Aquatic Invasive Species and Implications for Management and Research," 72 *Fed. Reg.* 45046, 45047 (Aug. 10, 2007). Most invasive species introductions are human-induced. Peter M. Vitousek, C. D'Antonio, Lloyd L. Loope, and R. Westbrooks, "Biological Invasions as Global Environmental Change," *American Scientist* 84, no. 5 (1996): 468–78.

16. 16 U.S.C. § 1531(b).

17. 16 U.S.C. § 1522(a)(1).

18. 16 U.S.C. § 1533(a)(3).

19. 16 U.S.C. § 1533(f).

20. 16 U.S.C. § 1536(a)(2).

21. 16 U.S.C. §§ 1538(a)(1) and 1533(d).

22. 16 U.S.C. § 1536(b)(4).

23. 16 U.S.C. § 1539(a)(1).

24. National Research Council, *Science and the Endangered Species Act* (Washington, D.C.: National Academies Press, 1995), 111–23.

25. A comprehensive taxonomy and record of climate change litigation cases is available at Michael B. Gerrard and J. Cullen Howe, "Climate Change Litigation in the U.S.," http://www.climatecasechart.com.

26. Center for Biological Diversity, "Center for Biological Diversity Announces Climate Law Institute, Dedicates $17 Million to Combat Global Warming," press release, February 12, 2009, http://www.biologicaldiversity.org/news/press_releases/2009/climate-law-institute-02-12-2009.html.

27. The discussion of the policy pitfalls of climate change "mitigation litigation" in this section is drawn with permission from J.B. Ruhl, "Climbing Mount Mitigation: A Proposal for Legislative Suspension of Climate Change 'Mitigation Litigation,'" *Washington & Lee Journal of Energy, Climate, & Environment* 1, no. 1 (2010): 71–91.

28. J.B. Ruhl, "Climate Change and the Endangered Species Act: Building Bridges to the No-Analog Future," *Boston University Law Review* 88 no. 1 (2008): 31–58.

29. 16 U.S.C. 1536(a)(2) (2000). The provision also requires that "[i]n fulfilling the requirements of this paragraph each agency shall use the best scientific and commercial data available."

30. 16 U.S.C. 1536(b)(3)(A).

31. All the definitions discussed in the text are found in 50 C.F.R. § 402.02 (2006).

32. The considerable distance between the action and the species is not determinative. The FWS consultation regulations define "action area"—the geographic scope of the consultation analysis—as "all areas to be affected directly or indirectly by the Federal action and not merely the immediate area involved in the action." 50 C.F.R. §402.02 (2006). Thus, the analysis is not limited to the "footprint" of the action, nor is it limited by the action agency's authority. Rather, it is a biological determination of the reach of the proposed action on listed species.

33. Regulation by the FWS and NMFS comes in the form of the agencies specifying "reasonable and prudent" alternatives to the action as proposed. 16 U.S.C. § 1536(b)(3)(A). Presumably, in the climate change mitigation context this would mean placing caps on emission levels.

34. Anna T. Moritz, Kassie R. Siegel, Brendan J. Cummings, and William H. Rodgers, Jr., "Biodiversity Baking and Boiling: Endangered Species Act Turning Down the Heat," *Tulsa Law Review* 44, no. 1 (2009): 228.

35. 73 *Fed. Reg.* 28212 (May 15, 2008).

36. U.S. Department of the Interior, "Secretary Kempthorne Announces Decision to Protect Polar Bears under Endangered Species Act," press release, May 14, 2008.

37. 73 *Fed. Reg.* 28, 306 (May 15, 2008) (interim rule); 73 *Fed. Reg.* 76, 249 (Dec. 16, 2008) (final rule).

38. Solicitor, U.S. Department of the Interior, "Guidance on the Applicability of the Endangered Species Act's Consultation Requirements to Proposed Actions Involving the Emission of Greenhouse Gases," October 3, 2008; U.S. Geological Survey, "The Challenges of Linking Carbon Emissions, Atmospheric Greenhouse Gas Emissions, Global Warming, and Consequential Impacts," May 14, 2008.

39. 50 C.F.R. § 402.02.

40. Ibid.

41. Ibid.

42. 50 C.F.R. § 402.03(b)(2).

43. 50 C.F.R. § 402.03(b)(3)(i).

44. Office of the Press Secretary, The White House, "Memorandum for the Heads of Executive Departments and Agencies Re: The Endangered Species Act," March 3, 2009.

45. 2009 Omnibus Appropriations Act, Pub. L. 111–8, Division E, Title IV, § 429 (2009).

46. 74 *Fed. Reg.* 20421 (May 4, 2009).

47. Greenwire, "Endangered Species: Some See EPA's Climate Proposal Prodding Interior on ESA," April 23, 2009, http://www.eenews.net/public/Greenwire/print/ 2009/04/23/4; and Alan Kovski, "Interior Nominee Agrees Climate Change Fits Poorly in Endangered Species Rules," *Environment Reporter*, 40 (2009): 622.

48. U.S. Fish and Wildlife Service, "Salazar Retains Conservation Rule for Polar Bears, Underlines Need for Comprehensive Energy and Climate Legislation," press release, May 8, 2009, http://www.fws.gov/news/NewsReleases/showNews.cfm?newsId=20FB90B6-A188-DB01-04788E0892D91701.

49. 16 U.S.C. § 1532(6).

50. 16 U.S.C. § 1532(20)

51. 16 U.S.C. § 1533(d). This would require no more than adding the term "climate-threatened species" to section 4(d).

9

Protecting Endangered Species at Home and Abroad: The International Conservation Effects of the Endangered Species Act and Its Relationship to CITES

Michael De Alessi

While the Endangered Species Act (ESA) provides for the legal protection of threatened and endangered species within the United States, international protection of threatened and endangered species rests primarily with the Convention on International Trade in Endangered Species of Wild Fauna and Flora (CITES). CITES protects endangered species by monitoring, regulating, and sometimes prohibiting trade of threatened and endangered species as well as of their parts and products; the ESA also has provisions to protect foreign endangered species by banning trade in them. The ESA and CITES both came into force in 1973, and both employ the species-specific approach to protecting threatened and endangered species that was favored at that time. Both rely on restrictions and penalties for harm to species rather than on incentives to protect species and their habitats. The U.S. Fish and Wildlife Service (FWS) and the National Marine Fisheries Service (NMFS) are the agencies responsible for implementing the ESA and for carrying out U.S. responsibilities under CITES.

The ESA and CITES have been much praised and criticized—and, given their similar histories and approaches, it is not surprising that the praise and criticism of each have much in common. It is difficult to evaluate the overall effectiveness of the ESA and CITES. Defenders point to the dearth of extinctions of protected species as evidence of success, while critics cite the lack of species recoveries or removal from endangered status as proof of failure. Both the ESA and CITES are often criticized for their reliance on protective measures that, at least in some cases, also create incentives that undermine the goal of species protection and recovery.

I will argue that the species-specific approach of ESA and CITES is fundamentally flawed. Both ESA and CITES neglect the need to protect ecosystems as a whole, and both create potentially perverse incentives for those whose actions affect threatened and endangered species. While it is impossible for the U.S. government alone to change CITES, the ESA could be reformed both to better protect foreign endangered species and to push CITES toward protecting habitats and ecosystems rather than single species.

In this chapter I examine the relationship of the ESA to CITES, the similar trajectories they have followed, and the criticisms they have met. I offer case studies of elephants, rhinoceros, sea turtles, crocodiles, and a failed for-profit conservation effort in Australia to show some of the complexities and problems endemic to the CITES approach, and conclude with suggestions for reform of the ESA's foreign listings.

The History of CITES

The earliest antecedent to CITES was the 1900 London Convention Designed to Ensure the Conservation of Various Species of Wild Animals in Africa which are Useful to Man or Inoffensive, whose very title revealed its imperial and anthropocentric approach. This Convention never came into force but set the stage for a focus on trade restrictions as a way to protect threatened wildlife.[1] Momentum slowly built until the International Union for the Conservation of Nature (IUCN), an intergovernmental organization, passed a resolution at its 1963 meeting calling for the international regulation of trade in endangered species.[2] At the same time, IUCN created its Red List of endangered species. Still prominent in international conservation circles today, the Red List was an inspiration for the first official list of endangered species in the United States published by the FWS in 1967.[3] Seventy-eight species were listed as endangered, but inclusion on the list did not trigger any protective measures. To add some teeth to the list, Congress enacted the Endangered Species Conservation Act of 1969,[4] which prohibited the import or export of species officially listed by the FWS as endangered, and also called for the negotiation of an international treaty regulating trade in wildlife and wildlife products.[5] In response to that call, a meeting was held in Washington, D.C. in 1973 which produced CITES. The United States immediately signed CITES, which came into force in 1975.

CITES regulates the international trade of animals and plants by placing endangered and threatened species into three appendices, which impose varying degrees of trade restriction.[6] Appendix I lists species threatened with extinction; CITES prohibits commercial trade of these species. Appendix II lists species that are threatened or whose populations are declining toward threatened status; CITES requires permits for import and export of these species. Appendix III lists species at the request of member nations who want to monitor trade more closely; CITES does not require trade permits for these species but does require increased monitoring of their trade. Inclusion in appendices I and II are voted on at Conferences of the Parties, which are held every two to three years, while any member state may add species to appendix III at any time. By 2008 the three CITES appendices contained approximately 28,000 species of plants and 5,000 species of animals, of which over 600 animals and almost 300 species of plants were included in appendix I.[7] As of 2009, there are 175 parties to the convention, making it one of the most widely ratified international treaties.[8]

Foreign Species on the Federal Endangered Species List

Endangered species are protected by CITES, but U.S law has also protected foreign threatened and endangered species. Although the original 1967 FWS list of endangered species contained only species native to the United States, the 1969 Endangered Species Conservation Act required the FWS to add foreign species to the list, and import and export restrictions were imposed on all species on the list. The 1973 CITES treaty also imposed trade restrictions on endangered species, and when the Endangered Species Act passed later that same year it made the Secretary of the Interior, through the FWS, responsible for enforcing CITES in the United States. Thus, while the ESA continued to list foreign species as endangered, it also became the legal enforcement mechanism for CITES restrictions on trade. This means that the FWS reviews and issues import and export permits, works directly with U.S. Customs on enforcement, and is the primary agency responsible for scientific assessments and advocacy of U.S. positions at conferences of the parties to CITES.[9]

There is significant overlap between the foreign species listed on the ESA as threatened and endangered and the CITES appendices. However, ESA foreign listings are more broad than CITES because they may include species not threatened by trade, whereas CITES listings primarily consider the effects of trade. As a result, the ESA foreign lists are extensive; in fact, 574 of the 1,214 animals (but only 3 of the 750 plants) listed as threatened or endangered under the ESA are considered "foreign" by the FWS.[10]

How ESA listing may protect foreign species. Since the only real teeth of the ESA's foreign listings is to ban their importation, and CITES already regulates trade in these species, one might reasonably ask why the ESA lists species that are not threatened by trade. Foreign listing under the ESA, however, allows the FWS to provide funding for international conservation efforts.[11] Specifically, Section 8 of the ESA, "as a demonstration of the commitment of the United States to the worldwide protection of endangered species and threatened species," authorizes the use of funds and personnel to assist in "the development and management of programs" in foreign countries "necessary or useful for the conservation of any endangered species or threatened species listed" under the ESA.[12]

Moreover, the ESA listing of foreign species may be important symbolically. In 2006, for example, the Center for Biological Diversity sued the FWS over its failure to list 56 endangered bird species from around the world.[13] In 2009, the FWS settled the case, agreeing to list 31 bird species.[14] Of those 31 species, only 3 were already listed by CITES (one in each appendix) and had been so since the 1980s.[15] While most of these species are critically endangered, the non-CITES-listed species among them do not appear to be threatened by trade. Nevertheless, listing these species drew attention to their imperiled situation, as noted by a Center for Biological Diversity press release that underscored the importance of the listings of these foreign birds, not for the trade protections or conservation funds generated but simply for "increased international recognition of those species' urgent plights."[16]

Nevertheless, serious doubts must be raised about the degree to which foreign species are protected through ESA listing. Of all of those foreign animals listed as endangered by the FWS, only six have been removed and officially listed as recovered by the FWS.[17] Three are Australian kangaroos, which were never endangered but were considered threatened by the FWS because of inadequate monitoring of trade in their hides and meat.[18] In fact they are Australia's most abundant species of kangaroo and, according to the Australian Department of Foreign Affairs and Trade, the combined populations of these three species has varied between 15 and 50 million animals over the past 25 years, with the fluctuations due more to seasonal variation than harvesting.[19] The other three foreign species removed from the ESA lists are bird species from Palau which were endangered after military operations during World War II but which have since recovered to close to their original population numbers.[20] Four other foreign species have been downlisted from endangered to threatened: the red lechwe (an African antelope species), two crocodile species (the Nile crocodile and the Australian saltwater crocodile[21]), and the yacare caiman[22] (a species similar to a crocodile). One more species, the Indian flap-shelled turtle, was removed from the list due to data error (it was determined that the species was not endangered or threatened after all).[23]

In each of these cases, the ESA has had no apparent effect on international conservation efforts. In the case of the kangaroos, ESA listing almost certainly spurred Australia to publish better data on markets for kangaroo products but, interestingly, none of the truly endangered species of kangaroo (such as the woylie, Australia's smallest and rarest kangaroo, and the bridled nail-tailed wallaby) were listed, only those with a commercial trade in their hides. So the ESA followed the CITES model in this case, ignoring the most endangered species because their products were not exported, focusing instead on what turned out to be a sustainably harvested species. In the case of the red lechwe, the FWS simply followed the lead of CITES, removing the species after it was downlisted from CITES appendix I to appendix II in 1979. In the cases of the Nile crocodile and the Australian saltwater crocodile, ESA downlisting was a response to successful ranching programs. In the case of the yacare caiman, ESA downlisting concurred with the CITES listing under appendix II and "to promote the conservation of the yacare caiman by ensuring proper management of the commercially harvested caiman species."[24]

How ESA listing may further imperil foreign species. ESA listing of foreign species may in fact have detrimental effects on conservation because, unlike CITES, the ESA does not allow for well-regulated and monitored trade. Well-regulated trade can help threatened and endangered species recover. Such was the case with the Nile crocodile, which the U.S. listed as endangered in 1970 and which was on appendix I of CITES when it came into force in 1975. In 1983, however, CITES moved the Zimbabwe population of Nile crocodiles to appendix II to allow for sales from commercial ranching operations, and moved the crocodile populations of nine other African countries to appendix II in 1985. These moves were supported by the IUCN Crocodile Specialist Group as a likely means of propagating the species.[25] The U.S. did reclassify the ranched Zimbabwean populations of Nile crocodile from endangered to threatened status in 1987 (and downlisted the wild population in 1988), but the rest of the appendix II populations were not reclassified until 1993. Due to FWS procedural issues, trade was not allowed into the United States, even from Zimbabwe, until 1996.[26]

The commercialization of the Nile crocodile appears to be a great conservation success story, and there is little doubt that the species has rebounded in countries with ranching programs. In recent years, CITES proposals for increased trade from countries with ranching operations like Botswana, Madagascar, and Malawi have all been accepted.[27] The Nile crocodile case highlights an important difference between CITES and the ESA on international trade. CITES allows for downlisting to appendix II (and therefore, trade of) threatened and endangered species if it can be shown that trade is *not detrimental* to the survival of the species. The ESA, on the other hand, requires that permits to import threatened and endangered species will only be issued when it can be demonstrated that trade will result in *enhancing the survival* of the species.[28] This distinction creates a different burden of proof, making the ESA significantly more restrictive and possibly hampering international efforts, even if sanctioned by CITES, to use markets to create positive incentives for conservation.

This distinction may be especially detrimental to ranching and captive breeding programs that are either within the United States or rely on transshipment through the United States. A recent court case, for example, found that FWS was in violation of the ESA when it issued an export permit to the captive breeders of three African antelope species, the scimitar-horned oryx, the addax, and the dama gazelle, which are endangered in their native ranges.[29] The case repeatedly cited the enhancement standard as key to its findings that individual species could not be permitted for export and that each farm or breeder must be individually evaluated. Similarly, in the case of the Cayman Turtle Farm (discussed below), the higher standard of the ESA prevented shipment of turtle products through U.S. ports, seriously undermining the breeding program of the turtle farm,[30] which, if successful, may have matched the conservation success of the farming and ranching of the Nile crocodile.[31]

The ESA trade restrictions and the regulation of world trade. The listing of foreign species under the ESA currently bans their import into and export from the United States regardless of whether a species is also listed on CITES appendix I. However, the ability of the United States to prohibit trade unilaterally is limited by the General Agreement on Tariffs and Trade (GATT) and the World Trade Organization (WTO). Two previous U.S. efforts to unilaterally impose trade restrictions were challenged under GATT and the WTO. The first challenge came in 1991, when Mexico won a GATT ruling against a U.S. effort to impose a trade ban against Mexican tuna because those tuna were not caught using the same dolphin-safe methods that the United States had imposed on its tuna fleet under the aegis of the U.S. Marine Mammal Protection Act.[32] The United States did not appeal this GATT ruling.

In the second case, the WTO ruled in 1998 against U.S. efforts to restrict imports of shrimp from some Asian countries that were not caught in ways that protected sea turtles.[33] The U.S. rationale for this restriction was that every species of marine turtle affected by shrimping was listed as endangered under the ESA.[34] In 2001, after the United States applied its policy evenly to all shrimp imports and made other changes to satisfy the WTO that restrictions were about protecting turtles and not the U.S. shrimping industry, the WTO accepted the trade restriction.[35] In both the original 1998 ruling and the successful 2001 appeal, the WTO explicitly underscored the importance of the listing of all of the relevant marine turtle species on appendix I of CITES to the legitimacy of the U.S. trade restriction.[36] Although the U.S. restriction on trade of an ESA-listed foreign species was eventually upheld by the WTO in this turtle case, the fact that marine turtles were also listed on CITES appendix I appears to have been a crucial factor in the WTO's acceptance of the trade restriction. The turtle case was also a special one because it aimed to protect turtles indirectly, not by banning imports of turtles or turtle products (which CITES already covered), but by altering fishing methods for shrimp that might adversely affect turtle populations. As a result, special legislation, wholly separate from the ESA, was required to implement the trade restrictions on shrimp.[37]

Thus, there are many reasons to doubt that foreign species are protected by being listed under the ESA as threatened or endangered. Although such listing allows the United States to fund conservation efforts abroad and draws attention to imperiled species, the six foreign listed species that have been officially classified as recovered were not saved by their ESA listing, and the most notable application of an ESA-style import ban to indirectly protect sea turtles required its own special legislative action. In some cases, trade restrictions that follow ESA listing of a species have undermined conservation efforts, while in other cases those restrictions have been challenged under GATT and by the WTO. The WTO, which eventually sanctioned U.S. turtle policy, has explicitly stated its belief that multilateral environmental agreements such as CITES are "the most effective way to deal with international environmental problems."[38] Of course, CITES, GATT, and the WTO have their critics too, some of whom make the reasonable claim that difficulties of monitoring compliance in other countries render the protection of turtles in other countries toothless.[39]

Limits to the Effectiveness of CITES

The relationship of trade to conservation lies at the heart of a fundamental contradiction in the CITES approach to protecting endangered species: the incentive structure it creates relies on prohibitions, punishments, and deliberate reduction of the market value of endangered species. But this is in contradiction with the positive biodiversity value that merits species protection. As others in this volume have shown, the tension between lowering market values in pursuit of conservation values makes administration of the ESA problematic; this same tension is found in the administration of CITES. It is certainly true that by successfully restricting trade in certain species, those species will in turn have less value in the market and so less effort will be spent hunting or harvesting them. This approach is especially well suited to state-managed lands and preserves, which are already being managed for conservation and where reducing the rewards to poaching and corruption will likely have positive effects. On communal or private land, however, devaluing species reduces the rewards to successfully protecting or propagating those species. It may also reduce interest in providing wildlife habitat, hastening, for example, the conversion of land to other uses such as agriculture.

The CITES approach is further undermined by the fact that among the greatest threats facing the conservation of endangered species worldwide, trade is overshadowed by habitat loss and degradation and by invasive species.[40] However, because its sole power is to restrict international trade, CITES is powerless to impel governments and landowners to protect habitat. There is nothing in CITES to prevent those who would "flood habitat with a hydroelectric dam, log it, level the hillsides of a road, build a golf course on the site, or burn the jungle to the ground for agricultural purposes."[41]

There is also nothing CITES can do to prevent internal markets from operating. Internal markets may not be important in small countries, but in places like China, where CITES trade bans have done little to decrease demand for animal parts used in traditional Chinese medicine, they may completely undermine CITES trade restrictions. For example, despite the listing of tigers on appendix I of CITES and evidence from a number of NGOs that farmed tiger parts are indistinguishable from illegally caught wild tiger parts, tiger farms are booming in China.[42] Currently, Chinese law prohibits any trade in tiger parts, but China has submitted requests to CITES to downlist farmed tigers, and the numbers of both the farms and the tigers on them are growing rapidly, up to 4,000 tigers by 2007.[43]

Finally, devaluing species by limiting their trade may not only compromise efforts by landholders and legitimate entrepreneurs; it has also in some cases limited the budgets of state wildlife agencies (discussed in further detail in the elephant and rhino examples below). Moreover, this approach is antithetical to conservation through commerce, which has proved effective in the conservation of some species like the Nile crocodile.

Those charged with administering the ESA and CITES recognize these problems, and have tried, with varying degrees of success, to address them (the ESA approach, the Safe Harbor program, is discussed elsewhere in this volume). For example, CITES distinguishes between discrete populations of some plants and animals, such as the crocodile populations mentioned above. However, the difficulty in distinguishing between CITES-legitimated products and CITES-trade-banned products—such as the difference between wild and farmed tigers in China—is extremely difficult and expensive.

Measuring Success

In light of these limits to the effectiveness of CITES, it is necessary to assess how successfully CITES has protected threatened and endangered species. While at first glance it appears plausible to apply a simple metric of success, such as whether population estimates have increased or decreased or whether species have either recovered or been downlisted from endangered, in fact performance measurement is notoriously difficult. Species may be kept on endangered lists even after their numbers have rebounded because of the research funding and attention their endangered status brings or, in the case of the ESA, the indirect habitat protection that listings provide. Downlisting also requires an evaluation of what effect the removal of ESA or CITES protections will have, which by its nature is conjectural.[44]

On the thirtieth anniversary of CITES, a United Nations Environmental Programme press release pointedly cited two (and only two) examples of species recovered under CITES, the South American vicuña (a small member of the camel family) and the Nile crocodile.[45] Highlighting the recovery of the vicuña and the Nile crocodile not only underscores the small numbers of CITES-listed species recoveries; it also highlights the importance of commercially driven captive breeding programs, which drove the recovery of both species.[46] In an opening address to the 2002

CITES meeting in Chile, Jaime Quiroga, the Chilean agriculture minister, proclaimed that the effectiveness of CITES was "demonstrated by the fact that no species covered by CITES has yet become extinct."[47] A recent U.S. Government Accountability Office review of international wildlife protection, however, stated that "it is difficult to directly link protections provided under the Convention to improvements in a species' status in the wild."[48]

Given the difficulty in evaluating the effect of CITES on a wide range of species that face diverse challenges to their survival, case studies may be the best way to evaluate the relative effectiveness of restrictive trade measures that treat market values as conservation liabilities versus regulated trade programs that treat positive market values as conservation assets. In the case studies of well-known, charismatic species below, at least, it appears that when sustainable harvests are possible, the negative consequences of treating species as liabilities are significant.

Elephants. Every few years the debate at CITES between those who believe in increasing the value of species through trade and those who believe in devaluing species by banning their trade crystallizes around the African elephant. When CITES moved the Africa elephant to Appendix I in 1989, all trade in elephants and elephant parts was banned, despite the fact that populations were not endangered in a number of southern African countries. Elephant populations were certainly dwindling in some countries in Africa, but in other countries, especially in southern Africa, elephants were suffering from overpopulation. Elephants historically roamed far and wide, but human settlement now often forces them to stay in more defined areas, where elephant populations can wreak ecological havoc. Chobe National Park in Botswana, for example, resembles a moonscape in some areas due to elephant overpopulation.

Prior to the 1989 ban on trade in elephants and their parts and products, ivory was sold by a number of southern African countries to raise money for the activities of their wildlife departments. Some governments deliberately culled elephants, and eventually they were able to successfully plead their case with CITES to get permission to sell ivory internationally on a limited basis. With promises that funds would go to wildlife management and community development, in 2003 Botswana, Namibia, and South Africa were granted permission by the parties to CITES for one-time ivory sales of twenty, ten, and thirty metric tons respectively. (This was the second time that CITES had permitted such a one-time sale: in 1999, Botswana, Namibia, and Zimbabwe sold almost fifty metric tons of ivory to Japan for about five million dollars.)

While there is evidence that the CITES ban successfully reduced demand for ivory, especially in the West,[49] the effects of the ban on elephant populations is less clear. Following the ivory ban in 1989, elephant numbers continued to decline in countries (such as the Congo and Sudan) where poaching was the biggest threat to elephants, while elephant numbers continued to increase in countries (especially Botswana, Zimbabwe, and South Africa) where populations were previously healthy.[50] This led one scholar to conclude recently that in Africa "factors other than legal ivory trade were the cause of elephant population changes," particularly political stability and less corrupt law enforcement.[51]

Even if CITES succeeded in destroying the market value of elephant ivory, it would not necessarily follow that elephants would be protected. To the poor Africans who live in or around elephant habitat, elephants are often viewed as a nuisance, trampling crops and humans, knocking over houses, and generally wreaking ecological and economic havoc. And if the people living with elephants do not see any value in them, they will either convert their habitat to something they do value or impede the efforts of wildlife authorities trying to protect elephant populations. It may be that in case of elephants, the best hope for their protection is the alleviation of poverty and the reform of domestic and international institutions that have encouraged poaching and habitat conversion—areas in which CITES plays only a small part.

Rhinos. Rhinos are another charismatic African species that has suffered from poaching, as their horns are valued both as ceremonial dagger handles in Yemen and for traditional Chinese medicine. There are two main species found in Africa, the white rhino and the black rhino. CITES banned the trade of white rhino parts at its first conference of the parties in 1975, and black rhinos were added to Appendix I at its next meeting in 1977.

Even after the ban, black rhino numbers fell precipitously, dropping 95 percent between 1970 and 1994.[52] By 1994, the black rhino was closer to extinction than ever before. According to South African economist Michael 't Sas-Rolfes, the CITES trade ban "had no discernible positive effect on rhino numbers, and did not seem to stop the trade in rhino horn. If anything, the Appendix I listings led to a sharp increase in the black market price of rhino horn, which simply fueled further poaching and encouraged speculative stockpiling of horn."[53]

At the same time, the white rhino continued its remarkable recovery from near extinction, particularly in South Africa. In the early 1900s, the white rhino was believed to be extinct in South Africa before a single population of fewer than 100 animals was discovered in Natal. The Natal Parks Board was established in 1947, and by the 1980s it had taken a different approach to rhino conservation than the rest of the continent—it commercialized them.[54] In 1986 the Board began holding auctions to sell live white rhinos to private landowners both for trophy hunting and game viewing. Revenues were used to fund park activities, including the protection and breeding of white rhinos, and the white rhino population increased rapidly both inside the parks on private lands, where by 2000 at least 20 percent of the white rhinos in South Africa resided.[55] In this case, treating rhinos as a commodity seems to have been the key to their recovery.

The Cayman Turtle Farm. Around the world, all seven marine sea turtle species, including the green sea turtle, are on CITES Appendix I and listed as either endangered or threatened on the IUCN Red List.[56] The primary threats to marine sea turtles are habitat loss (particularly on beaches where they lay their eggs) and both direct and indirect fishing pressure. Jacques Cousteau proclaimed decades ago that "if the green sea turtle is to survive, it must be farmed," and in the late 1960s a former chicken farmer decided to farm green sea turtles in the Cayman Islands.[57] In the 1970s, the Cayman Turtle Farm began ranching the turtles, collecting eggs from the wild and then rearing the turtles on the farm. The farm also released chicks back into the wild to supplement the natural populations on which the farm depended.

The green sea turtle was listed in CITES Appendix II when the convention came into force in 1975, moved to Appendix I in 1977, and added to the U.S. endangered species list in 1978. The farm was on its way to becoming a closed system, but because it was collecting eggs in the wild, concerns were raised about its effect on wild populations. The farm primarily traded with the United Kingdom, which was considered domestic trade by CITES because the Caymans were a dependency of the United Kingdom.[58] The ESA listing in 1978, however, effectively ended this trade because it stopped all transshipments through Miami, the only viable port at the time for shipments from the Caymans to the United Kingdom.

The farm fought the trade restriction in the U.S. courts, but ultimately failed when the court found that the Cayman Turtle Farm had not demonstrated its *positive* contribution to the conservation of wild sea turtles.[59] Other conservationists at the time, and even some detractors who primarily objected to the commercialization of the turtles, disagreed, believing that the farm could be an important part of sea turtle conservation.[60] At the time of the U.S. ruling, the wild population of green sea turtles in the Caribbean and Gulf of Mexico was estimated to be around 5,000 animals. When the farm went bankrupt in 1979, it had close to 100,000 green sea turtles in captivity. The farm was subsequently taken over by the Cayman government and is now run as a popular tourist attraction with about 10,000 turtles on site.[61] Had the ESA standard been less stringent, and only demanded that trade not be detrimental to the species, it is likely that the shipments would have been allowed.

Earth Sanctuaries Ltd. While not a direct example of the effect of CITES on conservation, Earth Sanctuaries Ltd. (ESL) is another international endangered species story worth mentioning. Set up by an academic mathematician in the late 1960s, ESL began as a small private wildlife reserve outside of Adelaide, Australia. It evolved over thirty years into an ambitious effort to tap into Australia's financial markets to save endangered species and to own and manage vast protected areas encompassing every representative native species and habitat in Australia.[62]

Australia has one of the highest rates of mammalian extinction in the world, largely because species there evolved in isolation from the rest of the world's continents and so were ill equipped to deal with the introduced predators and competitors that came with European settlement. ESL was a pioneer in conserving species through the eradication, rather than control, of introduced species, most notably cats, foxes, and rabbits. ESL was set up as a for-profit company because its founder, John Wamsley, believed in demonstrating that markets could resuscitate species rather than just keeping them on life support, and that conservation could be profitable.

And for a time it was. When ESL started buying land, building feral-proof fences, and reintroducing native species, endangered Australian species like woylies, rufous bettongs, long-nosed potoroos, and Southern brown bandicoots thrived in ESL's reserves. Some species, like the Eastern quoll, could only be seen in mainland Australia in one of ESL's sanctuaries. Species like the quoll drew paying visitors, especially to Warrawong, ESL's first, small-scale sanctuary near Adelaide.

ESL's business plan included specific target numbers for species recovery, as well as for land acquisition. After great success early on, ESL set its sights on larger sanctuaries, including Scotia, which covered a vast area—over 160,000 acres—of the remote bush. Fewer visitors were willing to trek out into the Outback, which only strengthened ESL's resolve that tapping into financial markets was the only way to access the kinds of funds needed to protect wildlife on the scale they envisioned. Thus, in May 2000, Earth Sanctuaries Ltd. was listed on the Australian Stock Exchange, earning the distinction of being the world's first publicly listed company whose "core business is conservation."[63] While the offering resulted in a significant inflow of cash to ESL, the stock price soon fell and ESL eventually went under. Its wildlife sanctuaries are now owned and managed by nonprofit environmental organizations.

ESL made two mistakes. One was to overreach and underestimate the importance of being close to population centers and a steady stream of visitors. ESL tried to fix that by selling Scotia and acquiring smaller sanctuaries closer to Sydney and Melbourne. Along with bad luck—the initial public offering coincided with a worldwide dip in financial markets—there was another huge hurdle that ESL faced: valuing its assets. Despite great success in protecting and propagating endangered and threatened species, there was no real way to value those species in its financial reports. In Australia, just as in the United States under the ESA, even domestic trade in endangered species is illegal, even between zoos or other conservation sanctuaries. Without even a limited market, it was impossible under current accounting standards to put endangered and threatened species in the asset column, and so the Australian equivalent of Wall Street never took ESL seriously.

ESL certainly faced other financial problems; for example, no doubt the markets in other zoos and conservation reserves is a small one. But still, ESL is a clear case where the existence of some market value in endangered species would have helped to nurture an ambitious conservation effort with a proven track record of species recovery. It is also another example where less strict criteria for trade—based on the assumption that markets and trade need not be detrimental to conservation—could have protected threatened and endangered species.

Lessons Learned and the Convention on Biological Diversity

Each of these case studies demonstrates the potential benefits of conservation through commerce as well as the possible harm caused to species protection efforts when species are treated as liabilities instead of assets. CITES has recognized the success of a number of ranching and breeding programs, including the Nile crocodile and the South African white rhino farms. However, it has only inconsistently applied the lesson of successful farming programs: for example, CITES accepts farming reptilians of the crocodile family but not of the sea turtle family.[64] And even when farming is allowed under CITES, there is still little or no effect on the habitat for these species in the wild, let alone the other species which depend on that habitat. Of course, captive breeding has its limitations, principally the lack of positive effect on habitat. However, for species in decline, captive breeding has proven crucial in a number of recoveries.[65]

CITES has also recognized that conservation will be more likely in developing countries when the people who live with wildlife see benefits from that wildlife—but this recognition has rarely fostered community-based programs. In the case of the African elephant, support for communal conservation was one reason for the allowance of one-time sales of ivory in countries like Botswana, Namibia, and Zimbabwe. There is no doubt that some of this money has trickled down to local communities, but just how much corruption may taint these government-to-government sales is an open question.

One of the most notable responses to both the primacy of habitat to conservation and the importance of community-level conservation has been the

1992 Convention on Biological Diversity (CBD), which followed the United Nations Conference on Environment and Development in Rio de Janeiro the same year. The CBD prioritizes sustainable development and puts conservation in a different context than CITES. Specifically, its preamble recognizes "that economic and social development and poverty eradication are the first and overriding priorities of developing countries."[66] In addition the Secretariat of the CBD has a program specifically aimed at highlighting "the importance of positive incentives" to conservation and development.[67]

One of the tenets of the CBD is that it grants to sovereign nations property rights over natural resources within their borders. Of course, that does not mean that those resources are then well managed, but it is at least an attempt to create positive incentives for conservation on an international scale.[68] In its administration of the ESA, the FWS has also begun to recognize the importance of habitat and the potential negative incentives created by land-use restrictions. It would do well to recognize those same problems in international species conservation as well.

Conclusions and Suggested ESA Reforms

CITES has been described as "the most direct international manifestation of the ESA."[69] ESA reform that recognized, or even facilitated, conservation through commerce would almost certainly have wide-ranging effects on CITES. Such changes to the ESA might include:

- Recognize the limitations of listing foreign species under the ESA and get rid of them. For funding international research, the FWS should use CITES/IUCN Red List priorities and FWS discretionary authority.

- If foreign listings and import restrictions remain, then relax the language of the ESA to fit the CITES standard. That is, allow trade when it is not detrimental to species populations (the CITES standard for Appendix II species) rather than allow trade only when it demonstrably enhances the survival of species populations.

- As long as the foreign threatened and endangered species are protected by trade restrictions rather than by other measures, some FWS funding should go to methods of differentiating between populations from different countries, between wild and farmed species, and between species that are protected on private and communal lands.

The ESA and CITES are fundamentally intertwined and flawed. The only reason to shoot a goose that lays golden eggs is out of fear that if you don't get that goose, someone else will, and if you'll never see those golden eggs, you might as well at least get a decent meal out of it. But if a person, family, village, community, or even sometimes a nation has assurances that it can hang onto those eggs, the goose will be carefully tended. Economically valuable species are in danger when they are free for the taking, but when they are not free for the taking, the higher their value the more effort will be put into protecting and propagating them. And indeed, any conservation efforts will be for naught if the underlying problem of habitat protection is not addressed. The ESA has formally recognized the problem of perverse incentives for both species and habitat protection domestically but not internationally. CITES has recognized that trade can be good for species conservation, but the CITES framework cannot fundamentally differentiate between populations at risk from trade and those that may benefit from it. Thus, CITES trade bans invariably have mixed results, reducing poaching in one place while reducing profit-seeking conservation efforts in another.

To date, the ESA has only exacerbated the problem by unilaterally listing foreign species and invoking its own trade restrictions, which are even stricter than CITES. To have a more positive impact on international species protection, the ESA must back off its own unilateral standards, put more effort into assisting in the differentiation between populations at different levels of risk, and push CITES to recognize the fundamental importance of protecting whole habitats and ecosystems rather than single species.

Notes

1. Peter H. Sand, "Whither CITES? The Evolution of a Treaty Regime in the Borderland of Trade and Environment," *European Journal of International Law* 8 (1997): 31–32.

2. Carlo A. Balistrieri, "CITES: The ESA and International Trade," *Natural Resources & Environment* 8 (Summer 1993): 33.

3. "Endangered Species," *Federal Register* 32:48 (March 11, 1967), 6.

4. Pub. L. No. 91–135, 83 Stat. 275 (1969).

5. Michael J. Bean, "The Endangered Species Act: Science, Policy, and Politics," *Annals of the New York Academy of Sciences* 1162 (2009): 370.

6. Pervaze A. Sheikh and M. Lynne Corn, "The Convention on International Trade in Endangered Species of Wild Fauna and Flora (CITES): Background and Issues," *CRS Report for Congress RL32751* (Washington, D.C.: Congressional Research Service, February 5, 2008).

7. CITES Secretariat, http://www.cites.org/eng/disc/number_species.pdf. (accessed October 20, 2009).

8. Ibid.

9. United States Government Accountability Office, "Protected Species: International Convention and U.S. Laws Protect Species Differently," GAO-04-964 (September 2004).

10. U.S. Fish and Wildlife Service, "Listed species: foreign species" downloaded from http://ecos.fws.gov/tess_public/pub/SpeciesReport.do?lead=10& listing-Type=L, "Listed species: all animals" downloaded from http://ecos.fws.gov/tess_public/pub/listedAnimals.jsp, "Species Report: Plants" downloaded from http://ecos.fws.gov/tess_public/SpeciesReport.do, and "Species Report: Listed Plants" downloaded from http://ecos.fws.gov/tess_public/pub/listedPlants.jsp (accessed October 21, 2009).

11. The majority of these funds go toward the charismatic species programs through the FWS "Wildlife without Borders" program. In 2008, these funds amounted to almost thirty-two million dollars for specific species (African and Asian elephants, rhinos and tigers, great apes, and marine turtles), along with over two million dollars for regional funding (to Africa, Latin America and the Carribean, Mexico, and Russia), some of which includes endangered species

protection as well as money for wetlands and migratory bird conservation. See U.S. Fish and Wildlife Service, "Wildlife Without Borders: Multinational Species Conservation Funds 2004-2008," downloaded from FWS, "Regional Programs 2008 update," downloaded from http://www.fws.gov/international/DIC/regional%20 programs/pdf/regional_funding_2009_final.pdf (accessed October 15, 2009). http://www.fws.gov/international/DIC/pdf/mnscf_history_update_fact-sheet_2009_final.pdf (accessed October 15, 2009).

12. Endangered Species Act of 1973, Public Law No. 93-205, amended at 16 U.S.C. §§ 1531-1543.

13. Center for Biological Diversity, "Center Seeks Protection for 56 Vanishing Birds and Five Imperiled Butterflies Around the World," press release, November 16, 2006, http://www.biologicaldiversity.org/news/press_releases/56-birds-butterflies-11-16-2006.html.

14. Environment News Service, "31 Rare Birds From Around the World Protected Under U.S. Law," June 16, 2009, http://www.ens-newswire.com/ens/jun2009/2009-06-16-092.asp.

15. Information gathered from the CITES-listed species database, http://www.cites.org/eng/resources/species.html (accessed July 10, 2009).

16. Environment News Service, "31 Rare Birds."

17. U.S. Fish and Wildlife Service, "Delisting Report," downloaded from http://ecos.fws.gov/tess_public/DelistingReport.do (accessed July 9, 2009).

18. Robert J. Noecker, "Endangered Species List Revisions: A Summary of Delisting and Downlisting," *CRS Report for Congress 98-32* (Washington, D.C.: Congressional Research Service, January 5, 1998).

19. Australian Department of Foreign Affairs and Trade, "About Australia: Kangaroos," downloaded from http://www.dfat.gov.au/facts/kangaroos.html (accessed October 16, 2009).

20. Noecker, "Endangered Species List Revisions."

21. Ibid.

22. U.S. Fish and Wildlife Service, "yacare caiman," http://ecos.fws.gov/speciesProfile/profile/speciesProfile.action?spcode=C004 (accessed July 14, 2009).

23. Noecker, "Endangered Species List Revisions."

24. "Reclassification of Yacare Caiman in South America From Endangered to Threatened, and the Listing of Two Other Caiman Species as Threatened by Reason of Similarity of Appearance," 65 *Federal Register* 87 (May 4, 2000), 25867–81.

25. Jon Hutton, "Who Knows Best? Controversy over Unilateral Stricter Domestic Measures," in *Endangered Species Threatened Convention: The Past, Present and Future of CITES*, ed. Jon Hutton and Barnabus Dickson (London: Earthscan, 2000), 57–66.

26. Ibid.

27. Henriette Kievit, "Conservation of the Nile Crocodile: Has CITES Helped or Hindered?" in *Endangered Species Threatened Convention: The Past, Present and Future of CITES*, ed. Jon Hutton and Barnabus Dickson (London: Earthscan, 2000), 60-61.

28. Sheikh and Corn, "CITES," 11.

29. U.S. District Court for the District of Columbia, *Friends of Animals et al. v. Ken Salazar, Secretary of the Interior; Rebecca Ann Cary et al. v. Rowan Gould, Acting Director, Fish and Wildlife Service et al.*

30. Robert J. Smith, "Private Solutions to Conservation Problems," in *The Theory of Market Failure: A Critical Examination,* ed. Tyler Cowen (Fairfax, Va.: George Mason University Press, 1988), 341–60.

31. Webb, "Are All Species Equal?" 98–106.

32. General Agreement on Tariffs and Trade, "United States—Restrictions on Imports of Tuna," June 16, 1994.

33. World Trade Organization, "United States—Import Prohibition of Certain Shrimp and Shrimp Products WT/DS58/R," May 15, 1998.

34. Gregory Shaffer, "United States—Import Prohibition of Certain Shrimp and Shrimp Products. WTO Doc. WT/DS58/AB/R," *The American Journal of International Law,* vol. 93, no. 2 (April 1999): 507–14.

35. World Trade Organization, "United States—Import Prohibition of Certain Shrimp and Shrimp Products WT/DS58/RW," June 15, 2001.

36. Elizabeth R. DeSombre and J. Samuel Barkin, "Turtles and Trade: The WTO's Acceptance of Environmental Trade Restrictions," *Global Environmental Politics* 2, no. 1 (February 2002): 12–18.

37. "Revised Guidelines for the Implementation of Section 609 of Public Law 101–162 Relating to the Protection of Sea Turtles in Shrimp Trawl Fishing Operations," 64 *Federal Register* 130 (July 8, 1999): 36946–52.

38. World Trade Organization, "Understanding the WTO: The Environment: A Specific Concern," downloaded from http://www.wto.org/english/theWTO_e/whatis_e/tif_e/bey2_e.htm, July 8, 2009.

39. Lori Wallach and Patrick Woodall, *Whose Trade Organization? A Comprehensive Guide to the WTO* (New York: The New Press, 2004).

40. See Jonathan Baillie, Craig Hilton-Taylor, and Simon Stuart, eds, *2004 IUCN Red List of Threatened Species. A Global Species Assessment* (Gland and Cambridge: International Union for Conservation of Nature, 2004); Brian Groombridge ed., *Global Biodiversity: Status of the Earth's Living Resources* (New York: Chapman and Hall, 1992); Michael Hoffmann, Thomas Brooks, Gustavo da Fonseca, Claude Gascon, Frank Hawkins, Roger James, Penny Langhammer, Russel Mittermeier, John Pilgrim, Ana Rodrigues, and Jose Maria da Silva, "Conservation Planning and the IUCN Red List," *Endangered Species Research* 6 no. 2 (May 7, 2008), 1–13.

41. Eric Hansen, *Orchid Fever: A Horticultural Tale of Love, Lust, and Lunacy* (New York: Vintage Books, 2001), 17.

42. Eric Dinerstein, Colby Loucks, Eric Wikramanayake, Joshua Ginsberg, Eric Sanderson, Josh Seidensticker, Jessica Forrest, Gosia Bryja, Andrea Heydlauff, Sybille Klenzendorf, Peter Leimgruber, Judy Mills, Timothy G. O'Brien, Mahendra

Shrestha, Ross Simons, and Melissa Songer, "The Fate of Wild Tigers," *Bioscience* 57, no. 6 (June 2007), 508–14.

43. Ibid.

44. Holly Doremus and Joel E. Pagel, "Why Listing May Be Forever: Perspectives under the U.S. Endangered Species Act," *Conservation Biology* 15, no. 5 (October 2001), 1258–68.

45. United Nations Environmental Programme, "Wildlife Treaty Comes of Age—CITES Celebrates 30 Years of Achievement," press release, July 1, 2005, http:// www.unis.unvienna.org/unis/pressrels/2005/envdev865.html.

46. See Webb, "Are All Species Equal?" 98–106; and Desmond McNeill, Gabriela Lichtenstein, and Nadine Renaudeau d'Arc, "International Policies and National Legislation Concerning Vicuña Conservation and Exploitation," in *The Vicuña: The Theory and Practice of Community Based Wildlife Management,* ed. I. Gordon (New York: Springer Verlag, 2009), 63–79.

47. Jaime Campos Quiroga, "Opening Address to the Conference of the Parties," CITES COP 12, Santiago, Chile, November 3, 2002, http://www.cites.org/eng/cop/12/chile_open.shtml.

48. United States Government Accountability Office, "Protected Species: International Convention and U.S. Laws Protect Wildlife Differently," GAO-04-964, (September 2004), 12.

49. Michael 't Sas-Rolfes, "Assessing CITES: Four Case Studies," in *Endangered Species Threatened Convention: The Past, Present and Future of CITES*, ed. Jon Hutton and Barnabus Dickson (London: Earthscan, 2000), 69–87.

50. Daniel Stiles, "The ivory trade and elephant conservation," *Environmental Conservation* 31, no. 4 (2004): 309–21.

51. Ibid. 313.

52. See Michael De Alessi, *Private Conservation and Black Rhinos in Zimbabwe: The Savé Valley and Bubiana Conservancies* (Washington, D.C.: Center for Private Conservation, January 2000) http://www.rhinoresourcecenter.com/ref_files/1175861954.pdf.

53. Michael 't Sas-Rolfes, "Assessing CITES: Four Case Studies," 71.

54. Brian Child, "Parks in transition: biodiversity, rural development and the bottom line," in *Parks in transition: biodiversity, rural development and the bottom line* ed. Brian Child (London: Earthscan, 2004), 233–56.

55. Michael 't Sas-Rolfes, "Assessing CITES: Four Case Studies," 73.

56. See IUCN Red List online at http://www.iucnredlist.org/.

57. Robert J. Smith, "Private Solutions to Conservation Problems," in *The Theory of Market Failure*, ed. Tyler Cowan (Fairfax, Va.: George Mason University Press, 1988), 341–60.

58. Karen L. Eckert, Karen A. Bjorndal, F. Alberto Abreu-Grobois, and M. Donnelly, eds., *Research and Management Techniques for the Conservation of Sea Turtles*. IUCN/SSC Marine Turtle Specialist Group Publication No. 4 (1999).

59. *Cayman Turtle Farm v. Andrus,* 478 F. Supp. 125 (D.D.C. 1979).

60. Sam Fosdick and Peggy Fosdick, *Last Chance Lost?* (New York: Irvin S. Naylor, 1994).

61. Cayman Turtle Farm, "History," downloaded from http://turtle.ky/history.htm, (accessed July 9, 2009).

62. See Michael De Alessi, "Saving Endangered Species Privately: A Case Study of Earth Sanctuaries Ltd.," *Policy Study 313*, Los Angeles: Reason Foundation, August 2003.

63. Earth Sanctuaries Ltd. press release (May 2000).

64. Webb, "Are All Species Equal?" 98–106.

65. See Noel F. R. Snyder, Scott R. Derrickson, Steven R. Beissinger, James W. Wiley, Thomas B. Smith, William D. Toone and Brian Miller, "Limitations of Captive Breeding in Endangered Species Recovery," *Conservation Biology* 10, no. 2 (April 1996): 338–48.

66. Preamble to the Convention on Biological Diversity (1992), downloaded from http://www.cbd.int/convention/articles.shtml?a=cbd-00 (accessed August 19, 2009).

67. CBD Secretariat, "Overview of CBD Activities" (2009), downloaded from http://www.cbd.int/incentives/positive.shtml (accessed August 20, 2009).

68. Christopher Barrett, Katrina Brandon, Clark Gibson, and Heidi Gjertsen, "Conserving Tropical Biodiversity amid Weak Institutions," *BioScience* 51, no. 6 (June 2001): 497–502.

69. Carlo Balistrieri, "International Aspects of the Endangered Species Act," in *The Endangered Species Act: law, policy, and perspectives*, ed. Donald C. Baur and William Robert Irvin (Chicago: American Bar Association Publishing, 2002), 496.

Index

About the Authors

Jonathan H. Adler is Professor of Law and Director of the Center for Business Law and Regulation at the Case Western Reserve University School of Law, where he teaches courses in environmental, regulatory, and constitutional law. Professor Adler is the author or editor of four books as well as numerous book chapters and articles. Prior to joining the faculty at Case Western, Professor Adler clerked for the Honorable David B. Sentelle on the U.S. Court of Appeals for the District of Columbia Circuit. From 1991 to 2000, he worked at the Competitive Enterprise Institute, a free market research and advocacy group in Washington, D.C., where he directed its environmental studies program. He holds a B.A. magna cum laude from Yale University and a J.D. summa cum laude from the George Mason University School of Law.

Jamison E. Colburn has been a Professor of Law at the Pennsylvania State University Dickinson School of Law since 2008. He teaches environmental law, natural resources law, property, and administrative law. Prior to joining the faculty at Penn State, Colburn was an enforcement lawyer for the U.S. Environmental Protection Agency and a collaborating researcher with the Project on Public Problem Solving at Columbia University. Professor Colburn has published widely on public lands management, administrative law, wildlife habitat, and other conservation topics. He is a member of the American Institute of Biological Sciences and the Society for Conservation Biology and has served as a trustee of the Connecticut River Watershed Council. He holds a B.A. from the State University of New York, Plattsburgh, a J.D. from Rutgers University, an LL.M. from Harvard University, and a J.S.D. from Columbia University.

David Dana is the Clinton Professor of Law at Northwestern University School of Law. He is also co-director of Northwestern University's Institute for Sustainable Practices. A former environmental litigator, Professor Dana has written widely in property, environmental, natural resources, and constitutional law. He clerked on the United States Court of Appeals for the Ninth Circuit. Professor Dana earned a B.A. at Harvard University and a J.D. at Harvard Law School.

Michael De Alessi is a postdoctoral scholar at Stanford University. His Ph.D., from the Department of Environmental Science, Policy, & Management at the University of California, Berkeley, examined the environmental history, politics, and economics of fisheries policy in New Zealand. He holds an M.A. in marine policy from the Rosenstiel School of Marine and Atmospheric Science at the University of Miami, as well as an M.S. in management science and engineering and a B.A. in economics from Stanford. He is the author of *Fishing for Solutions* (Institute of Economic Affairs, 1998) and the former Director of Natural Resource Policy for the Reason Foundation in Los Angeles and of the Center for Private Conservation in Washington, D.C.

James L. Huffman is the Erskine Wood Sr. Professor of Law at Lewis & Clark Law School, where he served as Dean from 1983 to 2006. He has been a visiting professor at Auckland University in New Zealand, the University of Oregon, the University of Athens in Greece, and Universidad Francisco Marroquin in Guatemala. He was also a fellow at the Humane Studies Institute and a Distinguished Bradley Scholar at the Heritage Foundation. He is the author of more than 100 articles and chapters on a wide array of legal topics, including property rights and environmental law. Professor Huffman earned a B.S. degree at Montana State University, an M.A. from the Fletcher School of Law and Diplomacy at Tufts University, and a J.D. degree from the University of Chicago Law School.

Brian F. Mannix is the President of Buckland Mill Associates, an economic consultancy. From September 2005 to January 2009 he was the Environmental Protection Agency's Associate Administrator for Policy, Economics, and Innovation. He served the Commonwealth of Virginia as Deputy

Secretary of Natural Resources from 1996 to 1998. From 1987 to 1989 Mr. Mannix was the Managing Editor of *Regulation* magazine at the American Enterprise Institute. Mr. Mannix was at the federal Office of Management and Budget from 1981 to 1987, serving as Deputy Director of the Natural Resources Branch in the Office of Information and Regulatory Affairs. He has also worked for the U.S. Council on Wage and Price Stability and the Energy Department. Mr. Mannix earned A.B. and A.M degrees at Harvard University and an M.P.P. degree at Harvard University's Kennedy School of Government.

Jonathan Remy Nash is Professor of Law at Emory University School of Law. He is a prolific scholar in the fields of environmental law, international environmental law, property law, and the law of federal courts. Prior to joining the Emory law faculty, Professor Nash was the Robert C. Cudd Professor of Environmental Law at Tulane Law School. He has been a Visiting Professor at Hofstra University School of Law and the University of Chicago Law School, a Visiting Scholar at Columbia Law School, and a Postdoctoral Research Fellow at New York University School of Law's Center on Environmental and Land Use Law. He clerked for the Honorable Nina Gershon, Chief Magistrate Judge of the United States District Court for the Southern District of New York, and for the Honorable Donald S. Russell, Circuit Judge for the United States Court of Appeals for the Fourth Circuit. He received his B.A. summa cum laude from Columbia University, his J.D. magna cum laude from New York University School of Law, and his LL.M. from the Harvard Law School.

J. B. Ruhl is the Matthews & Hawkins Professor of Property at Florida State University College of Law, where he teaches courses on environmental law, land use, and property. Previous to joining the FSU faculty in 1999, Professor Ruhl taught at Southern Illinois University in Carbondale, Illinois (1994–98), and at the George Washington University Law School (1998–99). He has also taught at Harvard Law School, Vermont Law School, the Lewis & Clark College of Law, and the University of Texas School of Law. Professor Ruhl is a nationally regarded expert in the fields of endangered species protection, ecosystem services policy, regulation of wetlands, ecosystem management, environmental impact analysis, and related environmental and natural resources fields. Prior to entering full-time law teaching, Professor Ruhl was a partner in the law firm of Fulbright & Jaworski, L.L.P., practicing environmental and natural resources law in the firm's Austin, Texas office. He is an elected member of The American Law Institute. Professor Ruhl received B.A. and J.D. degrees from The University of Virginia, an LL.M. in Environmental Law from The George Washington University Law School, and a Ph.D. in Geography from Southern Illinois University.

R. Neal Wilkins is Professor of Wildlife Science and Director of The Institute of Renewable Natural Resources at Texas A&M University. His primary focus is management and conservation of land, water, and wildlife resources on private lands. Much of his work integrates science, policy, and economics for developing incentive-based conservation programs. Professor Wilkins holds a degree in Forestry from Stephen F. Austin State University, a Masters of Wildlife Science from Texas A&M University, and a Ph.D. in Wildlife Ecology from the University of Florida.